The Movement for Indian Assimilation
1860-1890

Dr. Henry E. Fritz is Associate Professor of American History at St. Olaf College in Northfield, Minnesota. He received the Ph.D. degree in 1957 from the University of Minnesota for a thesis entitled "The Humanitarian Background of Indian Reform" and taught for two years at the University of Wisconsin, Milwaukee, before accepting his current position. Professor Fritz teaches courses in Frontier Expansion and Twentieth Century United States; occasionally he offers a seminar on the Progressive Era. He has lectured over KTCA—the educational television station of the University of Minnesota—on the Indian, and on the uniqueness of American democracy, nationalism, and culture. His publications include an article in *The Chronicles of Oklahoma*, and reviews for the *American Historical Review* and for *Arizona and the West*.

The Movement For
Indian Assimilation, 1860-1890

by

Dr. Henry E. Fritz

Philadelphia . University of Pennsylvania Press

7340
Printed in the United States of America

The Movement for Indian Assimilation
1860-1890

Dr. Henry E. Fritz is Associate Professor of American History at St. Olaf College in Northfield, Minnesota. He received the Ph.D. degree in 1957 from the University of Minnesota for a thesis entitled "The Humanitarian Background of Indian Reform" and taught for two years at the University of Wisconsin, Milwaukee, before accepting his current position. Professor Fritz teaches courses in Frontier Expansion and Twentieth Century United States; occasionally he offers a seminar on the Progressive Era. He has lectured over KTCA—the educational television station of the University of Minnesota—on the Indian, and on the uniqueness of American democracy, nationalism, and culture. His publications include an article in *The Chronicles of Oklahoma*, and reviews for the *American Historical Review* and for *Arizona and the West*.

To

Dolores Moeller Fritz

Preface

This book is meant to answer a need for better understanding of federal Indian policy during the period of crisis in United States—American Indian relations following the Civil War. Many studies of the various tribes and of hostilities with them have been published, with little comprehension of Grant's "Peace Policy" or of the forces that established it. Previous works have not portrayed the "Peace Policy" as a phase of a Protestant movement for the assimilation of Indians, which culminated with the passage of the Dawes Act; nor has the Catholic reaction to this movement been adequately treated.

The sources given in the Bibliography are those which make a distinct contribution to the text, and no attempt has been made here to include all of the literature on Indian affairs for the post-Civil War period. Because earlier studies of the subject seemed unsatisfactory, the author has relied mostly upon the extensive primary sources.

It is impractical to name the many persons who have helped prepare the manuscript; their services were invaluable and are gratefully remembered. The author wishes to thank St. Olaf College for aid which made possible a summer research trip to several archives in the East, and especially to express appreciation to Professor Ernest S. Osgood, under whose guidance this study was begun in 1955 at the University of Minnesota.

H.E.F.

Preface

Contents

Contents

Illustrations and Maps

The following illustrations appear as a group following page 126.

Episcopal Bishop Henry B. Whipple, 1864.

A Caddo village, Indian Territory, 1870's.

Map from "The Christian Weekly," December 12, 1874, depicting the assignment of reservations to religious bodies.

Students at the Cherry Creek mission of the Dakota Native Missionary Society, Cheyenne River Reservation.

A company of Indian police, Dakota Territory.

A day school, Indian Territory, 1870's.

Standing Bear, Ponca Chief.

Map of reservations in 1884 prior to the Congressional Act of 1886, under which millions of acres were relinquished by northern tribes.

Map of reservations in 1888 depicting the immediate effect of the Congressional Act of 1886.

The Movement for Indian Assimilation
1860-1890

I

The Status of Indians and Indian
Affairs in the 1860's

THE STRUGGLE FOR empire in North America caused the United
States in its earliest years to adopt an Indian policy similar to
the one devised by Great Britain in colonial times. The English
in their final struggle with the French and through the uprising
of Pontiac had learned the importance of Indian allies, or at
least of the pacification of the native inhabitants, to the
conquest of territory. As early as 1755 they had appointed two
superintendents, later assisted by deputies or agents, who were
made responsible for good relations with the tribes much as
ambassadors were held accountable for international tranquil-
ity. They had, in 1763, established a boundary separating the
Indian's country from that of the white man, and had initiated
the practice of moving the line westward, to make room for an
expanding Anglo-American community—all of this by treaty.
They had, in 1764, adopted a fair-trade plan which recognized
the importance of commerce to Indian relations—but which
unfortunately was abandoned within four years because of
administrative cost.[1]

The United States borrowed from all of these precedents in
making her first policy toward the tribes, but did not make the
mistake of neglecting commerce. The famous factory system
authorized in 1796 provided for government trading posts
where Indians could receive manufactured goods at cost in

---

[1] Clarence W. Alvord, *Mississippi Valley in British Politics*, I (Cleve-
land, 1917), 183-228, 287-312 ; II, 61-89 ; Clarence E. Carter, "British
Policy toward the American Indians in the South, 1763-8," *English
Historical Review*, XXXIII (1918), 37-56 ; Max Farrand, "The Indian
Boundary Line," *American Historical Review*, X (1905), 782-91.

exchange for fur at fair market prices. Such posts, scattered in a wide arc along thousands of miles of frontier from Florida to the Great Lakes, helped prevent Spanish and British alike from gaining control of the native inhabitants. It was expedient to win the loyalty of the Indians for the reason that they were important to the outcome of the imperial contest, and the fur trade was a part of the scheme. No power could be quite certain that it would enjoy the privilege of exploiting the rich resources of the Western wilderness until loyal subjects inhabited it. Before white citizens could establish farms in the Mississippi basin and along the rivers of the Gulf, the best hope of making good the paper title to trans-Appalachia was to ensure that the tribes should be allied with the United States. The westward movement of the agricultural frontier, together with the Rush-Bagot Agreement (1817), the Convention of 1818, and the Adams-Onis Treaty (1819), left the Indians in a precarious situation, for they were then seen as a worthless obstacle to "manifest destiny."[2]

By the 1830's, the slackening of the struggle of European powers for empire in North America had made possible a profound change in United States Indian policy, since the government had less motivation to woo the Indian as an auxiliary and more reason to clear the tribes from land needed for national development. Most important of the several features of the revised policy was the removal of the eastern tribes to the "Great American Desert" which, it was thought, would never be desirable for white settlement, and the assignment to them, in perpetuity, of lands sufficient for their subsistence. Legislation defined the Indian country, forbade unauthorized white men to infiltrate or to encroach upon it, and provided for Indian self-government. The concept that these

---

[2] Royal B. Way, "The United States Factory System for trading with the Indians, 1796-1822," *Mississippi Valley Historical Review*, VI (1919), 220-35.

tribes should be dealt with as if they were national entities was not changed. Public treaties were to be made with them, agents were to be appointed in the stead of ambassadors, and delegations of Indian chiefs were to be received at Washington.[3]

Through the alternation of persuasion and force, the removal policy resulted in the transportation of the bulk of the Eastern tribes beyond the Mississippi River and in their establishment on the edge of the Great Plains, within the bounds of what later became the states of Kansas and Oklahoma. However, as the line of settlement moved up to the Indian country and as lines of travel crossed and recrossed the trans-Mississippi West, the concept of maintaining an area of exclusive Indian occupation became more difficult to apply. By the late sixties it had become impossible; cattlemen and farmers with no regard for the Indians' patrimony were swarming onto the plains, determined to have every acre of land that might yield a profit.[4]

The policy of the federal government had not kept up with changing conditions, for it would soon be impossible to remove the tribes beyond the limits of the frontier. White intrusion was breaking down their self-government; non-intercourse laws of the United States were inadequate. For the Indians, caught as though in the jaws of a huge vise which pressed upon them from the Pacific region as it did from the prairie plains of the Middle West, life had become desperate. The destruction of the cultures of the last great tribes in the mountains and on the plains—squeezed by the more stable and respectable elements of Anglo-American society bearing down from opposite directions; robbed, harassed, and confounded by fugitive fragments in

---

[3] Annie H. Abel, "The History of Events Resulting in Indian Consolidation West of the Mississippi," *American Historical Association Annual Report, 1906,* I (Washington, 1908), 233-450.

[4] Annual Report of the Commissioner of Indian Affairs, Senate Exec. Doc. No. 1, 32nd Cong., 1st Sess., Vol. 3, 273-74. Hereafter cited as Ann. Rpt. of Com. Ind. Aff.

their van—required only three decades.[5]

That Indian policy became obsolete was not the fault of the Indian Bureau or of the Interior Department, which by act of Congress in 1849 took over Indian management from the War Department. Commissioner George W. Manypenny demonstrated foresight, competence, and concern about the welfare of Indians when in 1854 he proclaimed the need for a new code of regulations. He stated that removal must cease, because it was rapidly becoming evident that there was no place in the West where the Indians could be placed with a reasonable hope that they might escape molestation. The Intercourse Law of 1834 would have to be revised, he said, because its provisions had been aimed at individual intruders rather than at organized expeditions. Such organized bands of white intruders were so fully equipped for both offense and defense that they were capable of overcoming not only any resistance that the Indians themselves might offer, but also any that the government of a western territory might be willing to provide.[6]

Succeeding commissioners also perceived the fallacies of the old system and likewise emphasized the need for a new policy. Charles Mix said in 1858 that removal from place to place had prevented the Indians from acquiring settled habits or a taste for civilized pursuits; that assignment of large areas to the tribes in common had forestalled an appreciation of individual property; that the payment of annuities had "not only tended to foster habits of indolence and profligacy, but constantly made them the victims of the lawless and inhuman sharper and

---

[5] Francis A. Walker, "The Indian Question," *North American Review,* CXVI (1873), 329-88; James B. Thayer, "A People Without Law," *Atlantic Monthly,* LXVIII (1891), 551. Walker wrote at the end of his term as Commissioner of Indian Affairs. Thayer was recognized as the leading scholar of constitutional law and the law of evidence.

[6] Senate Exec. Doc. No. 1, 33rd Cong., 1st Sess., Vol. 1, 261.

speculator." In 1862 the Secretary of the Interior, Caleb B. Smith, placed in question the wisdom of treating the tribes as "quasi-independent nations" and suggested that it would be much more realistic to regard them as wards of the government.[7]

It was obvious to these keen observers that the only practical and humane answer to the Indian problem was to assimilate the Indians into Anglo-American culture. The central question was, How could this be done? Here were a Stone-Age people, culturally separated from their white neighbors by more than three thousand years of accomplishment. Here was a primitive society about to be destroyed through the onslaught of one organizationally and technologically superior to it. Here were 325,000 individuals who were required within a few decades to adopt political, social, and economic institutions which it had taken western European civilization thirty centuries to develop. The alternatives to adjustment were cruel and undesirable: either death or parasitical existence upon a reservation.

Administrators of Indian affairs sought to deal with the problem within the old legislative framework. Provision in treaties for teachers, farmers, blacksmiths, and carpenters who were to educate the natives became common during the fifties and sixties. Agency posts were established within fixed reserves for the accommodation of the agents and their employees, who were made responsible for both the discipline and the instruction of the Indians.[8]

Commissioner William P. Dole thought this procedure was correct in theory but admitted that from the moment reservations were surrounded by white settlers there were glaring weaknesses in application. He expressed regret in 1862 that the

---

[7] Ann. Rpts., Senate Exec. Doc. No. 1, 35th Cong., 2nd Sess., Vol. 1, 354; House Exec. Doc. No. 1, 37th Cong., 3rd Sess., Vol. 2, 10.

[8] Ann. Rpt. of Com. Ind. Aff., House Exec. Doc. No. 1, 38th Cong., 1st Sess., Vol. 3, 129; Alban W. Hoopes, *Indian Affairs and Their Administration, 1849-1860* (Philadelphia, 1932), 48-49.

comparatively small tracts of land which had been set aside for the original inhabitants should have become objects of the white man's cupidity. Pioneers regarded Indians with contempt and subjected them to "wrongs, insults, and petty annoyances," which sometimes stirred them to retaliate. Justice was usually unobtainable because, to begin with, rights by treaty or under federal law were wholly unintelligible to a vast majority of the Indian population. Conversely, Indian crimes against members of the white race were met with swift punishment, and whole tribes suffered because of individual acts.[9]

Except where authority had been granted the tribes by treaty to mete out justice in their own way, federal law governed crimes committed by whites in the Indian country. But who was to testify in those instances where the laws were applicable? Certainly not the settler whose fingers itched for a deed to the red man's land, nor the miner who longed for the mineral wealth which lay beneath it! Except in liquor cases, Indians were not competent witnesses, and white juries were not likely to convict those culprits who were unfortunate enough to be placed on trial. A case reported by General Alfred Sully from Montana Territory in 1870 was typical. Two scoundrels named Veil and Fitzpatrick had stolen twenty ponies from Blood Indians on the Marias River; the thieves were followed, and with the aid of troops sent by General Philippe de Trobriand from near-by Fort Shaw most of the stock was recovered. Fitzpatrick was taken into custody by the United States marshal, but the grand jury at Helena refused to indict him. Indeed, one of the jurors was bold enough to imply that no wrong had been committed.[10]

It was just as difficult to establish the guilt of whiskey

---

[9] Ann. Rpts., House Exec. Docs. No. 1, 37th Cong., 3rd Sess., Vol. 2, 169-70 ; and No. 1, 38th Cong., 1st Sess., Vol. 3, 129.

[10] Felix S: Cohen, *Handbook of Federal Indian Law* (Washington, 1942), 364-65 ; Sully to E. S. Parker, Mar. 17, 1870, Bureau of Indian Affairs, Letters Received, National Archives. Hereafter cited as Cohen, *Handbook,* and as Bur. Ind. Aff., Ltrs. Rec'd. Veil and Fitzpatrick lived

peddlers who violated the ban on liquor, even though in 1864 Indians were made competent witnesses by federal law where such persons were on trial. The Superintendent of Indian Affairs for Washington Territory wrote in 1867 that he had only recently succeeded, against much local opposition, in getting convictions in three out of fifteen cases brought before the court. The situation did not improve, for spirituous liquor was sold as cider and beer; selection of jurors was left to county sheriffs, who depended upon local popularity for their offices and often chose persons who were themselves guilty of offenses against the Indians. These panels were used by the United States courts. In the Southwest, the reaction of the frontier to the prosecution of liquor sellers was violent. In 1872, at a trial in La Mesilla, New Mexico Territory, involving the federal prosecution of Felix Trujillo and others who were accused of selling whiskey to the Mescalero Apaches, Chief Cadette appeared as witness for the plaintiff. Neither he nor the interpreter completed the one hundred and twenty-five mile journey back to the agency at Fort Stanton. Cadette's horse was found grazing in a canyon near the body of his master, and only the head and clothing of the interpreter were discovered."

State and territorial courts had no jurisdiction in litigation involving the relations of Indians and whites or among the Indians themselves which arose within the boundaries of reservations. The correction of abuses in this category was wholly up to the federal government. But, as has already been stated, one of the fundamental concepts of past policy had been that of tribal capacity for self-government. Therefore the constitutional authority of the United States which was plenary on Indian reservations had been held in check since 1817 by specific

---

at Sun River Crossing, about four miles from Ft. Shaw; the ponies were recovered there.

" 13 U.S. Stat., 29; T. I. McKenny to N. G. Taylor, June 4, 1867, Bur. Ind. Aff., Ltrs. Rec'd.; Ann. Rpts. of the Board of Indian Commissioners (1871), 113-14 (1873), 221-22.

provisions in Indian legislation exempting relations between members of the tribes from federal jurisdiction. The continued assumption of self-government, as the frontier swept into the far West, surrounding Indians both on and off reservations, was a grave mistake. General Philip H. Sheridan wrote in 1869 that the power of a chief among the plains tribes depended upon his willingness to make war, and furthermore that "there is no code in any tribe which enables a chief to exercise authority, nor is there any system of punishment to compel obedience." General William T. Sherman endorsed Sheridan's letter and stated that all the tribes were then "engaged in the same general system of wandering & Stealing." Colonel Henry A. Morrow, who was stationed at Fort Buford in Dakota Territory, reported that the conduct of roaming Yanktonai for several years past had demonstrated the powerlessness of Chief Black Eye to exercise control, and also that any attempt to compel their return to the tribe would drive them into open hostility and alliance with the Unkpapa camp. A committee of Colorado citizens made a similar assertion in regard to the Indians in their vicinity, so that one gets an impression of drifting bands with no particular allegiance raiding and pillaging over the high plains.[12]

White encroachment tended to destroy whatever authority the chiefs and head men were accustomed to wield. George Bonga, an intelligent Negro of mixed blood, who had lived among the Chippewa from childhood and had served them as interpreter, said the chiefs were "mere ciphers & tools for the Rowdies," and thought it would be impossible to accomplish anything for the Indians' benefit without simple laws and the means to enforce them.[13]

---

[12] Cohen, *Handbook,* 146 and 364 ; P. H. Sheridan to E. D. Townsend, July 12, 1869, War Records, National Archives ; H. A. Morrow to O. D. Greene, Dec. 4, 1869, and G. W. Lane to Andrew Johnson, July 5, 1866, Bur. Ind. Aff., Ltrs. Rec'd.

[13] Bonga at Crow Wing, Minn., to Vincent Colyer, Feb. 10, 1870, Bd. of Ind. Com., Ltrs. Rec'd, National Archives.

The breakdown of tribal government was widespread. Locality and stage of cultural development made little difference. The mission Indians of southern California experienced difficulties in common with more primitive tribes. Because of the early influence of Spanish padres, these people were considerably advanced in civilization, having, since the abandonment of the missions, farmed small patches of land along streams where irrigation was possible. Charles Maltby, the Superintendent for Indian Affairs in California, visited them in 1866 and found that a few lazy and drunken Indians, together with white men of low character, were obstructing the efforts of Chief Manuel Cota to prevent traffic in liquor and the auction of their squaws for prostitution. Assisting these degenerates was an unprincipled lawyer from Los Angeles, who, for a fee and other considerations, had agreed to aid in the deposition of Cota. Special agent Stanley had been continually harassed in the performance of his duties by this clique, which had gone to the extent of instituting, in the district court of Los Angeles County, a suit for six thousand dollars in damages against both the agent and the chief, in favor of an Indian who had been whipped for stealing by the latter's order. It did not help much that some respectable citizens commended Cota for his extraordinary intelligence, good character, and laborious struggle to improve the condition of his people. These Indians had no reservation and, as Maltby asserted, the power of an agent or superintendent to prevent abuses in such a case was nil, while any attempt to prosecute the offenders under the state laws would fail.[14]

Although tribes on reservations were better off than those outside them, the boundaries of such tracts were so poorly guarded that they did not afford an adequate asylum; and tribal government, whatever its former efficacy, deteriorated through contact with white culture. The agents were the first to become

---

[14] Maltby to D. N. Cooley, Apr. 13, 1866, Bur. Ind. Aff., Ltrs. Rec'd.

aware of the consequences because they were responsible for Indian deportment; some, in the absence of legislative arrangements, made improvisations. Agent John L. Smith, among the Oto and Missouri in Nebraska, in 1866 appointed a police force of six braves to see that everything was "kep strate." The chief agreed to the payment of the force out of tribal annuities because he wanted Indian theft stopped and whiskey shops closed. But it is not known to what extent Smith's subrogation was successful.[15]

Unfortunately, a great number of the superintendents and agents who held office in the 1860's were not concerned about the welfare of their charges. It will be convenient to discuss the superintendents separately and then take up the agents in connection with the more general topic of fraud.

There had developed the practice of appointing the governors of western territories as ex-officio Indian Superintendents. This did not work well because the interests of the two positions were antithetical. The territorial governor was usually concerned with the development of his area in favor of white settlers, and the Indian superintendent was supposed to be dedicated to the red man's welfare. Taking into account the speed with which the frontier moved, the temperament of the western pioneer, and the very sharp adjustment which the Indian was asked to make, it was necessary to compromise the interests of one office in favor of the other.

When Senator J. W. Nesmith of Oregon inquired into the condition of the Nez Percé of Idaho Territory in 1865, Caleb Lyon was governor and ex-officio Indian superintendent. By a treaty concluded with these Indians ten years earlier, they had been assigned a reservation which included the Clearwater River and its tributaries in Idaho Territory, and which stretched westward across the Snake into small portions of Oregon and

---

[15] E. B. Taylor to D. N. Cooley, Oct. 20, 1866, with Smith to Taylor, Sept. 17, 1866, encl., Bur. Ind. Aff., Ltrs. Rec'd.

Washington Territories. Provisions had been made for the establishment of agricultural and industrial schools, and, by the Indians' request, for the exclusion of liquor. Neither provision had been fulfilled and, during the four years immediately preceding, the reservation had been overrun by miners and farmers who were moving eastward from the coast. Buildings had been erected. Lands had been enclosed. Roads, towns, and counties had been laid out. Even the capitol of the Territory had been located within the reservation. And the settlers now expected the federal government to make a new treaty by which the Indians should relinquish what white men had no legal right to possess. No wonder that the Nez Percé chiefs objected. It is amazing that their patience endured so long. Agent O'Neill, a competent official, was doing all that he could to pacify them, but he had been entirely destitute of funds for a full year and the treaty employees had not been paid for eighteen months. Consequently, they had been forced to accept a discount of from forty to fifty per cent on their vouchers in return for personal necessities. Thus, the credit of the Indian Bureau was utterly destroyed. All sorts of merchandise were being sold upon the reservation in open violation of the Intercourse Law, and the merchants in Lewiston claimed the right to this trade on grounds that the federal government was collecting taxes on the goods. O'Neill, the only agent in the Territory, was powerless. He was bound by regulations to conduct all of his correspondence with the Interior Department through the superintendent for his district. Caleb Lyon had been out of Idaho for a considerable part of the year, but even when the Governor was present, Indian affairs were managed with complete disregard for both the rights of the Indians and the laws of the United States concerning relations with them. His carrying on of negotiations with a member of the tribe for the purchase of land on which to establish "New Lyonsdale" was characteristic of most territorial officials.[16]

Lyon was no novelty in his unfitness to manage Indian affairs. Governor G. C. Smith gambled away the funds of the Montana superintendency, while E. M. McCook of Colorado Territory was animated by a desire to open the Ute reservation for the benefit of mining interests and to get appropriations from Congress with which to satisfy the claims of citizens to damages from Indian raids. Upon being relieved of his Indian duties in 1871, McCook agreed that "The interests of the people of the territory, the general government, and the Indians would be better subserved, by separating the offices of governor and superintendent as widely as possible."[17]

Politics often interfered with Indian management. Missouri's Frank Blair was responsible for the replacement of Colorado's first governor and superintendent, General William Gilpin, who understood Indians and spoke their language. Gilpin's main fault was friendship with John C. Fremont, a bitter enemy of Blair's. His successor was John Evans, an Eastern politician whose diplomatic ineptitude was responsible for the Chivington massacre of November 1864. That the Cheyenne and Arapaho were willing to make peace did not matter; the Governor's wisdom in raising a one-hundred-day volunteer regiment at federal expense had to be demonstrated. Thus a short-sighted view that troops enlisted to kill Indians must kill them caused a merciless slaughter at Sand Creek, and in its wake a costly uprising which threatened to close the plains route connecting

---

[16] Charles J. Kappler, ed., *Indian Affairs: Laws and Treaties,* II (Washington, 1904), 528-31. Hereafter cited as Kappler, *Laws and Treaties.* "Report of the Joint Special Committee of Congress on the Condition of the Tribes," Senate Rpt., No. 156, 39th Cong., 2nd Sess., Appendix, 8-10.

[17] G. B. Wright to N. G. Taylor, June 11, 1868 ; C. T. Speer at Denver to Adjutant General, U.S. Army, Feb. 12, 1871 ; J. N. Trask at Los Pinos agency, Colorado Territory, to F. A. Walker, Feb. 13, 1872, with news clipping of Governor's annual message encl., Bur. of Ind. Aff., Ltrs. Rec'd.

Denver with Omaha and Kansas City. No influence was more detrimental to the Indian service than politics.[18]

This interference of politics with Indian administration meant fraud. The term "Indian ring" described any corrupt group which designed to steal from the red man, and numerous such rings were scattered over the country wherever there was an opportunity to exploit Indian annuities. Three principal figures were usually included: the politician, the agent, and the contractor or trader. This triumvirate was interdependent. The politician used his influence to install the agent, who in turn selected a contractor willing to share the Indian annuities which were often paid in cash. Presidential appointments of Indian agents had to be confirmed in the Senate. The Senators were not likely to approve a candidate who was opposed by delegates from the state or territory of his assignment. There was no competition in the purchase of supplies; a single contractor or firm was given a monopoly of the trade. Furthermore, agencies were located in distant places where they were not subject to scrutiny. They were remote from the surveillance either of the Indian Bureau or of intelligent and conscientious citizens, while the Indians were usually too ignorant to protect themselves from imposition and had no means of publicizing dishonesty even when they recognized it. Moreover the Indian bought on credit. Who was to prove at payment time whether the trader had supplied the goods for which he presented vouchers?

Commissioner George W. Manypenny had in 1854 recommended the annulment of all "contracts . . . made by Indian tribes . . . with claim agents, attorneys, traders, or other persons" and the immediate removal from the Indian country of any official or private individual who should in the future become a party to such transactions. The Minnesota legislature

---

[18] Fred Stanton at Denver to D. N. Cooley, Aug. 20, 1865, Bur. Ind. Aff., Ltrs. Rec'd.; Frederic L. Paxson, *The Last American Frontier* (New York, 1910), 259,

had petitioned President Buchanan in 1860 to complain about
roving Indians who were killing stock and game among the
settlements, and had urged "some action on the part of the
government, whereby the Indians may be paid in provisions
instead of money; the credit system abolished among the
traders, whereby the annuity is absorbed before being paid," in
order to remove the cause of their wandering and pilfering.
Minnesotans were becoming alarmed "that the Indians in a
moment of excitement and desire for revenge" might "commit
some high-handed outrage . . ."! The Minnesota massacre was
a little more than two years away.[19]

In 1865 Commissioner D. N. Cooley supposed the Department would not be startled by the novelty of his suggestion that
the agents and traders were often in collusion. He also called
attention to circumstances which engendered fraud, stating
that an innumerable list of applicants for the office of agent
was not proof that the salary of $1,500 was adequate to procure
high-class personnel; it was rather, he said, an indication of
outside income. No other explanation of why agents scurried to
Washington upon a change of administration will do. The
abuses were legion: agency buildings erected and sold to the
government for several times their cost, Texas cattle furnished
at prices of Northern beef, shorts substituted for flour, and
transportation accounts falsified.[20]

That corruption permeated the Indian service in the 1860's
was no secret. Even Governor Horace Austin, who sought the
removal of Minnesota's Indians to the west of the Red River,
deplored the fact that they were attended by "lying, cowardly,
thieving agents who only seek the place because it offers oppor-

---

[19] Ann. Rpt., Senate Exec. Doc. No. 1, 33rd Cong., 2nd Sess., Vol. 1,
229; Minnesota Memorial to Buchanan, Mar. 24, Bur. of Ind. Aff.,
Ltrs. Rec'd.

[20] Ann. Rpt., House Exec. Doc. No. 1, 39th Cong., 1st Sess., Vol. 2,
170; D. S. Stanley to J. D. Cox, Apr. 18, 1869, Bur. of Ind. Aff., Ltrs.
Rec'd.

tunities to plunder the Indians, . . . their superiors in everything
but the capacity for ineffable meanness." Any intention of
running an honest administration was almost certain to be
frustrated, for it was an unusual agent who could hold his
position against the trumped-up charges of an Indian ring.[21]

The condition of Indian affairs had become well enough
publicized by 1865 to prompt a Congressional investigation via
a joint special committee of the House and the Senate. Various
sections of the country were assigned to its members as they
ventured forth to collect data on the problem. After nearly two
years of work, Senator James Doolittle of Wisconsin submitted
their report. The Committee found that everywhere, except in
the Indian Territory, the red men were rapidly decreasing in
numbers. The major causes were disease, intemperance, war,
and starvation. The Indians' culture was being crushed by the
onslaught of white population from both east and west, while
the middle region was overrun by a class of adventurers who
recognized no law other than necessity and self-defense. In their
eager search for gold or fertile tracts of land, the boundaries of
Indian reservations were disregarded; wars followed in which
the Indians were overwhelmed if not exterminated. The building of two lines of railroad across the plains was in process—the
Union Pacific along the valley of the Platte and the Kansas
Pacific by way of the Smoky Hill. They would soon reach the
Rocky Mountains and sever the great range of the buffalo.
Those multitudinous herds would soon be killed off by hide
hunters and sportsmen to whom railroads made the bison
accessible. Two other routes were being projected: one in the
north from Minnesota to the upper Missouri, and the other in
the south from Arkansas by way of the Canadian. The game
was about to disappear, and with it the very foundation of the
Indian's way of life. All the powerful tribes of the plains must
inevitably vanish. There was in the Committee report a strong

---

[21] Austin to J. D. Cox, May 25, 1870, Bur. of Ind. Aff., Ltrs. Rec'd.

impression of "manifest destiny" as they in part ascribed the Indians' decrease to "the irrepressible conflict between a superior and an inferior race when brought in the presence of each other."[22]

These Senators and Representatives did not depend upon personal observation alone for what they reported. Men of integrity and long experience with Indian affairs were consulted: men like Colonel William Bent, Kit Carson, and Generals Pope, Carleton, and Wright, who were in command of the military departments of Missouri, New Mexico, and California respectively. The diseases of which they spoke were smallpox, measles, cholera, scrofula, and syphilis. The intemperance was produced by a veritable flood of whiskey, concerning which there is more correspondence among the letters received by the Commissioners of Indian Affairs between 1860 and 1890 than exists on any other subject. The wars, other than those among the Indians themselves, were in the majority of cases caused by the aggressions of lawless white men; on this Bent and Carson were in agreement. Death by starvation was the consequence of white appropriation of Indian hunting grounds, fisheries, and other sources of subsistence. Driven mad with hunger, many of the tribes became a nuisance to adjacent settlements, demanding and taking food wherever it was available. This, together with an addiction to drunken orgies, caused Western communities to demand their removal or at least their confinement pending other arrangements.

It had been stated over and over again that the Indian adopted the white man's vices much more readily than his virtues. What else could be expected when Anglo-American association with the tribes displayed so much vice and so little virtue?[23]

---

[22] Senate Rpt. No. 156, 39th Cong., 2nd Sess.
[23] Ann. Rpt. of Com. Ind. Aff., House Exec. Doc. No. 1, 38th Cong., 2nd Sess., Vol. 5, 149.

Perhaps it is impossible to select a typical reservation. On some, conditions were fairly good; on others they were appalling. In Oregon, on the eastern side of the coastal mountain range, was Grand Ronde, where more than a thousand Indians were concentrated, the remnant of eight tribes mostly from the Willamette and Umqua valleys. Having made treaties with the government, five of the tribes received annuities, while the rest were dependent upon what limited funds the superintendent could spare from appropriations for removal and subsistence. These annuities and these funds had proved insufficient to overcome an aversion to subsistence by agriculture, but they had been enough to cultivate a habit of depending upon charity. A few Indians farmed on a small scale, but the majority begged from surrounding settlements what the government failed to provide. Their persistent mendicancy multiplied opportunities for procuring whiskey, which in turn contributed to indolence, disease, and demoralization. Within a decade two-thirds of the number originally located at Grand Ronde in 1856 were already dead, prostitution among the women was universal, and syphilis and scrofula were so widespread that their eradication seemed impossible. These were the consequences of a relatively brief association with Anglo-American society. Although Grand Ronde was not representative of the general situation during the middle sixties, conditions there illustrate some effects of continuous white contact with primitive Indians, in conjunction with the pursuance of an obsolete federal policy.[24]

Teaching Indians the value of individual industry was a complicated task. Because farmers, blacksmiths, and carpenters were paid out of annuity funds, Indians regarded them as servants rather than as teachers. They were paid with the Indian's money, therefore it was their duty to perform the Indian's labor. This was a natural assumption on the part of the braves, whose aversion to toil was a tradition. With reference

---

[24] Senate Rpt. No. 156, 39th Cong., 2nd Sess., Appendix, 2-3.

to agriculture, early experiment with common fields had worked out badly. The parceling out of individual patches within the reservation was an improvement, but it was not the answer because the Indian had no assurance of continued possession. Lack of patents in fee simple permitted frequent removals, and Congress was notorious for its failures to provide promised annuities with which necessary equipment and supplies could be bought. All things considered, it was difficult for Indian personnel to be serious about their assignment.[25]

By the end of the sixties, the assimilation of the Indians had become imperative and, ironically, there was no time in the nineteenth century when it was more difficult. Their thorough-going education in a school of depravity was one thing. The location of many of them beyond the region of agriculture was another. But the most perplexing of the obstacles was the fact that time had run out. Every attempt of the past forty years to teach Indians the ways of western European civilization had been dissipated through Congressional lethargy and misdirection. Legislation to carry out educational programs and to cope with problems raised by the advancing frontier failed, despite prodding by the Indian Bureau, because the electorate was unconcerned about the red man's welfare. With the completion of a continental railroad in 1869, the movement of population into the vast spaces of the far West was ten times more rapid than the rate of progress which preceded it had ever been. Frontier movements always upset Indian affairs, and this forward thrust of immigrants destroyed in a single stroke whatever basis may have remained for the old policy. There was no possibility of hurriedly isolating the fierce plains tribes. The Sioux, Cheyenne, Kiowa, Comanche, and Apache were as determined to continue their nomadic tradition as Anglo-

---

[25] Stephen P. Riggs, "The Indian Question," *New Englander*, XV (1857), 260-61 ; Rpt. of Deficiencies in Appropriations for 1869, Senate Exec. Doc. No. 62, 40th Cong., 2nd Sess., Vol. 2, 3-10.

Americans were intent upon the conquest of their broad domain. Cultural divergence precluded mutual understanding and tolerance. Indians who agreed to adopt the white man's way became traitors, no less subject to attack than the invader. It was obvious that subjugation must precede assimilation, but the solution to the Indian problem was not reducible to naked military force, even had sufficient troops been made available. Open war would mean certain death to the solitary rancher, settler, or miner, and bring desolation to many valleys where "manifest destiny" had arrived. It would be utterly inhumane, extremely expensive, and, in view of guerrilla tactics used by mounted Indians, doubtful of success. No wonder Commissioner Nathaniel G. Taylor wrote in 1867 that the Indian problem had reached a crisis.[26]

Yet, in the same year, the joint committee of Congress which had investigated the condition of Indian affairs refused to recognize the need for a new policy. Instead, Indian troubles were attributed to abuses of the old system. The Committee's recommendations for the establishment of boards of inspection, for the endowment of agents and superintendents with the powers of circuit court commissioners, and for the receipt of Indian testimony in all court trials involving Indians, was an attempt at patchwork. Only the section of a proposed bill which provided for inspectors became law, and that in a modified form. Therefore, administrators of Indian affairs were left to handle a deplorable situation as best they could.[27]

---

[26] Rpt. on Indian Hostilities, Senate Exec. Doc. No. 13, 40th Cong., 1st Sess., 5 ; Rpt. of Indian Peace Commission, House Exec. Doc. No. 1, 40th Cong., 3rd Sess., Vol. 1, 504 ; Francis A. Walker, "The Indian Question," *North American Review*, CXVI (1873), 349.

[27] Senate Rpt. No. 156, 39th Cong., 2nd Sess., 8-9 ; 17 U.S. Stat., 463.

II

Roots of the Movement: Early Reformers
and Their Efforts

CONTRARY TO ACCEPTED opinion, the movement to reform
Indian administration and assimilate the Indians did not
originate among Eastern sentimentalists unfamiliar with the
difficulties. For the most part it grew out of the pleas of people
who moved to the western frontier, lived in close association
with the natives, and were shocked by the fraudulent and in-
different management of their affairs. Generally these reformers
had one characteristic in common: a genuine sympathy for
all humanity motivated by a deep-rooted Christian philosophy.

John Beeson, though not affiliated with any church organization, had Quaker sympathies. Coming to the United States
from England around 1830, he settled in Illinois, from which
"Oregon Fever" caused him and numerous other citizens to
move farther west in 1853. Late in September their wagon
train arrived in the Rogue River Valley, which was then a raw
frontier, sparse settlements having been established only in
the vicinity of its headwaters, while the lower and richer part
was occupied by Indians. The fertility of the soil, the mineral
wealth that lay in the gulches of some of its tributaries, and the
fact that it was the main thoroughfare between the Sacramento
and Willamette valleys, combined to make the Rogue River
land extremely desirable. Beeson located on one of the branches
in Jackson County and there, had it not been for a keen
conscience and deep religious conviction, might have spent the
rest of his life developing a farm like any ordinary settler whose
chief concern was the next crop.[1]

---

[1] Of greatest value for information on Beeson's reaction to ill-

He observed that among the thousands who crossed the plains there were many whose only faith was squatter sovereignty, and thought it unfortunate that a large percentage of Oregon's population had come from Missouri, where the Constitution was regarded as a device for subjugating the Negroes—an opinion easily extended to include the Indians. He read in a local newspaper that the natives had nothing in common with humanity but the form, and heard aspirants to public office recommend their extermination. Such declamation was common on the frontier, where Indians were regarded as inferior beings and justification for killing them was not a subject for heavy discourse.[2]

When the Rogue River War broke out in 1855, Beeson defended the Indians on the grounds that white people were the aggressors; he saw the war as a means of satisfying a desire for economic gain—the motive which brought most settlers west. There were benefits beyond the removal of the natives from the land. During the dry season, miners found employment by joining the "volunteers." Farmers supplied work animals and feed appraised at several times their value, and, as if to try the

---

treatment of Indians in Oregon is his *Plea for the Indians* (New York, 1858), which the author has studied intensively. Also consulted were Jasper L. Beeson, *Beeson Genealogy* (Macon, Ga., 1925), 7; T. W. Davenport, "Slavery Question in Oregon," *Oregon Historical Quarterly,* IX (1908), 325; W. C. Gould, Sec. of American Indian Aid Assn., to U.S. Grant, Nov. 28, 1873, and Beeson to R. B. Hayes, Oct. 15, 1877, with Beeson Memorial to the People of the U.S., Sept. 23, 1875, enclosed, Bur. Ind. Aff., Ltrs. Rec'd. Evidence of Beeson's Quaker leanings is to be found in his unmistakably strong admiration for William Penn and the early Quakers, coupled with the fact that his opponents referred to him as "Friend Beeson," and that his respect for the Indians' religion coincided with the position taken by the Hicksite Friends, namely that Indians should be allowed to worship according to their conscience. Furthermore, a large number of Beesons were Quakers.

[2] The climate of public opinion which Beeson described was reflected in the *Oregon Statesman* (Salem, Oregon), July 22, 1856.

limits of rascality, horses were sometimes foundered for the purpose of increasing the profit. The worth of a politician was measured by his ability to persuade the federal government to pay claims whether legitimate or not. Most men of conscience kept silent rather than risk public enmity; nonconformists were almost certain to be declared unpatriotic citizens.[3]

Beeson's nonconformity made him a traitor. For attempting to exercise freedom of speech and of press, he was summoned in May 1856 to a public meeting, at which the chairman read one of his letters from a spring issue of the *New York Tribune.* The editor of the *Sentinel,* a Rogue River paper, presented a manuscript by the same author which refuted Territorial Governor Curry's proclamation that "the Indians commenced the war without just cause." This, together with other pleas for the natives, constituted proof that the writer was an enemy of the people. Several speeches of a violent character were delivered, and when Beeson tried to reply the chairman declared him out of order, saying that the object of the meeting was not to hear him speak but to pronounce judgment on what he had written. Resolutions were adopted which stated that such writings "were the products of a low and depraved intellect, and that it was the duty of every good citizen to stop their circulation."

Because it appeared that the "volunteers" were determined on vengeance, Beeson fled to the capitol of the Territory at Salem, where he was refused an interview with the Governor, and where he learned in dismay that both the *Oregon Statesman* and the *Pacific Christian Advocate* had published the *Sentinel's* version of affairs in the Rogue River Valley. Very few Oregon newspapers were willing to print anything sympathetic to the

---

[3] Major General John E. Wool, Comdr. Mil. Dept. of the Pacific, to Isaac I. Stevens, Gov. of Washington Territory, Feb. 12, 1856. This letter was printed in the *Oregon Statesman,* Apr. 15, 1856, together with Stevens' scathing reply, and supported Beeson's contention that the "volunteers" were murdering innocent Indians.

Indians, and Beeson soon went to San Francisco, where his efforts to draw attention to the Indian question through the press also met with little success. He left California in September 1856, bound for New York City by way of Panama, hoping that in the East his cause would receive a fair hearing. Unfortunately, public interest was then absorbed with bloody Kansas and the presidential election. Negro slavery was the favorite issue, and would not surrender its primacy until after the Civil War.

In *A Plea for the Indians,* published privately in 1858, Beeson argued that it was not civilization which was destroying the original inhabitants, "but the more highly energized Savageism that creeps under its mantle, usurps its prerogative, and does unspeakable wrongs . . . in its name." Considering the liberal tradition of the United States, it was ironical for citizens to demand the extermination of the natives; to at least offer an equivalent for what was taken from them seemed more appropriate. Indians, he said, should receive instruction in every phase of the culture which was displacing their own: Anglo-American economy, democratic self-government, and the Christian religion.

During the Civil War, Beeson visited President Lincoln on numerous occasions and addressed several letters to him, the last of which contained a prophecy: "If you are firm in Justice towards the Indians, Your sunshine on earth will grow brighter and never set, but if you fail to be prompt in Justice, Your Sun will go down to rise no more." Lincoln is said to have replied: "My aged Friend. I have heard your arguments time and again. I have said little but thought much, and you may rest assured that as soon as the pressing matters of this war is [sic] settled the Indians shall have my first care and I will not rest untill Justice is done to their and to your satisfaction.'"

---

⁴ Quoted in Beeson to E. P. Smith, June 25, 1873, and Beeson to R. B. Hayes, June 5, 1879, Bur. Ind. Aff., Ltrs. Rec'd.

From his headquarters at Cooper Institute in New York City, Beeson continued his reform activities through the seventies. As a means of facilitating the consolidation of tribes in the Indian Territory in 1873, he sponsored a proposal to teach Indians a universal language; but because of a lack of funds, or so ran the official explanation, the Bureau of Indian Affairs did not adopt it. Up to that year he had made eight trips to Washington and had spent a part of seven winters there lobbying for the red men. No reform measures can be attributed to Beeson's influence, but his early agitation of the Indian question was the beginning of a long struggle which culminated with legislation of the middle eighties.[5]

Far more important was Henry B. Whipple, an Episcopalian clergyman who was elected Bishop of Minnesota in 1859. After having held a parish at Rome, New York, from 1849 until 1857, and having worked among less-favored residents of Chicago's south side for two subsequent years, Whipple established a home at Faribault in 1860. The Protestant Episcopal church already had a mission among the Mississippi Chippewa at Gull Lake, founded in 1852 by the Reverend James Lloyd Breck. Together with Breck, Whipple visited Gull Lake in the spring of 1860, and during the same year began another mission among the Sioux. The firsthand knowledge of Indian affairs which he gained through personal observation was augmented by frequent correspondence with John J. Enmegahbowh, an Ottawa who was ordained a deacon and sent as an Episcopal missionary to the Chippewa shortly before the Bishop came to Minnesota.

Upon returning from Gull Lake, Whipple addressed a letter to President Buchanan in which he outlined the Indian prob-

---

[5] E. P. Smith to Beeson at Cooper Institute, July 7, 1873, Bur. Ind. Aff., Ltrs. Sent; Beeson Memorial to Congress on Improvement of the Indian Tribes, Apr. 1, 1874, Senate Misc. Doc. No. 94, 43rd Cong., 2nd Sess.; Beeson to R. B. Hayes, May 16, 1879, Bur. Ind. Aff., Ltrs. Rec'd.

lem and made remedial suggestions. The decimating effects of whiskey distressed him most: "In my visits among them my heart has been pained to see them so utterly helpless and fast melting away before a curse our own nation presses to their lips." Liberal distribution of whiskey made good Indian government impossible and caused annual cash annuities to disappear almost as quickly as they were paid. Agents had no means of enforcing federal legislation which forbade the peddling of liquor to Indians; the army, because it was under the direction of a separate department and because reservations were numerous and widely scattered, was not an effective deterrent. Occasionally U.S. marshals made arrests, but partiality in the courts often allowed the guilty to escape. The federal policy of treating the tribes as self-governing nations was mistaken; it would be better to regard Indians as wards and undertake their assimilation. Law enforcement was a fundamental requirement and would be more feasible if United States commissioners with power to try violators of federal Indian legislation were stationed in the vicinity of reservations and if the Indians were concentrated on fewer reserves, thus expediting the task of keeping whiskey peddlers and other degenerates out. Were annuities paid in kind according to the Indians' needs rather than in cash, it would be evidence that the government had a real concern for their welfare. Once civilized means of subsistence were supplied, practical Christian teachers could instruct them in agriculture and other arts of civilization. In recognizing the obsolescence of the policy of dealing with the tribes as if they were semi-independent nations and in recommending the wardship theory, Whipple was more than a decade ahead of Congress, which did not end the treaty system until 1871, and then only in name.[6]

The Bishop was unknown at Washington, and letters of introduction elicited no reply. Undaunted, in March 1862 he

---

[6] Whipple to Buchanan, Apr. 9, 1860, Bur. Ind. Aff., Ltrs. Rec'd.

wrote to President Lincoln, again emphasizing the necessity of a new policy. That political patronage had a corrupting influence on Indian administration was not missed by him: "The Congressional delegates desire to reward John Doe for party work, and John Doe desires the place because there is a tradition on the border that an Indian agent with Fifteen hundred dollars a year can retire upon an ample fortune in four years. The Indian agent appoints his subordinates from the same motives, either to reward his friends' service or to fulfill the bidding of his Congressional patron." No wonder that Indian funds were squandered by fraudulent contracts and that the schools were a sham. Whipple called for an end to the system of political appointments and stated that "every employee ought to be a man of purity, temperance, industry, and unquestioned integrity." Good schools were an absolute necessity and would require competent and dedicated teachers. Many of his earlier suggestions were repeated or elaborated upon: because law and order was a requirement of Indian assimilation, the federal government must establish legal machinery on consolidated reservations; tribal annuities should be paid in goods; aid given in the building of houses; agricultural implements furnished; and land distributed individually to tribal members with inalienable patents.[1]

Lincoln sent Whipple's letter, together with the one he had written to Buchanan, to the Secretary of the Interior, Caleb B. Smith, and requested that he give their contents special consideration. Smith sent copies to the committees on Indian affairs in both Houses of Congress, and recommended three changes: isolation of the tribes from white contact by concentrating them on reserves of sufficient extent to provide a farm for each Indian, abolition of the credit system of trading with the natives, and payment of annuities with "goods, pro-

[1] Henry B. Whipple Letter Book, 1861-1864, Minnesota Historical Society, St. Paul.

visions and agricultural implements, at cost prices." The Secretary was alarmed lest, should Indians continue to buy on credit, the remainder of their lands should be absorbed by fraudulent claims; but he doubted whether a reform of the Indian service were possible because it would require the co-operation of Congress, which seemed unlikely.[8]

At this time Cyrus Aldrich of Minnesota was chairman of the House Committee on Indian Affairs, and Senator Martin S. Wilkinson, also of Minnesota, was serving on the Indian Committee of the Senate. Both of them wrote to Whipple. Aldrich said that he was not aware that the condition of the Indians in his state was any worse than that of other Indians elsewhere in the West, or that their affairs were more mismanaged. He agreed that the current system for managing Indian matters was defective in numerous respects, but pointed out that, having been developed by past administrations, it was based upon considerable experience and observation. What should be done was a question more easily asked than answered. Moreover, Whipple's letters contained nothing "more than general allegations and undefined charges." Certainly the Bishop could not have ascribed dishonesty or incapacity to agents at present employed in Minnesota, for whose appointment Aldrich considered himself responsible! And so far as any elaborate schemes in regard to civilizing the Indians were concerned, the Minnesota Representative retorted that in his opinion it was very questionable "whether under the most favorable circumstances the native aborigine 'to the manor born' is capable of attaining a high or even mediocre state of civilization."[9]

The tone of Wilkinson's epistle was much the same. Allusions to abuses in the service, of course, had reference to Buchanan's administration. These had now been remedied, since the

---

[8] Smith to Whipple, Mar. 31, 1862, Whipple Papers.
[9] Aldrich to Whipple, June 12, 1862, Whipple Papers.

Senator had been "somewhat instrumental in procuring the appointments of the present Superintendent & Agents in Minnesota. . . ." If the Bishop had some specific charges to make which he could sustain by the testimony of respectable witnesses, then some action would be taken. The trouble was not with persons; it was the system that needed attention, but to frame a new one would require considerable time and thought. The Indian question was embarrassing; perhaps the Bishop knew of a solution that would remove all of the difficulties. True, the schools were a sham, but this only proved that the government was squandering its money on the enterprise. "So long as an Indian feels that his mode of savage life is preferable to the civilization of his white neighbor, just so long your efforts to educate him will prove abortive, because education in no wise aids him in the gratification of savage ambition." Endeavors to civilize or Christianize "an idle race of Barbarians" could not succeed until the latter had been induced to labor and until they had adopted the objects of white men. Both Aldrich and Wilkinson introduced bills, but also indicated that they were too much occupied with Civil War business to spend much time on Indian matters. Considering the anti-Indian sentiment among their constituents, this was a convenient excuse.[10]

While Minnesota representatives were saving their political shirts by these evasions, the horrible vision of a massacre which had been portrayed in the Minnesota legislature's memorial to the President of March 24, 1860, materialized. Congress and the treasury delayed the annuity. Four insolent braves whose request for whiskey was denied murdered five settlers at Acton; Little Crow gave them protection and there followed the Sioux uprising of August 1862. Another cause of this catastrophe,

---

[10] Wilkinson to Whipple, May 8 and Aug. 11, 1862, Whipple Papers. The latter contains the statement: "We are slowly recovering from the effects of the recent disasters in front of Richmond."

which took the lives of several hundred pioneers, is seldom mentioned: the fact that since the beginning of the decade settlers in the vicinity of New Ulm had occupied the southern portion of the Sioux reserve.[11]

During the aftermath of that dreadful event, Whipple distinguished himself by showing compassion both for the victims of the massacre and for the Sioux. On the one side he attended the wounded and consoled the bereaved; on the other, he published articles in the St. Paul newspapers pointing out that the Indians had exercised the only means of defense left to them. His articles only served to infuriate the frontier population, but he stood his ground and through a personal visit to Washington succeeded in saving most of 303 braves whom a military commission at Mankato had condemned to the hangman's rope. He could not, however, prevent the expulsion of the Santee Sioux from the state; some of them were moved to Lake Traverse and Devil's Lake in Dakota Territory, and others to Niobrara in Nebraska Territory.[12]

In November 1862, Whipple enlisted the services of Senator Henry M. Rice, and through him presented to President Lincoln a memorial which carried the signatures of eighteen bishops of the Episcopal church. They asked for the appointment of "a commission of men of high character, who have no political ends to subserve," which should be given the responsibility for devising a more perfect system for administering Indian affairs. The President was impressed with the document, and called the attention of Congress to the subject in his annual message: "I submit for your especial consideration whether our Indian

---

[11] William Pfaender at New Ulm to Lincoln, Apr. 3, 1861, encl. petition with 32 signatures, Bur. Ind. Aff., Ltrs. Rec'd. The petitioners were settled on the reservation and asked the federal government for protection from the Santee Sioux. Kenneth Carley, *The Sioux Uprising of 1862* (St. Paul, 1961), 17-18.

[12] *Saint Paul Pioneer*, Dec. 3 and 17, 1862; *Saint Paul Press*, Dec. 4, 1862.

system shall not be remodeled. Many wise and good men have impressed me with the belief that this can be profitably done."[13]

Rice was not in agreement with Whipple's view that the captive Sioux should be treated as prisoners of war rather than as murderers, but he promised the Bishop his hearty support on the question of reform. At the same time the Senator thought that there was little cause for optimism because his term of office was about over. Retiring members generally had little influence, and little would be achieved unless other Senators supported his proposals. Rice's appeal to the Indian Committee in open Senate for consideration of the President's declaration went unheeded; in the midst of the Civil War Lincoln found time for the Indian question, but Congress did not. Yet one thing was accomplished before Rice left Washington: in keeping with Whipple's views, he wrote the Mississippi Chippewa Treaty of 1863, which provided for a board of visitors made up of Christian men, to attend to the payment of annuities, at least one-half of which were to be distributed in kind. Also, the board was to report on the qualifications and moral deportment of personnel assigned to the Chippewa agency. It is interesting that all of Rice's service was performed within the lame-duck period and that the Senator did not want his work publicized.[14]

Whipple served on the early Boards of Visitors and thus was afforded additional opportunities for observing the management of Indian affairs. He became particularly concerned that there was already a movement afoot, under the nominal leadership of the wily Chippewa chief, Hole in the Day, to break up the Chippewa treaty which had just been made. On this he commented:

The secret of this constant intermedling [sic] with treaties is that

---

[13] Rice to Whipple, Nov. 19 and 27, 1862, Whipple Papers; Richardson, *Messages*, VI, 132.

[14] Rice to Whipple, Nov. 19 and 27 and Dec. 4, 1862; Feb. 7 and Mar. 18, 1863, Whipple Papers; Kappler, *Laws and Treaties*, II, 841.

it is the surest way to unlock the treasury. The chiefs—the traders—the interpreters—the outsiders all have their palms crossed with "the siller" and the political manager knows how to use them all. The poor Indian goes to Washington and someone feeds him with fine promises, he is told he & his are to become like prosperous white men he saw on his way hither—he thinks all these pledges are in the bond—he goes home & the story is told in wigwam and council. Then comes defered [sic] hope—his lands gone his hunting grounds lost—his annuity & civilization funds taken—no government—no law—no home, irritation & fire water do the rest—he becomes an outlaw and at length only a choice of deaths is before him and he rushes with the madness of a demon into massacre & murder.[15]

Whipple shifted his appeal to the Commissioner of Indian Affairs, William P. Dole, saying that it was not new treaties which were needed, but "Christian manliness to fulfill old ones." Congress must pass the necessary appropriations to make this possible, and the tribes must be provided with government. Protect Indians from the "harpies" who goad them to madness and murder; give them homes and property; educate their children; devise a just system for trade; and appoint agents who "fear God and are ashamed to steal." This, together with the conversion of the tribes to Christianity, was the formula for Indian assimilation which the Bishop repeated over and over again.[16]

In October 1864, support came from an unexpected quarter. Brigadier General Alfred Sully, who commanded the North-Western Indian Expedition sent to make a show of force among the Teton Sioux, wrote from Dakota Territory that the easiest way to exterminate a wild Indian was to civilize him. As a

---

[15] J. Usher, Sec. of the Interior, to Whipple, May 9, 1863, Whipple Papers, names the first Board of Visitors. Other members were Catholic Bishop Thomas L. Grace and Rev. Thomas S. Williamson of the Presbyterian church. The quotation is from a copy of Whipple to W. P. Dole, Nov. 24, 1863, Thomas S. Williamson Papers, Minnesota Historical Society, St. Paul.

[16] *Ibid.*

means of bringing white culture to the tribes, he proposed a partnership between the government and the missionary societies. Although adult Indians were incapable of adjustment to a different mode of life, a wise program might acculturate the next generation. Certainly a policy aimed at the eventual incorporation of the natives within Anglo-American society would have greater merit than a war of extermination; for, aside from humanitarian considerations, to hunt down and shoot everything that wore a blanket would be extremely expensive. Sully believed that many Indians among the hostiles would voluntarily live near military posts if provision were made for their subsistence. The braves would make excellent scouts and soldiers for the purpose of compelling the roaming bands to surrender—the General had already directed fifty friendly Yankton Sioux, whose usefulness against the hostiles was proved, to erect lodges outside Fort Rice. Similar camps at each of the military posts in Dakota would serve as nuclei for the collection of Indians who might desert the hostiles on the basis that the government would supply their needs. The presence of the military would assure good order, and missionaries could come to the posts and establish schools where Indian boys and girls could receive a vocational education and perhaps, from the example of their teachers, learn something of Christian virtue."

General Sully was of the opinion that the maintenance of peace with the tribes was possible if the government adopted a just policy and furnished them with honest agents and traders. That very autumn, on his way down to Fort Randall, he encountered most of the Yankton Sioux headed north to hunt with the hostile bands because their annuities had not been delivered, and he dreaded the reports of the white man's

---

" Copies of Sully at Camp opposite Farm Island on the Missouri River to Asst. Adj. Gen., Mil. Dept. of the N. W., Oct. 7, 1864, and Sully at Ft. Sully to Asst. Adj. Gen., Mil. Dept. of Mo., Sept. 14, 1865, Bd. Ind. Com., Ltrs. Rec'd.

"justice" which they would spread. He knew that theirs was no isolated case, for at Crow Creek the Indians had also been starved out. Besides paying annuities promptly, Sully thought that three things might be done to assure subsistence: let the three senior officers at the military post nearest each agency serve as a "Council of Administration" and report the worth of supplies delivered, make trade competitive by requiring at least two independent contractors on every reservation, and disallow claims growing out of the extension of credit.[18]

Whipple's position was sustained elsewhere. In reply to a questionnaire circulated by the joint committee of Congress which investigated Indian affairs between 1865 and 1867, Superintendent W. H. Waterman of Washington Territory stated that only Christian influence could save the Indians from extinction. Intemperance and prostitution were prevalent among the natives under his jurisdiction, and especially where they were located in the vicinity of towns. A majority of deaths were traceable to "licentious intercourse with debased white men who induce them to the practice . . . with intoxicating drinks." Where agencies were located at a great distance from commercial centers and where they were run by Christian men, the situation was much improved. He alluded to a particular agency with a missionary agent and Christian employees which had "less of immorality, less of disease, less decay, more industry, more agriculture, more mechanical art, better habitations, and in every respect more of the comforts of civilized life . . . than any other in the territory." The superintendent wished that all agencies might be similarly administered, and suggested the propriety of appointing United States commissioners to try federal Indian cases, of conducting schools on a manual labor basis, of paying annuities in supplies rather than

---

[18] Copy of Sully at Milwaukee, Wis., to Asst. Adj. Gen., Mil. Dept. of the N.W., Nov. 22, 1864.

in money, and of allotting land in severalty with an inalienable title.[19]

Since 1863 Whipple's plan for the creation of "a commission of men of high character" to devise a new system for the management of Indian matters had been supported by William Welsh, an Episcopalian and a merchant in Philadelphia. Following Lincoln's message to Congress, Welsh had gone to Washington to aid Rice in his appeal to the Senate. Both men understood, however, that the test of any policy would be made in the field. Working together in 1866, they succeeded in having a bill introduced which provided for boards of inspection selected from among candidates nominated by the various religious denominations. All the tribal reservations from Minnesota westward would be included within five districts, with a board responsible for each district. The inspectors would make annual visits to the agencies, examine accounts, try violators of the law, remove delinquent agents, and make recommendations for improvement of the service. Other provisions would sanction Indian testimony in all courts where Indian matters were on trial; give inspectors, superintendents, and agents the authority of circuit court commissioners; and raise agents' salaries to $1,800 per year. The boards of inspection appear to have been a projection on a national scale of the Chippewa board of visitors, with added powers and significance. The essential parts of the bill were recommended by the joint committee of Congress which submitted its report early in 1867.[20]

Another champion of this measure was Samuel F. Tappan, whose activity lends weight to the thesis that Indian reform was largely a matter of Christian conscience, nurtured in the

---

[19] Waterman to Senator James R. Doolittle, Aug. 31, 1865, Bur. Ind. Aff., Ltrs. Rec'd.

[20] Rice to Whipple, Feb. 3, 1863; copy of Whipple to Sec. of the Interior, June 1, 1866; and Welsh to Whipple, Apr. 15, 1870, Whipple Papers; *Congressional Globe* (Mar. 19, 1866), 485-86. Whipple referred to these inspectors as "a board of commissioners . . . who fear God."

East, reacting in the West. A youthful Boston chair-maker during the early fifties, Tappan was incensed by the forcible return of Negro refugees to the South and, with encouragement from such notables as William Lloyd Garrison, Theodore Parker, and Wendell Phillips, joined the first company of Massachusetts emigrants to Kansas, where he figured importantly in the free-state movement. Then, in 1860, he moved on to Colorado Territory, which during the Civil War awarded him the rank of lieutenant colonel in the 1st Cavalry Regiment. Once the slaves were emancipated, Tappan found an outlet for his reform energies in behalf of the Indians. Writing to William Windom, chairman of the House committee on Indian affairs, he contended that the inspection bill would supply exactly what was needed: "Some tribunals where the Indians can be heard and those who do them wrong can be punished, where the Indians can obtain justice if in the right and be punished if in the wrong. A tribunal having control and supervision of our Indian Affairs in the respective districts, to establish the policy to be pursued, to inspect the acts of Indian Agents and . . . if guilt is discovered to suspend from office the criminal."[21]

The inspection bill also won the enthusiastic endorsement of the Society of Friends, and, after extensive modification, finally became law in 1873. More significantly, the fight over it produced an alliance between the Episcopal and Quaker organizations of far-reaching importance to the cause of assimilation. From 1866 forward, Bishop Whipple corresponded regularly with Benjamin Hallowell, the Quaker educator of Sandy Spring, Maryland, who led the Hicksite group in the movement to secure justice for the Indian. Hallowell's interest in humani-

---

[21] Tappan to Windom, May 22, 1866, Bur. Ind. Aff., Ltrs. Rec'd.; Daniel L. Tappan, *Tappan-Toppan Genealogy: Ancestors and Descendants of Abraham Tappan of Newbury, Massachusetts, 1606-1672* (Arlington, Mass., 1915), 52-53. There are several references to Tappan's participation in the free-state movement in William E. Connelley, *History of Kansas,* 2 vols. (Chicago, 1883).

tarian movements was long established, as he had been one of the founders in 1827 of an organization to secure legal rights for Negro slaves. For more than thirty years prior to the Civil War the Quakers, whose sympathy for the red man was a tradition, were almost completely occupied with black emancipation; but the freeing of the slaves allowed them, as it did Colonel Tappan, to devote their reform energies to the Indians' cause. The aid of the Friends proved invaluable to the general effort at Washington, and to Bishop Whipple in his work among the Chippewa of Minnesota.[22]

The Chippewa board of visitors had not been a panacea for corrupt practices. George Bonga reported from Leech Lake in 1866 that since the Treaty of 1863 ". . . they have kept the annuitie goods & Money pretty straight," but suggested that there was still much fraud in utility, transportation, and school funds. He also complained of the trading monopoly which had been awarded to the firm of Aspinwall, Ruffee, and Nash, and stated that four months after the appointment of Edwin Clark as agent, his position had been largely usurped by Charles Ruffee. When Clark, in 1866, was forced to vacate his office, Ruffee maneuvered himself into the position, but encountered the opposition of Whipple, who used his personal friendship with Secretary of the Interior Orville H. Browning to get the contractor removed before the Senate voted on confirmation. Having thus interfered with the "spoils system," Browning named an agent of the Bishop's choice, Joel Bassett. Reared a Quaker in New Hampshire and a man of strong religious convictions, Bassett was independent of church dogma; a talented administrator, he eventually became prominent in the lumber and flour milling industries of Minnesota. His confirmation by the Senate owed much to lobbyists from the Society of Friends. For chief clerk Bassett chose James Bean, who was also of

---

[22] 17 U.S. Stat., 463 ; Hallowell to Whipple, May 31, 1866, and Hallowell to James Bean, Mar. 15, 1867, Whipple Papers.

Quaker background; but the filling of lesser offices with reliable personnel proved very difficult. As was typical of any attempt at honest administration, rumors were soon circulating that Bassett and his employees were guilty of numerous misdemeanors, the most serious of which was that of colluding to profit from the contract for the removal of the Mille Lac band of Chippewa to White Earth. An investigation by special agent A. S. Paddock in 1868 found that "Bassett could not have made any money . . . to divide with anyone"; the only sworn evidence was an affidavit of D. L. Mous presented at Washington by Charles Ruffee. But this did not settle the question; the Indian ring was determined to have the agent ousted; whiskey dealers poisoned the Chippewa mind and defamatory stories were spread in St. Paul. In compliance with a request from Whipple, the Interior Department sent a second investigator, A. Jobe, who offered an opinion that Ruffee had inspired and organized the whole trouble. Still the Indian ring remained unbeaten; upon learning in December 1868 that the Chippewa were starving on their new reservation at White Earth because traders would not deliver supplies, the Bishop instructed Bassett to resign.[23]

Through a voluminous correspondence and seven visits to Washington on the Indians' behalf, Whipple had gained much respect. Horatio Seymour, twice governor of New York and Democratic nominee for President in 1868, had commended his views on Indian affairs to Andrew Johnson, and Interior Sec-

---

[23] Bonga to Whipple, Oct. 21 and Nov. 14, 1866; copy of Whipple to D. N. Cooley, Sept. 18, 1866; Browning to Whipple, Nov. 9, 1866; copy of Whipple to Bassett, Nov. 14, 1867; Bassett to Whipple, Nov. 15, 1867; Whipple to Browning, Dec. 17, 1867; photostat of Whipple to "My Dear Friend" (Browning), July 26, 1868; S. G. Wright, missionary at Leech Lake, to Whipple, Aug. 19, 1868; Bonga to Whipple, Aug. 22, 1868; Paddock to Whipple, Aug. 28, 1868; photostat of Whipple to Browning, Dec. 21, 1868, Whipple Papers; Jobe to N. G. Taylor, Oct. 24, 1868, Bur. Ind. Aff., Ltrs. Rec'd. A sketch of Bassett's life is in Isaac Atwater, ed., *History of Minneapolis*, I (New York, 1893), 539-43.

retary Browning relied upon him that year to help prevent the transfer of the Indian Bureau to the War Department. Even Congress extended him recognition, for in July 1868 he was named supervisor of appropriations for the Sisseton and Wahpeton Sioux, who had been removed after the Minnesota massacre to Dakota Territory. This appointment meant that Whipple's contention that Indians should be given incentive to labor was placed on trial; other than aid to the sick and aged the money was for the purchase of agricultural implements, clothing, groceries, and other provisions to benefit those Indians who were endeavoring to raise crops.[24]

The Lake Traverse experiment, as we may call it from the location of most of the Santee in Dakota, was not a simple proposition. Even though these particular Sioux had not participated in the Minnesota massacre, their annuities had been confiscated following that event and their suffering had been extreme. No buffalo entered their region during the summer of 1868, and though ducks and geese were plentiful in the autumn, they were not able to procure meat that could be preserved for winter use. Some of them had tried to farm, preparing the ground with knives and sticks, but most of the small amount of seed furnished by the Indian Bureau had arrived too late in the season. By November the diet of many was limited to bark and roots; if they were not provided subsistence on the government's bounty, death from starvation seemed certain.[25]

It was obvious that the first requirement was to feed and clothe these Indians—an undertaking which alone might absorb the $45,000 appropriated by Congress. The problem of getting provisions to the reservation before winter set in was critical

---

[24] Copy of Seymour to Johnson, Nov. 15, 1866 ; Browning to Whipple, Dec. 26, 1868, Whipple Papers ; 15 U.S. Stat., 217 ; Kappler, *Laws and Treaties,* II, 958.

[25] 1st Lieut. Charles E. Jewett at Fort Wadsworth to Whipple, Nov. 16, 1868, Whipple Papers.

and, to meet this emergency, Whipple secured the aid of General William T. Sherman, who permitted him to purchase supplies at cost from the Army commissariats at Forts Ransom, Totten, and Wadsworth. He was also granted permission by the Indian Bureau to buy in an open and therefore competitive market, thus attaining a threefold bargaining advantage in price, quality, and deliverability of goods. As a business agent, the Bishop was extraordinary: several firms were persuaded to sell at cost, one of them donated five hundred dollars, and another "neglected" to send a bill for twenty-five kegs of nails.[26]

Apparently, many of these Sioux were willing to labor. Dr. Jared W. Daniels, their physician prior to 1862 and Whipple's representative at Lake Traverse, said that he had never witnessed "such complete & universal humiliation," and did not doubt the sincerity of many who expressed a desire to cultivate the land. General J. G. Wistler offered the same opinion concerning the bands at Devil's Lake near Fort Totten: "They are ready to go to work & there should be some reliable person here to show them how." Under Whipple's supervision, the alternative for able-bodied male Indians was to labor or receive no rations. Once axes, handsaws, and other tools were furnished, the Sisseton and Wahpeton Sioux spent the winter splitting rails and cutting logs in preparation for a permanent settlement.[27]

The Bishop pledged that it was the government's design to provide them with means to cultivate their land, and Congress was induced to appropriate an additional $60,000, with which agricultural necessities were purchased in the spring. At Devil's Lake the Indians prepared the ground with hoes, and crops

---

[26] Copy of Whipple to "My Dear Friend" (Browning), Sept. 9, 1868; telegram from Sherman at St. Louis to Whipple, Sept. 14, 1868; N. G. Taylor to Whipple, Aug. 18, 1868; photostat of Whipple to J. W. Smith, 2nd Auditor of the U.S. Treasury, Jan. 25, 1869, Whipple Papers.

[27] Daniels to Whipple, Nov. 17, 1868; Wistler to Whipple, Dec. 5, 1868; photostat of Whipple to Browning, Jan. 25, 1869, Whipple Papers.

were planted in the proper season; at Lake Traverse, using work cattle and plows, more than three hundred acres were placed under cultivation. So impressed was the Indian Bureau that in July Daniels, who had acted merely as Whipple's liaison officer, became agent. Had it not been for drought and grasshoppers, one hundred and forty out of sixteen hundred Sioux might have been self-supporting by 1871. As it was, their crops were destroyed annually until 1878 when with seventeen hundred acres under cultivation the Indians reaped an abundant harvest. Except that the region was not entirely suited to agriculture, there can be little question but that Whipple's approach to the problem of Indian assimilation was correct. After thirty-six years of experience, James McLaughlin, one of the best agents who ever served in the West, called it "a wise arrangement."[28]

By the end of the sixties, the Bishop's health was impaired and he went abroad to seek medical care. Fortunately the reform of Indian administration had gained enough supporters so that it did not suffer during his absence. Even Horace Greeley, editor of the *New York Tribune,* to whom Whipple had written at great length in 1867, had been stirred to make a quest for articles on the status of Indian affairs. Of most importance to the success of the movement, however, was the Society of Friends. Their enthusiasm for Indian assimilation had won Whipple the honor of addressing the Quaker conven-

---

[28] 15 U.S. Stat., 315; photostat of Whipple to J. W. Smith, Jan. 25, 1869; Daniels to Whipple, Apr. 24, 1869; Peter Sutherland, farmer at Fort Totten, to Whipple, May 21, 1869; Daniels to Whipple, June 22, 1869; copy of E. S. Parker to Daniels, July 13, 1869; Daniels to Whipple, Jan. 4, 1871, Whipple Papers; Ann. Rpt. of agent Daniels, House Exec. Doc. No. 1, 42nd Cong., 2nd Sess., Vol. 3, 947; Ann. Rpt. of agent E. C. Hooper, House Exec. Doc. No. 1, 45th Cong., 3rd Sess., Vol. 9, 536-37. Francis A. Walker, "The Indian Question," *North American Review,* CXVI (1873), 362-63, substantiates the fact that these Indians had made considerable progress in agriculture. The quotation from James McLaughlin appears in *My Friend the Indian* (New York, 1910), 23. McLaughlin was agent at Standing Rock.

tion at Baltimore on October 31, 1867, and the alliance between the two churches which that event suggested was instrumental in launching the "Peace Policy" for which the years of Grant are famous.[29])

---

[29] Whipple to Horace Greeley via "My Dear Brother" (George Whipple), Feb. 28, 1867; B. Hallowell to Whipple, Nov. 12, 1867; Grenville M. Weeks, physician at Red Lake, to Whipple, Mar. 13, 1868; photostat of Whipple to Browning, May 20, 1869; J. D. Cox to Whipple, Oct. 4, 1869; copy of H. H. Sibley at St. Paul to W. S. Hancock, Comdr. Mil. Dept. of Dakota, Oct. 26, 1869, Whipple Papers. Whipple's letter to Greeley circulated and was read before a meeting of the Society of Friends; Greeley invited Weeks to write a series of articles for the *New York Tribune* for which Weeks credited the Bishop's influence.

III

Making Grant's "Peace Policy"

THE GOVERNMENT BEGAN in 1865 to make contracts with the various missionary societies for the maintenance of Indian schools for teaching agricultural and mechanical arts. This was a continuance of a plan for federal aid to Indian education begun with the American Board of Commissioners for Foreign Missions as early as 1818. The chief clerk of the Indian Office reported in 1825 that there were thirty-eight denominational schools east of the Mississippi River, and in Arkansas and Missouri, through which the government expended an Indian civilization fund amounting to only $13,550. Sixteen of these institutions were run by the American Board of Commissioners for Foreign Missions, seven by the Baptist General Convention, six by the United Foreign Missionary Society, and two by the United Brethren. The Methodist and Episcopal churches, the Society of Jesus, the Cumberland Missionary Board, the Society for Propagating the Gospel, the Western Missionary Society, and the Synod of South Carolina and Georgia each had one. Commissioner William Medill had written in 1847, "In every system which has been adopted for promoting the cause of education among the Indians, the Department has found its most efficient and faithful auxiliaries . . . in the societies of the several Christian denominations." Federal aid had been provided for academic education. Now, in the post-Civil War period, the government was seeking the cooperation of missionary groups in its program of vocational instruction.[1]

There was nothing revolutionary about a partnership

---

[1] Ann. Rpts., Senate Exec. Docs. No. 2, 19th Cong., 1st Sess., Vol. 1, 89-92 ; and No. 1, 30th Cong., 1st Sess., Vol. 1, 749. Arkansas was then a territory.

between church and state for the purpose of preparing Indians to adopt Anglo-American culture. (The churches had been partners all along, and the government came to rely upon them more completely as the need to assimiliate the Indians grew.) The first of the vocational-education contracts was concluded with the Indiana Yearly Meeting of Friends for a school among the Shawnee in Kansas) For many years prior to 1832, when the Shawnee were removed from Ohio, the Friends had maintained a mission among them, and since 1835 they had also undertaken rudimentary academic education. With encouragement from the Reverend E. E. L. Taylor of the Baptist Home Mission Society, who was named special agent to inquire into the condition of Indian schools and into possibilities for educational advancement, a concentrated effort was made, in 1866 and 1867, to bring other religious groups into this work. The terms offered by the Interior Department were that each denomination should agree to provide the Indian pupils with "a good English Education, teach the boys the use of Agricultural Implements and tools, the girls sewing, knitting, and housewifery, and to furnish Board, clothing, medicine, medical attendance, books, stationery, and to do whatever may tend to advance them in knowledge and promote their well being." In return for these services, the government would furnish a school house surrounded by one hundred and sixty acres of land, and seventy-five dollars per annum for each Indian student received by the particular society.[2]

The specifications of these contracts bear close resemblance to suggestions made by Alfred Sully in 1864. The General had

---

[2] Quart. Rpt. of Elisha Parker, Supt. of Friends Manual Labor School at Friends Mission, July 1, 1865; Taylor to D. N. Cooley, Com. Ind. Aff., July 30, 1866; Jas. Harlan, Sec. Interior, to Cooley, Aug. 27, 1866; W. Hadley and Jas. Stanley to Enoch Hoag, Ind. Supt. at Lawrence, Kan., Dec. 30, 1869, Bur. Ind. Aff., Ltrs. Rec'd. Cooley to S. B. Treat, Corr. Sec. Amer. Bd. Com. For. Missions, at Boston, Sept. 13, 1866, Bur. Ind. Aff., Ltrs. Sent.

written: "I would propose that our Missionary Societies furnish the necessary missionaries and support them, and the Government pay all other expenses." Also, he proposed that the missionaries should "establish Schools, teach a certain number of young children and support and clothe them, learn [sic] the boys a trade or to farm and the girls to cook and sew and above all to be cleanly in their habits." Beyond Sully's advice, this approach to assimilation may be explained by the fact that the men who ran the Indian Bureau through most of this decade were churchmen. Among these were William P. Dole, James Harlan, Orville H. Browning, and Nathaniel G. Taylor. They were of the opinion that many of the difficulties which complicated Indian affairs could be alleviated through the implementation of Christian principles, and through the moral influence of Christian men, were such men placed in direct contact with the tribes on Western reservations.[3]

George Hyde has remarked that by 1865 Indian matters were controlled in Washington by visionaries with their heads in the clouds, who based their policy on the doctrine that "the Indians were always in the right and the frontier white population always in the wrong, that the Indians were good people who would never cause trouble if dealt with in a Christian spirit of kindness and forbearance." Hyde has written further: "These humanitarians and idealists were quite unconscious of the fact that a great crisis had come in the Plains region, where the tribes were determined to oppose any further encroachment on their lands and the whites were firmly bent on opening up the region to settlement." These statements are not in accord with the facts.[4]

Admittedly, Commissioner Dole wrote in his annual report for 1861 that the good effects which were derived from the

---

[3] Copy of Sully at Camp opposite Farm Island on the Mo. R., Dak. Terr., to Asst. Adj. Gen., Dept. of the N. W., Oct. 7, 1864, Bd. Ind. Com., Ltrs. Rec'd.

[4] *Red Cloud's Folk* (Norman, Okla., 1937), 136-37.

presence of missionaries among the tribes could more easily be imagined than described. His enthusiasm about this did convey the impression that the Indians could not avoid adaptation to the "white man's ways" in a short time; but within three years, Dole's optimism had given way to sober reflection upon the many difficulties which grew out of contact between the two races. He not only admitted that his efforts to define a new policy were incomplete, but declared "Indian civilization" the most perplexing of all political problems. His successor, D. N. Cooley, said in 1866 that the Indian troubles had continually increased as white population crowded westward, and Commissioner Taylor applied the term "crisis" to this situation in 1867.[5]

James Harlan, twice president of Iowa Wesleyan College and an active Methodist all of his life, was Secretary of the Interior in 1865. He believed that the churches could be of great aid to the Indian service by supplying a needed moral influence as well as vocational instructors. Yet he was not merely an idealist, since his concern was that the Indians should not become a perpetual burden to the white community by reason of their growing wants. Harlan had no mistaken notions of Indian goodness, for he had been reared on the Iowa frontier and spoke of their "perfidious conduct" in having made unprovoked war upon the United States in 1861. His successor, O. H. Browning, was of the opinion that the Indians were fully capable of adopting the white man's culture and that Christianity ought to be the crowning influence. It would take time; but he pointed out, "The arts of civilization . . . slowly displaced the primitive tastes and habits of our own race." He designed to teach the Indians habits of industry after they had been

---

[5] Ann. Rpts., Senate Exec. Doc. No. 1, 37th Cong., 2nd Sess., Vol. 1, 645; House Exec. Docs. No. 1, 38th Cong., 2nd Sess., Vol. 5, 149; and No. 1, 39th Cong., 2nd Sess., Vol. 2, 2. Rpt. on Ind. Hostilities, Senate Exec. Doc. No. 13, 40th Cong., 1st Sess., 5.

gathered upon reservations. In the transitional period, it was "more humane and economical to subsist Indians than to fight them." The frontier had characteristics which severely limited the application of this plan, but reflection upon twentieth-century history of Indian affairs causes Browning's "vision" to look like foresight.[6]

The crisis which had come on the plains meant war. Hostilities led to Chivington's butchery of the Cheyenne and Arapaho at Sand Creek near Fort Lyon, Colorado, in November 1864. The Indians sought revenge during the winter by raiding ranches and mail stations in the Platte Valley. This outbreak had become so serious by the spring of 1865 that eight thousand U.S. troops were withdrawn from the effective force then engaged in the final phase of the Civil War and sent against these plains tribes. In October, Generals William Harney and John Sanborn, accompanied by William Bent, Kit Carson, Jesse Leavenworth, and James Steele, met tribal representatives on the Little Arkansas River in Kansas and concluded a treaty of peace. The Cheyenne and Arapaho agreed to exchange their southeastern Colorado reservation for one in southern Kansas and in the Indian Territory between the Arkansas and Cimarron Rivers. A line from the mouth of Buffalo Creek on the Cimarron due north to the Arkansas was the western boundary. The object was to remove the tribes from the Colorado region, which was invaded by a host of prospective miners at the close of the Civil War.[7]

Frontier editors who clamored in their newspapers for extermination of the Indians were unrealistic. As Secretary Harlan pointed out, "The military operations of last summer have not

---

[6] Ann. Rpts., House Exec. Docs. No. 1, 39th Cong., 1st Sess., Vol. 2, vii, ix; and No. 1, 40th Cong., 2nd Sess., Vol. 3, viii, ix.

[7] Rpt. of the Ind. Peace Com., House Exec. Doc. No. 1, 40th Cong., 1st Sess., Vol. 2, 495; Kappler, *Laws and Treaties,* II, 887. The Cheyenne and Arapaho never occupied this reserve; by the Treaty of Medicine Lodge, 1867, they agreed to accept other lands south of Kansas and in 1869, by order of President Grant, were assigned a reservation in western Indian Territory. Colorado was then a territory.

occasioned the immediate destruction of more than a few hundred Indian warriors. Such a policy is manifestly as impracticable as it is in violation of every dictate of humanity and Christian duty." Financial considerations forbade such a plan, since it was estimated that the maintenance of each regiment of troops engaged in warfare with plains Indians entailed an expenditure of approximately $2,000,000 per annum. In the interest of economy, Congress was intent upon reducing the Army to a skeleton force.[8]

The Cheyenne and Arapaho treaty was scarcely signed when troubles arose in another quarter. News spread that the government intended to build the Powder River road in response to the demands of Montana citizens for a cheaper transportation link with their territory. This triggered a war with the Sioux. The route, which extended from the Oregon Trail along the North Platte River and through the rolling foothills of the Big Horn Mountains to Bozeman, was a threat to the game of that region. Hostilities lasting two years reached a climax in December 1866, when Captain W. J. Fetterman went in pursuit of an Indian war party which had attacked a wood-cutting detail near Fort Phil Kearney. Fetterman, along with his entire company of eighty men, was slaughtered. This victory spurred the Sioux to greater action, and their attacks became furious. Forts Reno, Phil Kearney, and C. F. Smith, meant to protect the new road, were virtually under siege by the spring of 1867. To make matters worse, trouble recurred with the Cheyenne and Arapaho, but under circumstances quite different from the account usually given. The military command of General W. S. Hancock, which found these tribes camped on the Pawnee Fork of the Arkansas River and burned two hundred of their lodges, along with one hundred belonging to the Sioux, was not attempting to overawe them and thus to prevent an expected

---

[8] Ann. Rpt., House Exec. Doc. No. 1, 39th Cong., 1st Sess., Vol. 2, viii.

outbreak of hostilities. Hancock's troops were stationed by this village five whole days before the burning took place on April 19. It was news of "the barbarous killing" by Cheyenne warriors of three guards at Lookout mail station on the Smoky Hill River which prompted Hancock's punitive action.[9]

Because the Army was compelled to muster all volunteers out of service by the end of 1866 and because the cavalry was especially shorthanded, the western commander, General William T. Sherman, was willing that peace commissioners should be sent among the hostile bands to induce the peaceably inclined to settle upon reservations. This was wholly a matter of strategy for, as Sherman wrote, it would "simplify the game." His concern was that the area between the Arkansas and the Platte should be cleared of Indians. It made little difference to him whether they were coaxed onto reservations or killed.[10]

Under pressure from both the military and the humanitarian groups, Congress passed a bill on July 20, 1867, providing for the appointment of a commission of military and civilian personnel to make peace with the plains tribes. The causes of conflict were to be resolved by treaty. The commissioners were to select one or more large districts where all the Indians east of the Rocky Mountains who did not reside on reservations could concentrate. Such districts were not to be near the main thoroughfares of travel, particularly the routes of the Union Pacific, the Northern Pacific, or the proposed Atlantic and Pacific Railroads. If the commissioners failed to secure peace,

---

[9] Copy of Hancock to Senator John B. Henderson, June 30, 1868, William T. Sherman Papers, Library of Congress. Fort Reno was on the Powder River; Fort Phil Kearney lay farther north, being 223 miles from Fort Laramie on the Oregon Trail; and Fort C. F. Smith was on the Big Horn River where the Powder Road swung westward around the northern end of the Big Horn Mountains toward Bozeman. Lookout station, six miles southwest of Hays City, Kansas, was a stage stop of the Butterfield Overland Dispatch.

[10] Two ltrs. from Sherman at Fort McPherson, Nebr., to Sec. of War Stanton, June 17, 1867, Bur. Ind. Aff., Ltrs. Rec'd.

the Secretary of War might accept the services of four thousand mounted volunteers from the states and territories for the purpose of ending hostilities by force."

The Army was represented on this commission by four officers of top rank: Lieutenant General W. T. Sherman and Brevet Major Generals William S. Harney, Alfred H. Terry, and C. C. Augur. The other members were Nathaniel G. Taylor, Commissioner of Indian Affairs; Senator John B. Henderson, Chairman of the Senate Committee on Indian Affairs; General John B. Sanborn, who had won recognition as a commander of volunteers during the Civil War; and Colonel Samuel F. Tappan, a reform-minded Congregationalist from New England, who had won his rank as a Colorado volunteer.

This Commission met at St. Louis in August 1867 for a preliminary conference. The members moved to adopt a plan similar to one proposed by General Sherman in November of the previous year, and elaborated upon by Commissioner Taylor in response to a Senate resolution of July 8 seeking advice on the question. This plan was to concentrate the Sioux, the Crow, and some others in the area north of Nebraska and west of the Missouri River, and to place the southern plains tribes (Arapaho, Cheyenne, Comanche, Kiowa, and Apache) in the western section of the Indian Territory. The object was to clear Kansas and Nebraska of hostile Indians where the pressure of frontier population was the greatest. On paper, at least, this was accomplished by the treaties of Medicine Lodge and Fort Laramie. An agreement was made with the Sioux only on condition that the United States stop building the Powder River road and that the three forts which guarded it near the Big Horn Mountains be abandoned. In addition to gathering the respective tribes upon reservations in the above-named districts, these treaties provided that each Indian was eventually

---

" 15 U.S. Stat., 17-18.

to obtain a separate allotment of land, and that the government should furnish clothing, agricultural implements, mills, schools or mission houses, agency buildings, and other essentials necessary to promote self-sustaining habits.[12]

Commissioner Taylor, who served as president of this delegation, had been a preacher. He was a graduate of Princeton and is said to have possessed great powers of oratory. In his absence for the work of the Peace Commission in 1867, his annual report was written by Acting Commissioner of Indian Affairs Charles Mix. It is likely that Taylor wrote the report of the Peace Commission and persuaded the generals to sign it. The tone of that document is such that it could not have come from the pen of any one of the military officers. With reference to the situation of the Cheyenne and Arapaho prior to the treaty of 1861, signed at Fort Wise in south-eastern Colorado, the report reads as follows:

These Indians saw their homes and hunting grounds overrun by a greedy population, thirsting for gold. They saw their game driven east to the plains, and soon found themselves the objects of jealousy and hatred. They too must go. The presence of the injured is too often painful to the wrong-doer, and innocence offensive to the eyes of guilt. It now became apparent that what had been taken by force must be retained by the ravisher, and nothing was left for the Indian but to ratify a treaty consecrating the act.[13]

Such remarks, together with others suggesting a policy of conquering with kindness and doing "good to them that hate us," were the product of a mind schooled in Biblical thought.

---

[12] Rpt. on Ind. Hostilities, Senate Exec. Doc. No. 13, 40th Cong., 1st Sess., 17-18 ; Kappler, *op. cit.*, II, 977-89, 998-1015. The treaties with the southern tribes were signed at Medicine Lodge Creek, about seventy-five miles south of Fort Larned in Kansas, October 21, 1867. The stream empties into the Salt Fork of the Arkansas River. The treaties with the Sioux, the Crow, the Northern Cheyenne, and Northern Arapaho were signed at Fort Laramie on the North Platte River in Dakota Territory between April 29 and May 10, 1868.

[13] House Exec. Doc. No. 1, 40th Cong., 3rd Sess., Vol. 2, 489, 493.

The generals would hardly have expressed such sympathy for the Indian warriors who had proved worthy opponents of the United States Army. Nevertheless, their signatures are evidence that they were not averse to part of the content. It was not a case of "hard-headed realists" duped by dreamy-eyed humanitarians. The military men were sensible; some were even humanitarian, after the Indians had been defeated. They were disposed to give benevolent proposals a trial because there was no possibility of subduing the enemy with naked force.

The commissioners expressed a desire for a speedy settlement of all the western territories and for the development of their agricultural and mineral wealth "by an industrious, thrifty, and enlightened population." They understood that the Indians could not be allowed to stand in the way of these aims, but they challenged "the purity and genuineness of that civilization which reaches its ends by falsehood and violence, and dispenses blessings that spring from violated rights." As provided by Congressional act, the honor of the nation demanded that one or more districts should be set aside for the occupation of the tribes east of the Rocky Mountains. A territorial government should be set up in each district; if a strong military government were needed in the beginning, it should be accepted. The governor should have integrity and his salary should be sufficient to place him above temptation. Congress would establish courts and other institutions best suited to the condition of the Indian tribes. Agriculture and the mechanic arts should be introduced as rapidly as possible. Schools should be established and the children required to attend. Common use of the English language would diminish the prejudices of tribe against tribe. "The annuities should consist exclusively of domestic animals, agricultural implements, clothing, and such subsistence only as is absolutely necessary to support them in the earliest stages of the enterprise." After some progress was made in their instruction, "each head of a family should be encouraged to select and improve a homestead." The women should be taught sewing, knitting, and weaving. All this work could be furthered by the influence and aid of missionary associations and benevolent societies, whose representatives would come and live among the tribes.

Many of the bands might not willingly confine themselves to these districts, but in a short time the buffalo would disappear and starvation would compel them to abandon their nomadic ways. In the meantime a new generation reared on the reservations would adapt to the white man's culture and would have a restraining influence upon those who preferred to remain warlike. Progress would be slow, but that was no excuse for shirking an attempt to solve the Indian problem. A quarter of a century was the estimate given by the commissioners' report of the time needed for the transition.

The commissioners recognized that an obstacle to peace was the unwillingness of frontier people and of railroad builders to respect the provisions of Indian treaties. They also understood that the reform of the Indian service required more than the establishment of two major reservations in the plains region. They suggested a thorough revision of the Indian intercourse laws; the creation of a separate Indian Department and the extension of the commission's powers so that they might continue to meet with those tribes professing peace and persuade them to come within the land reserves that had been selected. In addition, they recommended remodeling of the trading system; discontinuance of the practice of employing territorial governors as ex-officio superintendents; and inspection of agency business so that dishonest and incompetent personnel might be discovered and discharged.

By 1873 the recommendations had been adopted, with the exception of those having to do with revision of the intercourse laws, a separate Indian Department, and extension of the commissioners' powers. It was tragic that the points which would have constituted to a large extent the inauguration of an enlightened Indian policy were rejected. A thorough revision of the intercourse laws would have involved a clear definition of the rights and duties of civilian and military personnel in the Indian service. Creation of a separate Indian Department would have fixed the responsibility for Indian administration upon a single individual in the government, and would have relieved the Secretary of the Interior of a work load which was already too great. It would have raised Indian matters to a higher level of prestige before both Congress and the country. Extension of the commission's powers to bring all the peaceful tribes within the proposed districts might have implied Congressional acceptance of the scheme for their control and instruction. Certainly it would have carried with it an obligation to feed those who were confined. This would have entailed the appropriation of large sums of money, and still larger sums if the entire program which the commissioners had advocated were written into law, to say nothing of innumerable hours of committee work. Generally speaking, congressmen were unwilling to accept such responsibility.

Moreover, steps taken in both the House and Senate early in 1870 to provide a government for the Indian Territory were discouraged by the vociferous opposition of the Choctaw and the Cherokee. These tribes regarded territorial government as a curse which would impose the absolute rule of foreigners and make them the prey of politicians and land speculators. To stop this movement they borrowed a phrase from the Declaration of Independence and wrote that to displace the General Council of the Five Civilized Tribes by instituting a territorial government would violate not only the treaties concluded with them in 1866, but also "the laws of nature and of nature's God!"[14]

---

[14] Resolution on Expediency of Establishing a Territorial Government over Certain Tribes, House Misc. Doc. No. 21, 41st Cong., 2nd Sess.,

Intelligent recommendations without Congressional support were useless. Secretary Browning warned in his report for 1868 that the provisions in the treaties concluded by the commissioners would not be worth the paper on which they were written unless Congress made sufficient appropriations for their execution. A year and a half later, Secretary Cox stated that the government had defaulted on its obligations because the House of Representatives refused to be bound by those engagements. Colonel D. S. Stanley wrote from Dakota Territory that the friendly Sioux at the Cheyenne and Grand River agencies were anxious to farm, and that their chiefs had inquired of him where all the provisions were which had been promised by the treaty concluded at Fort Rice two years earlier. From nearly every quarter, and especially with reference to the compacts made by the Peace Commissioners, there came reports that the Indians were dangerously unquiet and that they were upbraiding the government for its breach of faith.[15]

During the spring and early summer of 1868, the agent for the southern Cheyenne and Arapaho received supplies for the subsistence of his Indians, but later in the season provisions ran out and no more arrived. The treaty with the two tribes, like the one with the Kiowa and Comanche, allowed tribal hunting outside the bounds of their reservation south of the Arkansas River for as long as the buffalo were numerous enough to justify the chase. The Peace Commissioners had promised to supply arms and ammunition for this purpose. When arms were not forthcoming in time of need, some of the wilder spirits among the Cheyenne and Arapaho were angered, and when the belated

Vol. 1 ; Rpt. on Consolidation of Indian Tribes, Senate Rpt. No. 131, 41st Cong., 2nd Sess. ; Memorial of the Choctaw Nation, Senate Misc. Doc. No. 90, 41st Cong., 2nd Sess. ; and Petitions of the Cherokee Tribes, House Misc. Doc. No. 76, 41st Cong., 2nd Sess.

[15] Message on Ind. Treaties, Senate Exec. Doc. No. 57, 41st Cong., 2nd Sess., Vol. 2, 2-4 ; D. S. Stanley to E. S. Parker, Feb. 20, 1870, Bur. Ind. Aff., Ltrs. Rec'd.

rifles and cartridges were handed out by the agent in August, they spent their anger by raiding the white settlements of the Saline Valley in Kansas. This was the last straw for General Sherman. He believed that the Cheyenne and Arapaho had violated the treaty of Medicine Lodge and had begun outrages in a war without provocation. While he admitted that some of the Indians had not committed atrocities, the General declared that all of the Cheyenne and Arapaho were at war because the peaceable members had not restrained the hostile group and had not turned the criminals over to the agent as agreed. He maintained that the time had come to settle the question of Indian hostilities with a single stroke. Never before had the government been in such an advantageous position to destroy or humble the marauding Indian bands. After allowing the peacable members of the tribes a reasonable time to withdraw, he would solicit an order from the President, declaring all Indians residing outside the bounds of their reservations outlaws, and directing both soldiers and citizens to proceed against them as such. This was but a repetition of the plan which Sherman had advocated in November 1866, proposing the establishment of two districts, one north of the Platte and west of the Missouri, and the other south of the Arkansas and east of Fort Union, into which the tribes must either go or perish. General Sherman's interest was to make the central plains safe for travel and for homestead settlement. His proposed strategy won the approval of General Grant.[16]

Whether or not the Indians of the southern plains were given an opportunity to get within their reservations before the troops struck is of little importance. It was futile to ask starving people to reside at agencies which had no means for their subsistence. The Kiowa and Comanche, who late in September were still at

---

[16] Sherman ltr., Sept. 17, 1868, accompanying Ann. Rpt. of Com. Ind. Aff., House Exec. Doc. No. 1, 40th Cong., 3rd Sess., Vol. 2, 536-37.

peace, had been assembled on the Arkansas for several months awaiting the arrival of their annuities. They were destitute, and the agent for the Cheyenne and Arapaho tribes predicted that they could not avoid being involved in the hostilities. The agent was right. The tribes were forced to hunt, and the troops did not distinguish a friendly Indian from a hostile one. In a short time the United States was at war with nearly all of the wild tribes of the southern plains.[17]

In the meantime the members of the Peace Commission, with the exception of Senator Henderson, reconvened in Chicago and on October 9, 1868, adopted a set of resolutions which were sent to the President and to Congress. With General Sanborn voting on the side of the regular Army officers and with moral support from General Grant, who was present, the military had their way. They made several recommendations: Arrangements should be made at once to feed, clothe, and protect all Indians of the plains who currently resided or who should in the future locate permanently on their respective reservations. Indian treaties should remain in force only in those cases where the tribes restricted themselves to the boundaries therein described. The government should cease to recognize the tribes as domestic, dependent nations except as it might be required to do so by treaties already in existence. Thereafter all Indians should be individually subject to and protected by the laws of the United States "except where . . . it is otherwise provided in . . . treaties." Those clauses in the treaties made at Medicine Lodge in 1867 which allowed the Indians to hunt outside of their reserves should be declared void. The Army should be employed to compel Indians to go upon reservations, and the Indian Bureau should be transferred to the War Department.[18]

---

[17] E. W. Wynkoop to S. F. Tappan, Oct. 5, 1868, House Exec. Doc. No. 1, 40th Cong., 3rd Sess., Vol. 2, 826.

[18] Resolutions of the Peace Commission, House Exec. Doc. No. 1, 40th Cong., 3rd Sess., Vol. 2, 831-32.

Colonel Tappan was the most vigorous opponent of the military. He introduced a counter-resolution to the effect that only the guilty among the Cheyenne and Arapaho ought to be punished and held that the United States was certainly not justified in declaring war upon the Kiowa, Comanche, and Apache, who appeared at that moment to be in flight. He maintained that the Indians had done nothing which warranted the annulment of their treaties, and that those who were peaceful should be protected at all hazards. Only Tappan voted in the affirmative on this; Commissioner Taylor stood with him in favor of an independent Indian Department. Still, the advocates of the "kid glove" policy were overwhelmed by a vote of five to two. The generals, including Grant, were of one mind. They sought a practical solution to the problem of ending hostilities. Questions of justice and morality which complicated it must be put aside. Grant spoke for them when he said (as reported in the *New York Times*) "The settlers and emigrants must be protected, even if the extermination of every Indian tribe was necessary to secure such a result."[19]

By 1868, there were two major schools of thought about Indian assimilation. General Sherman was representative of the one which wanted to acculturate the nomads of the plains at the point of the bayonet. Because the Indians must be forced to work, this military group held that they should be managed by those best qualified to use force. Hence, the Bureau of Indian Affairs belonged within the Department of War. Commissioner Taylor represented the humanitarian school which wanted to coax the Indians on to reservations and send Christian teachers to prepare them for life in Anglo-American society. Indian affairs, in his view, ought to remain under the supervision of the Department of the Interior until a separate Indian Department was created.[20]

---

[19] *New York Times*, Oct. 11, 13, 16, 1868.
[20] Sherman to Generals Sheridan, Hazen, and Grierson, Dec. 23, 1868,

After Grant had been elected, but before he took office, the representatives of seven yearly meetings of the Society of Friends met in Baltimore and prepared a memorial. It was based upon the most informative documents available, including the report on the condition of the Indian tribes by the joint special committee of Congress in 1867 and the report of the Indian Peace Commission in 1868. The Friends maintained that military supervision was not the answer. Though some of the ranking officers might have both the character and competence to administer Indian matters, the association of common soldiers with the natives would cancel all of their beneficial efforts. Instead of returning the Indian Bureau to the War Department, the Friends proposed to give it a separate status, as provided in a bill then before the Senate. Under such a law, the tribes could be consolidated, civilized, and governed. "Let the effort be made in good faith to promote their education, their industry, their morality. Invite the assistance of the philanthropic and Christian effort which has been so valuable an aid in the elevation of the freedmen, and render it possible for justice and good example to restore that confidence which has been lost by injustice and cruelty."[21]

With the memorial in hand, the Baltimore conference proceeded to Washington, where the members met with various influential officials; but their outstanding achievement was an audience with General Grant on January 25, 1869. The President-elect might well have thought himself the object of a

---

House Exec. Doc. No. 240, 41st Cong., 2nd Sess., Vol. 2, 177; Ann. Rpt. of Com. Ind. Aff., House Exec. Doc. No. 1, 40th Cong., 3rd Sess., Vol. 2, 462 & 478-79.

[21] House Misc. Doc. No. 29, 40th Cong., 3rd Sess., Vol. 1. Evidence that Quaker reform effort shifted from the Negro to the Indian after the Civil War is Jas. Harlan to O. H. Browning, Nov. 2, 1867, enclosing Enoch Hoag to Harlan, Oct. 28, 1867, and Memorial of Friends on Behalf of the Freedmen, Dec. 14, 1865, with commentary by Hoag thereon, Bur. Ind. Aff., Ltrs. Rec'd.

Quaker assault, because on the following day he was visited by another group of Friends from Philadelphia. The result of this lobbying was that on February 15 Grant's aide-de-camp, Brevet Brigadier General E. S. Parker, addressed letters to both the Orthodox and Hicksite organizations, asking them to supply lists of names of persons whom they would endorse as suitable candidates for the office of Indian agent. Parker also assured them that any efforts on their part to educate, to Christianize, or to improve the condition of the Indians would receive from General Grant all the encouragement and protection warranted by the laws of the United States.[22]

What the Friends had won from Grant was a concession to conduct an experiment. While the General was very cordial and considerate of their views, he was not convinced, nor did he intend to fill a large number of agency posts with Quakers. Both he and Parker, who became Commissioner of Indian Affairs, were too much in favor of military administration to allow such a conclusion. But neither had the Friends expected to be given the responsibility of selecting agents. Benjamin Hallowell stated that Parker's letter had caused him more anxiety than anything affecting the Hicksite Society in years. He was concerned that no members of the Friends should be placed in the Indian service without some safeguard against degenerate influences. For this reason he visited Washington on April 5, and proposed that the government assign an entire superintendency to his Society, giving it authority to appoint all of the employees from the superintendent down. Appointment of agents and superintendents would of course be subject to the approval of the President and to confirmation by the Senate. The Society would take care to choose men whose chief concern was the Indians' welfare rather than the promotion of sectarian

[22] Rayner W. Kelsey, *Friends and the Indians, 1655-1917* (Philadelphia, 1917), 167. Ely S. Parker was a Seneca Indian and the grandson of Chief Red Jacket of the Wolf Clan.

interests. All would be under the supervision of an executive committee of judicious members of the Friends Society who were to serve without compensation from the government. Both the President and the Secretary of the Interior, J. D. Cox, received the proposition favorably, and it was agreed that the Hicksite Friends should assume control of the northern superintendency, which embraced the whole of Nebraska. On the same basis the Orthodox group was given the central superintendency, including all of the Indian tribes in Kansas and the Indian Territory with the exception of the Five Civilized Tribes.[23]

It was clear that Grant had not been won over to the Quaker point of view, for he filled most of the agency posts with military officers. In his first annual message, while commending the experiment with Quaker agents, he said that Indian affairs could be more economically, more efficiently, and more honestly managed by the military than by civilians. The President was apparently more concerned about the welfare of a large surplus of military personnel left over from the Civil War than he was about the well-being of the Indians. Even after attaching sixty officers to the Bureau of Indian Affairs, the Army still had one hundred and fifty-six for whom no position could be found.[24]

But Grant had said in his inaugural address that he would favor any course in regard to the Indians which lent itself to "their civilization and ultimate citizenship." Around March 20, William Welsh and Samuel Hinman, an Episcopal missionary to the Santee Sioux, spoke at a meeting in Philadelphia which was attended by a number of eminent Quakers. At Welsh's suggestion, they appointed a joint committee of the two

---

[23] Parker's Plan to Establish Peace with the Indians, House Misc. Doc. No. 37, 39th Cong., 2nd Sess., Vol. 1, 1 ; Hallowell to Whipple, Apr. 6, 1869, Whipple Papers.

[24] Richardson, *Messages,* VII, 38-39 ; Ann. Rpt. of the Gen. of the Army, Sherman, House Exec. Doc. No. 1, 41st Cong., 2nd Sess., Vol. 2, 26-27.

churches which proceeded to Washington. In an interview with the President and Secretary Cox, the committee requested that the appropriations necessary to carry out the recent treaty with the Sioux be administered by a board of five citizens appointed by the Chief Executive and authorized to act jointly with the Secretary of the Interior. At this moment, the two Houses of Congress had reached a stalemate over the appropriations needed to execute all the treaties made by the Peace Commissioners, which made the mission of the church committee doubly important. Committee members talked with the most influential leaders in both the House and the Senate, and asked for $3,000,000 to be used toward keeping the Indians at peace and for promoting self-sustaining habits among them. In other than financial terms, they received far more than they sought. On April 10, the annual Indian appropriation bill became law. Congress had provided $2,000,000 for the purpose designated by the churchmen, and had authorized the President to organize a board of ten commissioners selected for their intelligence and philanthropy to exercise joint control with the Secretary of the Interior in the disbursement of the funds. The commissioners were to serve without pay but would be reimbursed for their expenses.[25]

The significance of this act is better understood when two facts are pointed out: all the members of the Board which it created were nominated by the various religious denominations, and one of their major functions was to advise the government of needed changes in Indian policy. At a conference held in Washington on May 26, 1869, the Board was asked to conduct an investigation and to make recommendations concerning all the issues which troubled Indian affairs. In every respect, this

---

[25] Richardson, *Messages,* VII, 8 ; Welsh to Whipple, Mar. 26, 1869, Whipple Papers ; 16 U.S. Stat., 40. Joint control proved unworkable ; William Welsh, the first chairman of the Board of Indian Commissioners, resigned the position in 1870 after failing to make good a claim to equal authority with the Secretary of the Interior over Indian affairs.

church-appointed body was the "commission of men of high character" with no political ends to serve, which Bishop Whipple had advocated since 1862.[25]

Grant's early policy of appointing Army officers as Indian agents failed when Congress passed a bill on July 15, 1870, forbidding military personnel to hold civil office. Besides the constitutional issue, the motive was a return to political appointments. Grant, under tremendous pressure, might have yielded to the politicians, but with support from the Board of Commissioners he stood firm and decided in favor of their plea that the agencies in question be awarded to the other Christian denominations on terms similar to those held by the Quakers.[27]

Since one of the considerations in proposing this system was to achieve harmony in relations between missionaries and agents, the Secretary of the Interior requested that the Indian Bureau furnish information on the location of Indian mission schools. Finding little data available, he instructed the secretary of the Board to draw up a sketch depicting the manner in which agencies should be allotted to the several missionary societies. Accordingly Colyer prepared a letter and a map which served as the initial guide. After a few changes because of errors, this is how the agencies were distributed: [28]

Religious Group	Names of Agencies and Location	Total No. Agencies	Total No. Indians
Hicksite Friends	Great Nemaha, Omaha, Winnebago, Pawnee, Otoe, and Santee in Nebraska	6	6,598

---

[26] A. C. Barstow to Senator Dawes, Feb. 13, 1881, Henry L. Dawes Papers, Library of Congress ; E. S. Parker to Members of Board, May 26, 1869, Bur. Ind. Aff., Ltrs. Sent.

[27] 16 U.S. Stat., 319 ; Vincent Colyer to the Reverend Mr. Anthon, June 25, 1870, Bd. Ind. Com., Ltrs. Sent.

[28] Ann. Rpt. of Com. Ind. Aff., House Exec. Doc. No. 1, 42nd Cong., 3rd Sess., Vol. 3, 460-62.

Religious Group	Names of Agencies and Location	Total No. Agencies	Total No. Indians
Orthodox Friends	Potawatomi, Kaw, and Kickapoo in Kansas; Quapaw, Osage, Sac and Fox, Shawnee, Wichita, Kiowa, and Upper Arkansas in the Indian Territory	10	17,724
Baptist	Cherokee and Creek in the Indian Territory; Walker River and Paiute in Nevada; and Special in Utah Territory	5	40,800
Presbyterian	Choctaw and Seminole in the Indian Territory; Abiquiu, Navajo, Mescalero Apache, and Tularosa in New Mexico Territory; Moquis Pueblo in Arizona Territory; Nez Percé in Idaho Territory; and Uintah Valley in Utah Territory	9	38,069
Christian	Pueblo in New Mexico Territory and Neah Bay in Washington Territory	2	8,287
Methodist	Hoopa Valley, Round Valley and Tule River in California; Yakima, Skokomish, and Quinault in Washington Territory; Warm Springs, Siletz, and		

Religious Group	Names of Agencies and Location	Total No. Agencies	Total No. Indians
	Klamath in Oregon; Black-feet, Crow, and Milk River in Montana Territory; Fort Hall in Idaho Territory; and Michigan in Michigan	14	54,473
Catholic	Tulalip and Colville in Washington Territory; Grand Ronde and Umatilla in Oregon; Grand River and Devil's Lake in Dakota Territory; and Flathead in Montana Territory	7	17,856
Reformed Dutch	Colorado River, Pima and Maricopa, Camp Grant, Camp Verde, and White Mountain in Arizona Territory	5	8,118
Congregational	Green Bay and Chippewa of Lake Superior in Wisconsin; Chippewa of the Mississippi in Minnesota	3	14.476
Episcopalian	Whetstone, Ponca, Upper Missouri, Fort Berthold, Cheyenne River, Yankton, and Red Cloud in Dakota Territory; and Shoshone in Wyoming Territory	8	26,929

Religious Group	Names of Agencies and Location	Total No. Agencies	Total No. Indians
American Board of Commissioners for Foreign Missions	Sisseton in Dakota Territory	1	1,496
Unitarian	Los Pinos and White River in Colorado Territory	2	3,800
Lutheran	Sac and Fox in Iowa	1	273
		73	238,899

Each denomination appointed an executive committee on Indian affairs and all nominations to the Indian service, from the agent down, were subject to the approval of these committees. The executive committees corresponded with the personnel under their jurisdiction, and occasionally visited the Indians assigned to them for purposes of inspection. Once a year they sent representatives to Washington for a meeting with the Board of Indian Commissioners. This afforded an opportunity to discuss general problems, and through that body to make the government aware of needed changes in administration or policy.

After the use of Army officers as Indian agents had been forbidden by Congress, the President seems to have become more favorably disposed toward the work of the churches. He assured William Welsh of his determination not to yield an inch to political or personal considerations in producing a thorough reform of the Indian service and pledged that the missionary effort to "civilize and Christianize" the tribes would be sustained to the full extent of his authority. Grant's promise was kept. While the politicians fought vigorously at times for the return of their "prerogative," they did not achieve their object until after the close of his second administration.[29]

Once Grant allowed the churches extensive official participation in Indian administration, the essential character of the "Peace Policy" was established. It was strictly an administrative policy because Congress had, in effect, responded to the Protestant demand for reform by unloading the whole Indian problem upon the churches. The $2,000,000 appropriation of April 10, 1869 was made for the purpose of keeping the Indians at peace, of bringing them upon reservations, and of encouraging their efforts at self-support. The representatives of two Protestant churches had asked for a similar appropriation, and these same churchmen had requested the appointment of a commission to supervise the expenditure of the funds for the Sioux. By the law of April 10, the President was empowered to create the Commission, but its authority was made as broad as the Indian question. Thus the Commissioners who were nominated by the Protestant churches were given the assignment of working out the details of a new system. This was a responsibility which the Indian committees of the House and the Senate should have assumed.

Both military and religious opinions were taken into consideration in making the new policy. One of the most important documents which the Board reviewed as they searched for a solution was a letter written by General Alfred Sully from Dakota Territory in 1864, wherein he suggested the protection of peaceable Indians near military posts, and their instruction by missionaries in the academic and vocational arts.[30] The plan finally adopted did constitute a concession to the views of

---

[29] Welsh to Whipple, Feb. 17, 1870, Whipple Papers; William Welsh, *Report of a Visit to the Sioux and Ponka Indians on the Missouri River* (Washington, 1872), 36.

Sherman and Grant. For the Indians who would not consent to go upon reservations, it meant war to the last man. The following order was issued on June 29, 1869, by General Philip H. Sheridan, who commanded the military division of the Missouri which embraced the entire plains region:

All Indians when on their proper reservations are under the exclusive control and jurisdiction of their agents. They will not be interfered with in any manner by military authority, except upon requisition of the special agent resident with them, his superintendent, or the Bureau of Indian Affairs in Washington. Outside the well defined limits of their reservations they are under the original and exclusive jurisdiction of military authority . . . All Indians . . . who do not immediately remove to their reservations, will be . . . treated as hostile, wherever they may be found, and particularly if they are near settlements or the great lines of communication.[31]

By November 1871 these instructions had been extended to include the military division of the Pacific as well, and throughout the remainder of Grant's term in office they were the basic tenet of Indian administration. Indians who did not go willingly to the reservations would be either driven there by force or exterminated in the process. Once on the reservation, the Christian agents and teachers could help them assimilate the white man's culture.[32]

This policy was suggested by the Board of Indian Commissioners. One of the "peace" agents stated that it was established upon the Board's recommendaton, and certainly the first chairman of that body was capable of advising such a course. In a report on the Sioux in 1872, William Welsh encouraged the building of the Northern Pacific Railway "as a military necessity, enabling the War Department to bring the lawless Indians of the North into subjection, and thus aid effectively the re-

---

[30] Copy of Sully at Camp opposite Farm Island on the Mo. R. to Asst. Adj. Gen., Dept. of the N. W., Oct. 7, 1864, Bd. Ind. Com., Ltrs. Rec'd.

[31] General Order No. 8, War Records, National Archives.

[32] General Order No. 10, Nov. 21, *ibid.*

ligious bodies charged with bringing Christian civilization to bear upon them."[33]

Because Western public opinion was opposed to constructive Indian legislation, to allow the military and the churches to proceed according to their respective ideas, one outside and the other within the reservations, was the best that could be done. Francis Walker, who left the Census Bureau to become Commissioner of Indian Affairs in 1871 and who understood the critical situation resulting from the rapid movement of population into the plains region, called the policy "shrewd" for several reasons. It would place conflict between troops and Indians in the light of disciplinary action rather than of war. It would reduce the number of hostile Indians whom the Army must subdue. The use of the military arm would involve no abandonment of the efforts on the reservations to promote self-sustaining habits, but rather would serve to cultivate, among the less enterprising tribesmen who might harbor thoughts of returning to their old ways, a growing respect for the government's power. Most important of all for the national welfare, it would entail the least possible danger to settlers on the plains who were subject to attack in the event of an Indian uprising.[34]

The "Peace Policy" was constructed from the more practical ideas of individuals opposed to one another. Sherman and Grant argued unrealistically that the Indians could best be instructed in the arts of Western civilization under the supervision of the Army. The truth was that military men, especially of the lower ranks, generally lacked the moral character, competence, interest, and patience which were necessary. Tappan and Taylor were idealistic in thinking that the tribes could be brought

---

[33] J. H. Stout to Vincent Colyer, Dec. 6, 1871, Bd. Ind. Com., Ltrs. Rec'd.; Welsh, *Report,* 28.

[34] Francis A. Walker, "The Indian Question," *North American Review,* CXVI (1873), 350-56.

upon the reservations by civil agents, because rebellious bands
were certain to resist. The rapid advance of frontier population
meant that hostile Indians must be removed at once. The
Army was capable of driving them upon the reservations. The
churches had men and women who were qualified to teach
their children. Under the "Peace Policy," the government
approached the Indians of mountain and plain with a Sharp's
Carbine in one hand and a Bible in the other.

The Board of Indian Commissioners, though originally
authorized for only one year, continued until 1934, and this
longevity owed something to a circular letter sent by Bishop
Whipple and William Welsh to religious organizations in every
state asking them to plead with their congressmen for permanent commissioners. Because the responsibilities of the Board
were exceedingly burdensome—especially the task of visiting
agencies to determine whether contracts were fulfilled—the
need for a separate board of inspectors was soon recognized.
Therefore the Episcopal inspection bill, which had been before
Congress since 1866, passed in February 1873. It provided that
the President, with the advice and consent of the Senate, should
appoint five inspectors who were to hold office in four-year
terms at a salary of three thousand dollars per annum. Different
inspectors were to visit each agency twice annually and were to
make a thorough examination of financial accounts, the condition of the Indians, and all important affairs on the reservations.
They were given the authority of law-enforcement officers and
could suspend unworthy personnel from the Indian service. In
passing this bill, Congress demonstrated economy-mindedness
by abolishing four Indian superintendencies and by allocating
the funds formerly appropriated for their maintenance to pay
the inspectors. This was a wise provision because abolition of
the superintendencies eliminated the practice of allowing
Western governors to hold the offices and thus to exercise much
undesirable influence upon Indian affairs, whereas the inspect-

ors were a means of combating corruption. Like the Board of Indian Commissioners, the inspectors were nominees of the Protestant churches.[35]

It was because Protestant churchmen complained vociferously about Indian management, and because Congress failed to formulate an assimilation policy, that the problem was delivered to the religious denominations. Having temporarily rid themselves of an onerous responsibility, the legislators placed the church appointees in an anomalous legal position, for the Senate Judiciary Committee reported in December 1870 that "an act of Congress which should assume to treat members of a tribe as subject to the municipal jurisdiction of the United States would be unconstitutional and void." Thus the federal government had sovereignty over the land occupied by Indians but not over their persons. Yet Congress passed a bill on March 3, 1871, which abolished the legal foundation of the old policy by stating that "hereafter no Indian nation or tribe within the territory of the United States shall be acknowledged or recognized as an independent nation, tribe, or power with whom the United States may contract by treaty."[36]

Previously the legal position of an Indian agent had been that of a minister resident to a domestic, dependent nation. His status as such was hereby terminated, as was the legal recognition of Indian chiefs. Commissioner Walker described the situation which was created by this measure:

It is sufferance, not law, which enables the Indian Office . . . to administer its charge. While the Act of 1871 strikes down at a blow the hereditary authority of the chiefs, no legislation has in-

---

[35] 16 U.S. Stat., 360; circular ltr., Philadelphia, Oct. 2, 1869, Whipple Papers.

[36] Senate Rpt. No. 268, 41st Cong., 3rd Sess., 9; 16 U.S. Stat., 566. This inconsistency was not resolved until 1886, when the Supreme Court reversed the decision of the Senate Judiciary Committee: *United States Reports of Cases Adjudged in the Supreme Court*, CXVIII, 375-85. Hereafter cited as U.S. Rpts.

vested Indian agents with magisterial powers, or provided for the assembling of the Indian *demos*. There is at this time no semblance of authority for the punishment of any crime which one Indian may commit against another, nor any mode of procedure, recognized by treaty or statute, for the regulation of matters between the government and the several tribes. So far as law is concerned, complete anarchy exists in Indian affairs. . . . [37]

Agents did continue to exercise authority on the reservations, but throughout the period of church management this was largely made possible by force of habit, by the tendency of Indian communities to homogeneity, by the fact that the Indians were dependent upon their agents for the distribution of annuity goods, and by administrative ingenuity.

The motive for ending the treaty system was attainment of equality of the House of Representatives with the Senate. House members were disgruntled about the treaties made by the Peace Commission of 1867 because they had been given no opportunity to approve or object to their provisions. How then could they be expected to supply the appropriations required to execute them? Therefore, treaty-making with the tribes was denied by an amendment to the Indian Appropriation Act for 1871. The mode of dealing with the Indians was in fact unchanged, but thereafter it was done through "agreements," a form of compact which required the ratification of both Houses of Congress. It is to the credit of the legislators that in this same bill, they did one thing worth their while: all private contracts with Indians not approved by the Secretary of the Interior and the Commissioner of Indian Affairs were declared invalid. [38]

The "Peace Policy" of the Grant administrations was one phase of a Protestant crusade which reached a climax during the middle eighties with the passage of legislation looking to the solution of the Indian problem in the West. It was estab-

---

[37] Francis A. Walker, *op. cit.*, 335.
[38] 16 U.S. Stat., 570.

lished through Protestant influence in order to clear the Great Plains for white settlement, and to undertake Indian assimilation in a period when public opinion was against legislative reform favoring the Indian. The men who sought government adoption of the policy were aware of the enormity of the task. Their plan was practical. Contrary to the accepted view, the "Peace Policy" was not "a product of confusion regarding the proper course to pursue" but an intelligent attempt, in view of adverse circumstances, to deal with complex problems which were associated with the settlement of the western frontier. Among the many obstacles to its smooth application were the reaction of the Catholic Church, the attitude of the West, and the position of the military.[39]

[39] Loring Priest, *Uncle Sam's Stepchildren* (New Brunswick, 1942), 183.

IV

The Reaction of the Catholic Church

THE CATHOLIC CHURCH took no part in the reform movement; the clergy were not interested in a federal policy to assimilate Indians unless it would aid the propagation of the Catholic faith. Toward this latter end the whole Catholic organization was oriented. Catholic solicitation of the government was always motivated by a concern for missionary activity and, in the early seventies, prospects of federal aid prompted the formation of a Catholic lobby at Washington.

It was unfortunate that the Catholics were not represented on the Board of Indian Commissioners. Although it seems doubtful that a Catholic commissioner could have worked in harmony with nine Protestants, who must certainly have opposed him, the exclusion of the Catholics from that body provided them with a cause for complaint. However, they did not reveal any interest in the Board until it became clear that the new system, worked out with the Commissioners' advice, had undesirable implications for the future of their missions. When the plan for the distribution of agencies to the various denominations was drawn up in August 1870, most of the Catholic hierarchy were attending the Vatican Council in Rome. Nevertheless, Father De Smet had twice declined an invitation to attend a meeting of the Board's executive committee during the previous May, giving as a reason his failing health and a previous intention of visiting the Sioux.[1]

---

[1] Peter J. Rahill, *The Catholic Indian Missions and Grant's Peace Policy, 1870-1884* (Washington, 1953), 46. In the spring of 1871, Father De Smet asked that the Indian Bureau promote "unison" among agents and missionaries on the reservations in Montana, Idaho, and Washington Territories; he strongly suggested that the transfer of the Blackfeet

When F. N. Blanchet, the Archbishop of Oregon, returned home in December, he became aware of the change in Indian administration through Grant's second annual message to Congress, wherein the President stated his determination "to give all the agencies to such religious denominations as had heretofore established missionaries among the Indians, and perhaps to some other denominations who would undertake . . . missionary work."[2] The Archbishop did not react to this news for a month, and then wrote as if he had no knowledge of the forces which had produced the changes or of the fact that most of the agencies had already been assigned. His preoccupation with missions was apparent in a letter to the Indian Bureau:

This wise plan will at last put an end to the sufferings of our . . . indian missions, which hitherto have remained under the control of protestant ministers or layman agents, notwithstanding our own efforts and the repeated . . . protestations of the Indians. . . . The friends of the old System, on losing the grasp of our catholic missions, may, no doubt, highly complain and condemn the change, but most certainly all upright and impartial men will rejoice. . . . Hoping that the time for a reformation is arrived and that the system proposed by our Excellent President is not a mere show of vain words, I beg justice for our catholic missions among the Indians in the state of Oregon.[3]

It was a profound shock for Blanchet to discover that the "shufflings of the methodists" had deprived him of the Umatilla, Grand Ronde, and Warm Springs agencies. A second letter, quite the opposite in tone from that of his earlier corres-

and Yakima agencies from Methodist to Catholic control would be favorable to "unison." It is clear that De Smet's great concern was that the Catholic church should be put to no disadvantage in seeking converts among the tribes: P. J. De Smet at St. Louis University to Robert Campbell, member of the Bd. Ind. Com., at St. Louis, Mo., April 18, 1871, encl. copy of De Smet to E. S. Parker, Mar. 27, 1871, Bur. Ind. Com., Ltrs. Rec'd.

[2] Richardson, *Messages,* VII, 109.

[3] Blanchet at Portland, Oregon, to E. S. Parker, Jan. 27, 1871, Bur. Ind. Aff., Ltrs. Rec'd.

pondence, declared that the new system was a great deal more dangerous to Catholic missions than the old one and upbraided the Board of Commissioners for their injustice, stating that nearly three-quarters of thirty-eight agencies recently allotted should have gone to the Catholics, whereas of this number they had actually received only four. His view was in keeping with the claim of the *Catholic World* in 1877 that forty of the seventy-two agencies originally distributed should have gone to the Catholics, including all of the fourteen which were given to the Methodists.[4] The Archbishop compared the "poor and miserable condition" of Indians under the care of the Protestants with those who had been subjected "to the christian rule" by the Jesuit Fathers. Then, in remonstrance, he asked:

How can the government expect that a true civilization may be given to our Indians by Sects, not christian but infidel? No we are not of those who think . . . all . . . denominations are equally good, though teaching doctrines diametrically opposed to each other. Woe to the Indians to whome these contradictory doctrines are taught by dissenting sects.[5]

In reply Secretary Columbus Delano stated that the Interior Department was "bound to view these 'dissenting sects' . . . in a more Catholic and charitable spirit," but promised that an effort would be made to secure equity for the Archbishop's church. Subsequent investigation proved that the assignment of Umatilla and Grand Ronde to the Methodists had been an error, as had been the assignment of Fort Hall in Idaho to the Catholics. Therefore, an adjustment was made whereby Umatilla and Grand Ronde were turned over to Catholic management and Fort Hall was surrendered to the Methodists. This two-for-one settlement did not quiet Catholic resentment, because their claim to other agencies such as Siletz in Oregon and

---

[4] P. Girard, "Our New Indian Policy and Religious Liberty," XXVI, 101-103.

[5] Blanchet to Parker, July 8, 1871, Bur. Ind. Aff., Ltrs. Rec'd.

Papago in Arizona Territory was much stronger than that of the Methodist church. Bishop J. B. Salpointe of Tucson succeeded in having the Papago agency transferred to Catholic management in 1874, but was out-maneuvered two years later when the Indian Bureau consolidated it with the Pima and Maricopa under the control of the Reformed Dutch. There are several reasons for supposing that Commissioner Edward P. Smith, a Congregational clergyman, may have been motivated by sectarianism in taking this action. It was Smith's administration which created the agency and assigned it first to the Methodists; the Commissioner was dissatisfied with the Catholic nominee for agent because he was adversely critical of his predecessor's management. Also, the Papago had little in common with the Pima and Maricopa; the reservations of these tribes were sixty miles apart, making it impossible for a single agent to deal with intruders; and a succeeding Commissioner found it necessary to recommend the re-establishment of the Papago agency after the "Peace Policy" was ended.[6]

The Catholics were dealt with unjustly in receiving only seven of the agencies, but their claim to forty of them was even more inequitable. That figure may be of some value, however, in estimating what would have been the breakdown had the "Peace Policy" been instituted by a Catholic rather than by a Protestant movement. It seems doubtful whether Archbishop

---

[6] Copy of Delano to Blanchet, July 31, 1871, Bd. Ind. Aff., Ltrs. Rec'd.; Delano to F. A. Walker, Dec. 19, 1871, Bur. Ind. Aff., Ltrs. Rec'd. Chas. Ewing to Delano, Jan. 20 and June 27, 1874; Ewing to Salpointe, July 2 and 15, 1874; John W. Cornyn, Papago agent, to Ewing, May 31 and Oct. 29, 1875; Cornyn to E. P. Smith, Oct. 30, 1875; Ewing to Sec. of Interior Z. Chandler, Mar. 27, 1876; Chandler to Ewing, Mar. 30, 1876 (mostly copies), Archives of the Bureau of Catholic Indian Missions, Washington D.C., hereafter cited as A.B.C.I.M.; Ann. Rpts. of Com. Ind. Aff. (1872), 461 (1885), xlvii (1886), xlii. There was considerable pressure from Tucson citizens in 1875 to have the Papago Indians removed to the Pima and Maricopa reservation; this was not done, nor was the Papago agency re-established.

Blanchet would have been willing to afford Protestants greater participation than Vincent Colyer recommended for the Catholics. In speaking of his decision to turn the agencies over to the various religious denominations, Grant had said that responsibility would be given to those who had previously taken part in Indian mission work and perhaps to some others. It was because no detailed information on Indian missions could be found in the Indian Bureau that Interior Secretary Jacob Cox turned to the secretary of the Board of Indian Commissioners for advice. From the report of the Commissioner of Indian Affairs for 1861, it would appear that the Catholics did not fare as badly as they claimed. Of seventy-seven missionaries then among the Indians, there were twenty-five Methodists, nineteen Catholics, nine Baptists, five Quakers, three Congregationalists, two Episcopalians, and one Lutheran. While the remainder were undesignated, a large number of them must have been Presbyterians, for Reverend John C. Lowrie reported in 1870 that his church had maintained 264 missionaries and assistants among the Indians in past years. According to these figures, the Quakers and Episcopalians received a disproportionate share of agencies, but statistics do not recognize that the "Peace Policy" was an outgrowth of their influence. If Father De Smet had not declined the repeated invitation of the Board's executive committee of May 1870, perhaps the Catholics would have been given more agencies than they were finally assigned.[7]

The Catholic view was that the Protestants saw in the "Peace Policy" an opportunity to spread "their propaganda among the Indians with little . . . cost to themselves," and to interfere with "the work of the Catholic Church among many of the tribes." Through ministers and laymen serving as agents and teachers

---

[7] Colyer to Cox, Aug. 11, 1870, Senate Exec. Doc. No. 39, 41st Cong., 3rd Sess., Vol. 1, appendix 25, 98 ; Ann. Rpt., Senate Exec. Doc. No. 1, 37th Cong., 2nd Sess., Vol. 1, 645 ; Lowrie, Sec. of Presbyterian Bd. of Foreign Missions, to Colyer, June 8, 1870, Bd. Ind. Com., Ltrs. Rec'd.

paid by the government, the Protestants would wield an auto-
cratic power and drive Catholic missionaries from the reservations. When the priests were gone, Catholic Indians would become Methodists, Baptists, Presbyterians, Quakers, or Unitarians—a process hastened "by judicious bribery and intimida-
tion." The Catholics suspected that the "Peace Policy" was not
original with Grant, and surmised that the men "behind the
throne" were motivated by sectarianism. They were averse to
the precept that sectarian differences were unimportant, and the
approach of Felix Brunot, second chairman of the Board of
Commissioners, who explained denominational Christianity to
Indians in terms of many roads leading to the same place, was
particularly odious. In this regard, Catholic blows fell hardest
upon the Unitarians, in regard to whom they declared that
according to the "doctrine of indifferentism" it did not seem to
make much difference whether one believed "that Jesus Christ
is God, or that he was simply a tolerably good but rather weak
and vain man."[8]

From the beginning, the "Peace Policy" was fraught with an
authoritarian struggle which recalled the bitterness of sixteenth-
century Europe and which grew worse as the seventies pro-
gressed. Such a result was farthest from the minds of those who
instituted the policy, for Secretary Cox had stated in July 1870,
that the government hoped to bring the management of agencies
"into strict harmony and accord" with educational and missionary endeavors. The misassignment of agencies was not owing to
an anti-Catholic plot; it was circumstantial. A rapid distribution
was essential to meet the necessity of replacing the military
agents, whose services Congress had terminated, and to avoid
the possibility of a return to political appointments. Cox had
hoped to arrange a meeting of the denominational representatives before the distribution was made, but this failed to come

[8] Girard, *op. cit.*, 99-100.

about, and the Interior Department dealt with the situation as best it could. It was not the Catholics alone who were slighted. Protest came immdeiately from the American Board of Commissioners for Foreign Missions, which had been given no agencies in spite of the fact that their organization was very active among the Sioux. Cox apologized for the oversight, but gave his assurance that he would guarantee "to *all* Missions the fullest protection and recognition, and . . . impose absolute fairness & impartiality upon the Agents selected." Following the Lake Traverse experiment, the A.B.C.F.M. received the Sisseton agency in Dakota. This Protestant society placed a representative on the Board of Indian Commissioners, but it never did receive an equitable share of the agencies.[9]

Although Catholic delegates attended the early annual meetings of religious representatives with the Board of Indian Commissioners, they did not feel comfortable on these occasions. The Catholic church regarded the Board as a council for Protestant propaganda, and consequently organized a separate Bureau at Washington in January 1873, "to defend Catholic Indian missions against the organized assault which has been made upon them." This Catholic Bureau of Indian Missions was composed of a commissioner, treasurer, director, and board of control, all of whom were appointed by the Archbishop of Baltimore. The Commissioner was a layman and was recognized by the government as the official representative of the Catholic church in all matters concerning Indians. For this important post, Archbishop J. Roosevelt Bayley chose Charles Ewing, an able attorney whose sister, Ellen, was the wife of the General of the Army, William T. Sherman. If political considerations were involved in this appointment, the judgment of the Archbishop was at fault. Sherman never liked the Catholic organization, but the *Catholic World* argued the Army's case

---

[9] Cox to Rev. S. B. Treat, Sec. of A.B.C.F.M., at Boston, July 19 and Sept. 3, 1870, Sec. of Interior, Ltrs. Sent, National Archives.

for a large military force. The treasurer, director, and president of the board of control were clergymen.[10]

Through this organization the Catholic church launched a counter-movement, the aim of which was not only to defend those missions already in existence, but to establish new ones at every opportunity. Posing as a champion of religious liberty and as an opponent of state churchism, the Catholic Bureau fought the "Peace Policy" wherever its application barred priests from ministering to the tribes. It would be a mistake to assume a metamorphosis of character; Commissioner Ewing never invoked these principles when Catholics were in control of reservations. He was, however, very regular in applying for the privilege of appointing agents when vacancies occurred, and constantly assembled evidence to support Catholic claims. Furthermore, many Indian petitions asking the removal of Protestant agents were prepared by Catholic missionaries and funneled through the Bureau to the Interior Department. Catholic efforts to seize agencies assigned to Protestants were bold and sometimes entirely unjustified; the most sweeping of Ewing's requests concerned all of California, when by admission of a local priest the Catholics had done nothing at Hoopa Valley, where the Methodists were in charge.[11]

[10] Girard, *op. cit.*, 107-108 ; E. Butler, "A Glance at the Indian Question," *Catholic World*, XXVI (1877), 201-202 ; Sherman to Ewing, May 29, 1878, Charles Ewing Papers, Library of Congress. Sherman's letter was provoked by the decision of his son, Thomas, to become a priest : "If they boast over . . . this conquest—well I won't threaten, but within the reach of your influence check them, for not only am I not a Catholic, but am . . . so bitter that written words can convey no meaning."

[11] Undated MSS by Ewing with Montana correspondence for 1873 ; M. Wallrath at Crescent City, Calif., to Ewing, July 16, 1873 ; Ewing to Delano, June 14, 1874 ; Bureau of Catholic Indian Missions' publications (Washington, 1874-1879), Nos. 1-17, A.B.C.I.M. John B. Monteith, Nez Percé agent, to Com. Ind. Aff., July 4, 1873 ; John Buffalo and A. John Buffalo at Red Cliff reserve, Wis., to Com. Ind. Aff., Nov. 25, 1875 ; Ewing to Chandler, June 14, 1876 ; J. B. A. Brouillet, director of Catholic Bureau, to Com. Ind. Aff., Mar. 15, 1877 ; W. T. Hughes, agent

The closing of reservations under Protestant control to Catholic missionary activity was not merely a reflection of sectarian bigotry. A larger cause was that priests, who recognized no superiors outside of their own hierarchy, incited disrespect for Protestant officials; no agent could tolerate a division of authority upon an Indian reservation and expect to maintain order. Until 1875 the government tried to uphold religious liberty. Commissioner Edward P. Smith, a Congregational minister, permitted the building of a Catholic church and school among the Nez Percé despite Presbyterian objections. But the principle became more and more difficult to apply because of the Catholic counter-movement, and the Interior Department was compelled to refuse the request of California Archbishop J. S. Alemany, for permission to build a mission at Round Valley. Inspector William Vandever reported that the Indians there, who were under Methodist supervision, were opposed to the establishment of a Catholic church, and advised that the judicious course was "to require each religious denomination to confine their efforts to the reservations especially assigned to them." In Vandever's opinion there could "be no co-alescence of Catholics with Protestants on the same reservation."[12]

Denominational conflict and the consequential abandonment of religious freedom upon the reserves was a most unhappy aspect of the "Peace Policy's" implementation. The situation was intolerably bad at Round Valley, where agent J. L.

at Standing Rock, Dak. Terr., to Com. Ind. Aff., Aug. 30, 1878; H. C. Bulis, special agent at Rosebud, Dak. Terr., to Com. Ind. Aff., Mar. 17, 1879; Ewing to Carl Schurz, Mar. 13, 1880, Bur. Ind. Aff., Ltrs. Rec'd.
[12] Ann. Rpt. of Com. Ind. Aff., House Exec. Doc. No. 1, 44th Cong., 1st Sess., Vol. 4, 524-25; Smith to Monteith at Lapwai agency, Idaho Terr., May 27, 1873, and Oct. 28, 1875, Bur. Ind. Aff., Ltrs. Sent; Smith to H. B. Whipple, Aug. 23, 1875, Whipple Papers; copies of Ewing to Delano, Apr. 5, 1875, and Vandever to Smith, June 4 & July 22, 1875, A.B.C.I.M.

Burchard justifiably removed a Mexican priest several times on grounds of insubordination; but nowhere did religious strife reach the proportions that it attained at White Earth in Minnesota.[13]

The government had begun to concentrate the Mississippi Chippewa at White Earth in 1868, and the first bands were accompanied there by a native Episcopalian missionary, Enmegahbowh, who had worked among them for a decade under the direction of Bishop Whipple. There was no Catholic mission and on grounds of sustained activity the Episcopal claim was obviously the strongest, but when the agencies were distributed, White Earth was placed under Congregational management, as was the Chippewa agency at Green Bay in Wisconsin. Despite this misassignment, relations between the two Protestant churches were amiable; it was because of Father Ignatius Tomazin, who was sent by the Catholic church as resident priest in the early seventies, that trouble brewed.[14]

The promotion of Edward P. Smith to the headship of the Indian Office caused the Catholic Bureau to press the Interior Department for the privilege of appointing his successor at the White Earth agency. In order to prevent Catholic control, the Episcopal Mission Board upheld its own claim, and in 1874 relinquished Fort Berthold agency in Dakota Territory to the Congregationalists in exchange for White Earth. But the Catholic effort to seize the agency persisted and was strengthened by the arrival of a band of Pembina Chippewa, who were largely Catholic half-bloods. Under the priest's direction, several petitions were circulated and sent to Washing-

---

[13] Copy of Vandever to Smith, July 2, 1875, A.B.C.I.M.

[14] Enmegabowh at Crow Wing to Bishop Whipple, Sept. 10, 1868, and at White Earth, Dec. 24, 1868, and June 6, 1872 ; copy of H. M. Rice at St. Paul to Wm. Welsh, April 2, 1873, Whipple Papers. Copy of Whipple to Pres. Grant, Nov. 11, 1875, Bd. Ind. Com., Ltrs. Rec'd. Rahill, *op. cit.*, 197.

ton asking for the transfer of the reservation to Catholic management; agent Lewis Stowe was charged with having shown partiality toward an Episcopal minority in the payment of annuities, while a large Catholic majority lived in distress. Indian testimony showed that some of the names on the petitions were attached without the knowledge of the Indians concerned, and an investigation in 1875 by General E. Whittlesey of the Board of Indian Commissioners found the administration of White Earth honest, economical, and intelligent. That Father Tomazin was overzealous in seeking to inculcate the "true faith" among the Chippewa is certain. Already a new Catholic church and school stood upon the reservation; a Catholic agent would benefit this work.[15]

The Catholic Bureau refused to accept the findings of General Whittlesey, and in Catholic circles stories of Protestant mismanagement circulated far and wide. At Las Vegas, New Mexico Territory, the *Revista Catolica* iterated the myth that $15,000 of appropriations for agriculture and housing had been used to build an Episcopal church at Wild Rice River, in which no religious services were held because the Protestants had converted only one Indian, "and him not with the word of God but by means of a sack of flour and a leg of pork." This ludicrous statement loses some of its humor when one reflects that Enmegahbowh reported the Catholic conversion of Episcopalians by the same means in 1873, remarking that all might become Romanists to save their poor mortal bodies.[16]

---

[15] Copy of Ewing to Bishop Thomas L. Grace at St. Paul, Mar. 15, 1873 ; Tomazin to Ewing, Nov. 13, 1874 ; Tomazin to Brouillet, July 30, 1875 ; Copy of E. P. Smith to Sec. of Interior Chandler, Dec. 3, 1875 ; A.B.C.I.M. Edward C. Kemble to Whipple, Mar. 25, 1872 ; Smith to Whipple, Mar. 5, 1873 ; Stowe at White Earth to Whipple, Jan. 28, 1875 ; copy of Ten chiefs at White Earth to Com. Ind. Aff. Smith, Jan. 28, 1875 ; Tomazin "To the Reverend Clergy and laity of the United States!", Sept. 8, 1875, Whipple Papers.

[16] Chandler to Ewing, Jan. 24, 1876, A.B.C.I.M. ; Whipple to Chandler,

To Bishop Whipple, the controversy at White Earth was very disturbing. So much was at stake: the reputation of his personal appointee as agent, the Episcopal mission, and the "Peace Policy" itself. He unburdened himself to Grant in the autumn of 1875, declaring that there was enough work for both Catholics and Protestants on the reservation and that a willingness of the priest to proceed in such a spirit would be welcomed. But the undoing of Episcopal accomplishments by a Catholic clergyman who informed Indians that they were bound for hell if they attended the Protestant church would not be tolerated. Whipple's good intentions were substantiated in that he advised the Commissioner of Indian Affairs that Catholic teachers should be employed in government schools attended by Catholic Indian children."

Religious strife continued to mount as the Indians' allegiance divided sharply between the two churches, and tension reached a climax in March 1877. Somewhat ironically, the cause was an estrangement of the Catholics themselves. When Father Tomazin sent his housekeeper, a half-breed Chippewa woman, away from the reservation pending the birth of an illegitimate child, the priest's co-worker, F. L. Gonzaga Maléssy, sought her return on behalf of relatives. Having thus incurred the priest's ire, Brother Gonzaga determined to leave White Earth, but could not procure his belongings from the mission. Reluctantly, agent Lewis Stowe agreed to intervene and, upon Tomazin's refusal to grant admittance, forced open a door; Gonzaga then removed his personal effects, together with a trunk containing furnishings for the mission, which he had purchased in Philadelphia on credit. The priest, who was

Dec. 29, 1876, encl. copy of H. Forrester at Santa Fe to Whipple, Dec. 9, 1876, which quoted from the Catholic paper, Bur. Ind. Aff., Ltrs. Rec'd.; Enmegahbowh to Whipple, Feb. 13, 1873, Whipple Papers.

" Copy of Whipple at New York City to Grant, Nov. 11, 1875, Bd. Ind. Com., Ltrs. Rec'd.; Whipple at Faribault to J. Q. Smith, Apr. 28, 1877, Bur. Ind. Aff., Ltrs. Rec'd.

furious because of this "sacrilegious outrage," summoned the Catholic Indians by ringing an alarm on the mission bell, and wrote a letter which was published in the *New York Sun,* accusing the agent of theft.[18]

Catholic Commissioner Ewing told the Indian Bureau that the charge bore the semblance of truth and requested an investigation. Simultaneously, however, he informed Bishop Rupert Seidenbush of St. Cloud that Tomazin was guilty of inciting the Chippewa against their agent and advised that the priest be removed from the reservation. Catholic Director J. B. A. Brouillet also entreated Seidenbush to transfer Tomazin in order to avoid the embarrassment of governmental proceedings and their reflection upon the church, but the Bishop refused to sacrifice the missionary, because his linguistic ability was indispensable to the winning of converts.[19]

In pursuance of instructions from the Commissioner of Indian Affairs, Stowe ordered Tomazin to leave White Earth not later that the first of May; but the priest refused to recognize the agent's authority, and continued to counsel the Indians adversely. Though the question of control thus became imminent, the Interior Department was as anxious as the Catholic Bureau to avoid a forcible removal; while Carl Schurz authorized coercion, he hoped that prompt action by the Catholic organization would preclude it. The Secretary made every possible concession: Ewing's request for an investigation was granted, and the suggestion of St. Paul Bishop Thomas L. Grace that former Senator Henry M. Rice serve on the commission of inquiry was accepted. Rice and William Lyon of the

---

[18] Ewing to J. Q. Smith, Mar. 21, 1877, encl. news clipping, Mar. 1st; Stowe to Smith, Apr. 10, 1877; F. L. Gonzaga Maléssy at Atoka, Ind. Terr., to Sec. of Interior Schurz, Nov. 19, 1877, Bur. Ind. Aff., Ltrs. Rec'd.

[19] Ewing to Seidenbush, Mar. 20, 1877; Seidenbush to Ewing, Apr. 6, 1877; Brouillet to Seidenbush, June 27 and July 13, 1877 (mostly copies), A.B.C.I.M.

Board of Indian Commissioners reported in favor of Stowe, but questioned the wisdom of leaving the agent in office because of the ill feeling against his administration which Tomazin had aroused among the Chippewa. No reason for further delay in the execution of the government's removal order being justified, Inspector Edward C. Kemble was assigned this disagreeable task. In defiance, the priest called upon the Indians to resist and argued that only Bishop Seidenbush could order him to leave the reservation. When a small military force was brought to the scene in October, however, he left under protest "on behalf of the Catholic people of the United States and all lovers of religious freedom." That the government did not send some other inspector than Kemble, who had served earlier as secretary of the Episcopal Indian Commission, was impolitic, but the total insubordination of the priest was ample cause for his expulsion.[20]

Both the Interior Department and the Catholic Bureau were shocked when Tomazin returned to White Earth in December and claimed victory over agent Stowe. Commissioner Ewing realized that the interests of all Catholic missions were dependent upon good relations with the government and had already abandoned all vindicative efforts. His determination to prevent a breach was seen two months later, when the priest committed the further indiscretion of leading a delegation of Chippewa chiefs to Washington with no sanction whatever. On that occasion, Ewing renounced him and stated that the Catholic Bureau condemned "all acts . . . wanting in proper respect to

[20] Stowe to J. Q. Smith, May 14, 1877; telegrams from Kemble at White Earth to Com. Ind. Aff., Sept. 17, 24, & Oct. 3, 1877; Tomazin at St. Paul to Carl Schurz, Oct. 15, 1877; Geo. W. DuBois at Faribault to E. A. Hayt, Com. Ind. Aff., Jan. 10, 1878; Bur. Ind. Aff., Ltrs. Rec'd. Copies of Rpt. by Rice and Lyon, Aug. 10, 1877, and of agent Charles Ruffee to Hayt, Apr. 23, 1878, Whipple Papers. Copies of Schurz to Com. Ind. Aff., May 22, 1877, and of Ewing to Schurz, July 2, 1877, A.B.C.I.M.

the officials of the United States." But this was not the last time that amity was threatened by the missionary. From a new field of labor at Red Lake, he again led chiefs to the Capitol in 1883, and again Bishop Seidenbush rejected a plea of the Catholic Bureau to remove him, so that the government was obliged to exercise force.[21]

The trouble at White Earth was representative of the authoritarian controversy at its worst, and resulted in the ending of the "Peace Policy" there. Regardless of Bishop Whipple's efforts to prevent it, agent Stowe was replaced by Charles Ruffee, who had won the patronage of such Minnesota politicians as Governor J. S. Pillsbury, Alexander Ramsey, and Representative J. H. Stewart. Ruffee's appointment was only part of a general turning back to the spoils system in Indian affairs during the administration of Rutherford B. Hayes, but there can be no doubt that, in Minnesota, Catholic opposition to Protestant management hastened the process. The Catholic church and the "Indian ring" were joined in a common endeavor for different purposes. Tomazin's machinations caused unrest among the Chippewa; and Congressman Stewart, who was allied with the Catholic Bureau, argued successfully that the imminence of an uprising required a change of agents.[22]

Ruffee was a Crow Wing merchant who had sought the office for more than a decade, and it may be supposed that his major motive was profit. Bishop Seidenbush, in not removing the priest whose rebellious conduct was responsible for the diffi-

---

[21] R. F. Hunter for Ewing to Bishop Grace, Sept. 12, 1877 ; Brouillet to Seidenbush, Dec. 6, 1877 ; Ewing to Hayt, Feb. 12, 1878 ; Ewing to Seidenbush, June 2, 1883 ; Seidenbush to Ewing, June 1883 ; Inspector Robert S. Gardner to Sec. of Interior, July 2, 1883 (mostly copies), A.B.C.I.M.

[22] Stewart to Ewing, July 26, 1877 ; copies of Pillsbury, Ramsey, *et al.*, to Schurz, Sept. 14, 1877 ; Pillsbury to Schurz, Sept. 18, 1877 ; Stewart to Schurz, Sept. 22, 1877, A.B.C.I.M. Stowe to Whipple, Oct. 12, 1877, Whipple Papers.

culties at White Earth, in not demanding the appointment of a Catholic agent to replace Stowe, and in not offering a substitute for denominational management, unwittingly aided the re-establishment of a system of Indian service appointments which was historically corrupt.

Bigoted competitiveness made the appointment of agency employees by various church groups incompatible with the practice of religious liberty. Official relations between church and state have always been destructive to freedom of worship, and the "Peace Policy" was not an exception. Protestant leaders tried to solve the Indian problem through the Board of Indian Commissioners, which provided a link between the Protestant denominations and the government. Fearing inroads upon their missionary field, the Catholic church likewise established a Bureau in Washington with which the government did business, whether pertaining to the assignment of agencies, to the awarding of school contracts, or to the allowance of missions. These two organizations at the Capitol were focal to the battle for the Indian mind which raged in the far West. No wonder that religious freedom became impossible to apply on the reservations.

By the late seventies it had become a rule of the Indian Bureau not to authorize missionary activity on reservations assigned to other denominations. Father Meinrad McCarthy, who in May 1879 tried to establish a mission near Red Cloud agency without the government's sanction, was ordered expelled, and Daniel Renville of the Dakota Native Missionary Society was denied entry to the Catholic-controlled Devil's Lake agency in January 1880. While the Protestants had paid no heed to the fate of Father McCarthy, limitation of religious liberty in the case of Renville brought an immediate protest from the American and Presbyterian Boards for Foreign Missions, which sponsored the native society. In response, Commissioner Roland Trowbridge requested the views of all the religious societies appointing agents and found that six of them approved the rule, two were noncommittal, and only the Catholic Bureau favored the removal of all restrictions. With such overwhelming support, Trowbridge saw no reason to change the regulation, and a subsequent petition of the director of the Catholic Bureau to establish a school at the Fort Peck agency in Montana was refused. Fort Peck was in the charge of the Methodists, who were very much opposed to admitting the Catholics, and the government's denial brought an appeal from director Brouillet to President Hayes which asked that the ruling be reversed and that the President acknowledge the constitutional "right of every christian church to exercise her ministry among the Indians wherever and whenever she pleases. . . ."[23]

The Catholic plea for religious liberty was founded more upon expediency than upon constitutional principle. From the same consideration the Protestants were reluctant to relinquish the advantage afforded by the Indian Bureau's ruling. But troubled conscience, together with Catholic support of a bill in Congress to give all denominations equal privileges, prompted them to initiate a return to freedom, and when the representatives of religious societies met with the Board of Indian Commissioners at Washington in January 1881, a Presbyterian memorial asking that "Indians be granted the same religious liberty which we claim for ourselves" and that reservations "be open to all religious societies who sincerely work for the elevation of the Indians" swung Protestant opinion behind it.

---

[23] Rahill, *Catholic Indian Missions,* 277 and 298-99. Alfred L. Riggs *et al.* at Santee agency, Neb., to Schurz, Feb. 11, 1880; John C. Lowrie for Presbyterian Bd. of Foreign Missions at New York to Schurz, Feb. 5, 1880; John Reid for Methodist Mission Bd. to Trowbridge, July 2, 1880; Brouillet to Pres. Hayes, Aug. 25, 1880, Bur. Ind. Aff., Ltrs. Rec'd. Hayt to Riggs, Jan. 3, 1880; Trowbridge to B. Rush Roberts *et al.,* Apr. 7, 1880; Trowbridge to Riggs, May 27, 1880, Bur. Ind. Aff., Ltrs. Sent.

The Protestant groups addressed separate but identical letters to the Secretary of the Interior, Carl Schurz, asking that the Indian Bureau's ruling be rescinded. Schurz agreed "that their request should be complied with . . . in all cases except where the presence of rival religious organizations would manifestly be perilous to peace and good order. . . ." But this did not satisfy director Brouillet, who in July 1882 repeated the Catholic demand for the removal of all restrictions. Schurz' successor, Henry M. Teller, capitulated and thus made it possible for the Catholic Bureau to become the most successful bidder for Indian school contracts during the eighties and nineties.[24] True to the prediction of Commissioner Ewing, made many years before, the Catholic church did "gather a good harvest" by going "upon the record for religious liberty," as the following table of expenditures for denominational contract schools illustrates:[25]

Year	Catholic	Presbyterian	Congregational	Friends	Episcopal
1886	$118,343	$32,995	$16,121	$ 1,960	None
1887	194,635	37,910	26,696	27,845	$ 1,890
1888	221,169	36,500	26,080	14,460	3,690
1889	347,692	41,825	29,310	23,383	18,700
1890	356,957	47,650	28,459	23,383	24,876
1891	363,349	44,850	27,271	24,743	29,910
1892	394,756	44,310	29,146	24,743	23,220
1893	375,845	30,090	25,736	10,020	4,860
1894	389,745	36,340	10,825	10,020	7,020
1895	359,215	None	None	10,020	2,160

[24] Copy of Brouillet to Archbishop John J. Williams of Boston, Aug. 24, 1880, A.B.C.I.M.; Ann. Rpt. of Bd. Ind. Com. (1880), 95-114. Lowrie to Schurz, Jan. 22, 1881; Schurz to Com. Ind. Aff., Feb. 17, 1881; Brouillet to Teller, July 28, 1882; Bur. Ind. Aff., Ltrs. Rec'd. Teller wrote his order in the margin of Brouillet's letter and transmitted it to the Indian Bureau on July 31, 1882.

[25] Copy of Ewing to Archbishop J. B. Purcell of Cincinnati, Apr. 30, 1874, A.B.C.I.M.; Ann. Rpts. of Com. Ind. Aff. (1891), 68 (1900), 25.

Year	Catholic	Presbyterian	Congregational	Friends	Episcopal
1896	308,471	None	None	None	2,160
1897	198,228	None	None	None	None
1898	156,754	None	None	None	None
1899	116,862	None	None	None	None
1900	57,642	None	None	None	None
Total	$3,959,643	$352,470	$219,644	$170,577	$123,346

Year	Methodist	Lutheran	Unitarian	Mennonite
1886	None	None	None	None
1887	None	None	$1,350	$3,340
1888	None	$ 1,350	5,400	2,500
1889	$2,725	4,050	5,400	3,125
1890	9,940	7,560	5,400	4,375
1891	6,700	9,180	5,400	4,375
1892	13,980	16,200	5,400	4,375
1893	None	15,120	5,400	3,750
1894	None	15,120	5,400	3,750
1895	None	15,120	5,400	3,750
1896	600	None	None	3,125
1897	None	None	None	None
1898	None	None	None	None
1899	None	None	None	None
1900	None	None	None	None
Total	$33,945	$83,700	$44,550	$36,465

One of the strongest of Catholic objections to the "Peace Policy" had been that it forced Catholic Indians to attend government schools staffed by Protestant teachers. Catholic missionaries believed that Indians could become civilized only if they were converted to "sterling Christianity." That they meant to augment their missionary activity by placing considerable emphasis upon education was already apparent during the seventies when the number of Catholic Indian schools was in-

creased from eight to thirty. The making of school contracts
with the government was a means of financing mission work as
well as of civilizing Indians, and with the return to political
patronage in the appointment of agency employees, the Catholic Bureau gave its attention almost entirely to such contracts.
Industrial boarding schools located on the reservations were
best suited from the Catholic point of view, to the instillment of
white culture, because next to pagan religion the greatest obstacle to the Indian's assimilation was his aversion to labor. In
view of the statistics given above it is no surprise that in 1892
the Presbyterians cried "Uncle," and called for the abolition of
the contract system. They could not compete with the Catholic
Bureau in lobbying for funds, and thus it was expedient to call
attention to the fact that the "appropriation of public money
for the support of sectarian schools" was contrary to the
fundamental principle on which American institutions rested,
"the separation of church and state."[26]

It was this very point that the Baptist Commissioner of
Indian Affairs, Thomas J. Morgan, had been making since his
taking office in 1889, and it was the reason that the Catholic
Bureau tried desperately to prevent his confirmation by the
Senate. The director of the Bureau, Father J. A. Stephan, was
determined that government support of Catholic Indian schools
not only should continue but should increase year by year. As
the table of expenditures shows, Stephan was very successful
through 1892, but in the meantime he had underestimated the
importance of maintaining good relations with the Indian
Office. Unlike Commissioner Ewing, who, in the interest of
amity, had refused to defend unworthy Catholics, director
Stephan was enraged in 1889 when the Superintendent of Indian

---

[26] Lawrence B. Palladino, S. J., *Indian and White in the Northwest*
(Baltimore, 1894), 83, 85, and 93 ; Rahill, *op. cit.*, 273-74 ; Brouillet to
Chandler, Dec. 24, 1875, Bur. Ind. Aff., Ltrs. Rec'd ; Ann. Rpt. of
Com. Ind. Aff. (1892), 178.

Schools, Daniel Dorchester, dismissed a large number of incompetent and otherwise unsuitable personnel, including several Catholics. He was particularly angered that Dorchester, a Methodist clergyman and president of the National Temperance League, ousted John Gorman from the education division on grounds of intemperance, insubordination, and inefficiency. The Catholic Bureau immediately found a place for Gorman on its staff, from which he repeatedly attacked the Harrison administration through the press. Whether or not there was any truth in Stephan's charges of gospel fanaticism and hypocrisy, his course of action was poor politics because it caused a severance of official relations with the government. In 1891, Commissioner Morgan ended the practice of making contracts for the education of Indian youth through the Catholic Bureau, and chose instead to negotiate directly with the Catholic schools. With the central Catholic organization thus deprived of much influence, with Protestants calling for an end to federal suppport because they could not compete, and with the Commissioner of Indian Affairs favoring nonsectarian education, a policy of increasing the number of government schools and of decreasing those conducted under contract froze the Catholics out by 1901.[27]

Because Catholic officials misinterpreted the motives of Protestant leaders who persuaded Grant to adopt denominational administration in preference to the spoils system, the Catholic reaction was a counter-movement in the interest of Catholic Indian missions. Again and again the charge of "bigotry" was made, and the *Catholic World* went so far as to declare that the Protestants had "itching palms." Certainly

---

[27] Stephan to Chas. Lusk, Sec. of B.C.I.M., July 27, 1889 ; Copy of Stephan to Senator Henry L. Dawes, Chm. of Sen. Com. on Ind. Aff., Dec. 19, 1889, A.B.C.I.M. Morgan to Presidential Secretary E. W. Halford, Sept. 3, 1889 ; Morgan to Sec. of Interior, Nov. 25 and 26, 1889, Benjamin Harrison Papers, Library of Congress. Ann. Rpts. of Com. Ind. Aff., Vol. 1 (1891), 161-64 (1900), 26-27 (1901), 26,

Bishop Whipple and Benjamin Hallowell, whose humanitarian spirit sparked the "Peace Policy," stand acquitted by the historian. The Protestant group as a whole would have been other than human had not some of its members been guilty of acting from self-interest and narrow sectarianism. But Catholics too lived in houses made of glass![28]

---

[28] Seidenbush to Brouillet, Aug. 6, 1877, A.B.C.I.M.; E. Butler, "A Glance at the Indian Question," *Catholic World*, XXVI (1877), 199.

V

The View of the West

WESTERN OPINION OF Indians and Indian affairs was determined by the desires of frontier population. Throughout the westward movement frontiersmen were interested in land because it was a means to wealth, or at least to material well-being. The inevitable consequence was that enmity grew between the original inhabitants and white people who came to take their patrimony. Frontier citizens learned quickly that the wilderness had a price beyond the monetary value fixed by the ever-changing public land laws. Indians fought to preserve home and mode of life; their guerilla tactics and barbaric ferocity in striking at the advancing settlements terrorized pioneer families. Anxiety, suffering, and sudden death were the real price of the land. The urge to conquer on the one side, and the instinct to defend on the other, caused mutual hatred and distrust to flourish between Indian and white in the West.

It made little difference where the West was; in Nebraska, Idaho or Arizona, the demands of citizens were the same: land, transportation links, protection from Indian attacks, and removal of the Indians. Most Western people considered the destruction of Indian tribes meritorious, and were unconcerned that the frontier left a wreckage of long-established primitive cultures in its wake. Incapable of sympathy for what was considered an inferior race, they held to an attitude determined by the spirit of adventure associated with the westward movement, by self--aggrandizement and the instinct for self-preservation.

No habitable plot of ground was so insignificant that white men did not want it. Indian reservations were especially prized, having the added attraction of a challenge to bold men who dared brook the displeasure of the government by encroaching upon them. One of the few reserves left in Kansas when Grant became President was the Kaw, a remnant of a huge tract recognized by treaty in 1825. The Ohio tribes had been settled upon it under the removal policy, and then mostly resettled in the Indian Territory to make room for expansion of the agricultural frontier. Pioneers thought of the Kaw Reserve as "one of the best tracts of land in the State," and wanted to establish farms there. Fifteen or twenty white families had already settled illegally, the surrounding community was stripping off the timber, and the United States marshal's office was unable to prevent such intrusion. Obviously the Kansas legislature, which sent resolutions to the United States Congress in 1870 and 1871 asking the abolition of all reservations in the state, was on the side of the intruders. The story was much the same at Round Valley in California, a reserve enveloped by a mountain barrier with a narrow outlet at one end. Stockmen, each claiming several square miles of range, were moving in to pasture cattle and sheep. These trespassers did not worry much about suits of ejectment brought against them in 1876 by agent J. L. Burchard; due process of law might require several years, while the use of the range would more than pay the expense of keeping the cases in court. Moreover, in the event of a decision to break up the reservation, their claims to the land would have priority. Neither in Kansas nor in California were the reserves abolished, but circumstances in both states explain why agents required military assistance to keep white people from stealing Indian land.[1]

Frontier citizens had no regard for justice when it was opposed to their self-interest. Rather, defiance of authority was

---

[1] Kappler, *Laws and Treaties*, II, 156-59 ; Resolutions, Senate Misc. Docs./No. 55, 41st Cong., 2nd Sess., and No. 69, 41st Cong., 3rd Sess. J. B! Gilliland at Emporia, Kan., to Pres. Grant, Feb. 14, 1871 ; Joseph Dunlap at Leavenworth, Kan., to Supt. Enoch Hoag, Feb. 14, 1871 ; Burchard to Com. Ind. Aff. J. Q. Smith, Apr. 13, 1876, Bur. Ind. Aff., Ltrs. Rec'd.

a common reaction to any attempt at law enforcement, as the "Boomer" movement proved. By 1879, "almost the entire population of southern Kansas" was "agog" for opening the Indian Territory to homesteaders. Within one year, an Oklahoma bill was before Congress and preparations for an organized assault on the land were in progress under the leadership of David L. Payne, formerly an assistant door-keeper at the U.S. House of Representatives. To prevent forcible entry, President Hayes issued two proclamations pro-viding for removal by the military of any persons who should illegally attempt to occupy the great Indian reserve. In open contempt, the *Kansas City Times* declared that executive orders were no bar to the settlement of lands ceded by the Five Civilized Tribes in 1866 for occupation by other Indians who, it was now certain, would not need them. There were "ten millions of acres of the finest agricultural public lands on the continent . . . awaiting . . . the hardy pioneer who would soon turn up the virgin soil, subdue the waste places, and make the land . . . blossom as the rose." Currently the Territory was a barrier to civilization and a refuge for highwaymen. No other President of the United States had dared prevent citizens from settling on the public domain. "On to Oklahoma!" Ten years, a relatively short time as the historian reckons, were required for the "Boomers" to obtain their prize.[2]

Curiously enough, the editorial in the *Times* was clipped and sent to President Hayes by an old settler who had lived in the Kansas City area since 1831. A one-time supporter of President Jackson, who had advocated Indian removal, this frontiersman was now on the side of the Indians, and would have denied succeeding generations the opportunity to profit from the

---

[2] John M. McNeil at Coffeyville, Kan., to Com. Ind. Aff. E. A. Hayt, May 6, 1879 ; B. B. Richards at Kansas City to Hayes, Feb. 19, 1880, encl. news clipping, Bur. Ind. Aff., Ltrs. Rec'd. Acting Com. Ind. Aff. E. Marble to Sec. of Interior, Mar. 30, 1881, Sec. Interior, Ltrs. Rec'd.

conquest of Indian land. If there was any integrity left in the white race, he wrote, the treaty should be kept. Had not the tribes been guaranteed reservations in perpetuity; did not the Indians, like the rest of humanity, require a place to exist? The "Boomers" were a lot of thieves! In old age it cost nothing to talk of justice and to reprimand one's juniors for base designs.

Western businessmen, like farmers and stockmen, meant to profit from the opening of Indian Territory to settlement. E. S. Mety of Wm. E. Storer & Co. at St. Louis saw in what was then "a barrier to the commercial interests of the Southwest" and a harbor for absconding debtors, a potential market and a bread-basket of raw agricultural products. In view of these considera-tions, there was ample reason for Mety to exceed the bounds of veracity and declare Oklahoma "the garden spot of the United States lacking . . . the garden," and to state that the land was of no more use to the Indians than an area two hundred miles farther west would be. Always, the frontier rationalized in favor of the white community.[3]

In remote middle regions where efficient transportation links with the rest of the nation were absent, farmers and ranchers sometimes welcomed an Indian reservation as a market for grain and beef. Along the Ruidosa and Bonito Rivers of New Mexico Territory, in 1867, were the widely scattered dwellings of sod-busters and cattle grazers—the advance force of Anglo-American civilization. In the hilly and mountainous country-side lurked the Mescalero Apache, whose depredations were the scourge of the best "lands for Agriculture and the raising of Stock . . . on the Continent." A plan of the citizens was to con-centrate these marauding bands on one-half of the military reserve at Fort Stanton, where they would come under the surveillance of soldiers and where the government would pay for their subsistence. Fort Stanton, already a market for local

---

[3] Mety at St. Louis to Hayes, Feb. 19, 1878, Bur. Ind. Aff., Ltrs. Rec'd.

produce, did become the agency of the Mescalero Apache, and the confinement of hungry Indians there was an economic benefit to the surrounding white community.[4]

Military installations, like Indian reservations, were an economic godsend until cheap transportation to distant markets arrived; but even more important, the presence of soldiers was balm to unsteady pioneer nerves. If no fort protected a given sector of the frontier, a request was soon sent to the government to have one built; if a post was manned by a skeleton force, the settlers asked for additional troops, cavalry preferred. The Nebraska legislature memorialized the federal government in 1873 that a fort was needed in the Republican Valley for the protection of lives and property, in order to facilitate the settlement of the southwestern portion of the state; Governor Furnas informed the Secretary of War that great fear of Indian hostilities was expressed in letters and petitions, making the building of a post advisable. Roaming bands of Sioux, sulking because desperadoes had murdered two braves, were threatening vengeance. No fort was built, but the General of the Army authorized cavalry to drive the Sioux within their Dakota reservation. Idaho citizens complained the same year that fifty soldiers stationed at Fort Boise were inadequate to provide security against large bands of Bannock, Shoshoni, and Umatilla whose summer depredations were retarding economic development; they wanted four companies of cavalry sent to keep the Indians on their reservations. Of the fact that the Army lacked enough troops of any kind, not to mention cavalry, to guard the entire frontier, there was little appreciation.[5]

---

[4] Petition of 210 citizens of N. Mex. Terr. to Supt. A. B. Norton, Jan. 22, 1867, Bur. Ind. Aff., Ltrs. Rec'd.

[5] Robert W. Furnas to Sec. of War, Feb. 13, 1873, encl. memorial of the Nebraska legislature and Sherman's endorsement, Feb. 21 ; petition of 750 Idaho citizens to Pres. Grant, June 13, 1873, War Records.

The West was military-minded about Indian affairs because westerners thought they saw in armed force an abrupt means of solving the Indian problem. Indians were a worthless obstacle to "manifest destiny" and were members of an inferior race doomed to extinction; the assimilation of "savages" was a totally unacceptable idea. Frontier citizens were quick to agree with Darwin that the progress of civilization was dependent upon the survival of the fittest. To talk of educating the denizens of mountain and plain was worse than nonsense; it was a transgression of natural law.

This attitude alone explains why the "Peace Policy" was unwelcome beyond the Mississippi River. But contempt for it there was heightened by misunderstanding. The very term "Peace Policy" was a source of irritation because the West favored war until the last Indian had "bitten the dust," or gone meekly to a reservation. Frontier folk read only the local newspapers, which with reference to Indian affairs were strongly biased. To most Westerners, the "Peace Policy" was a foolhardy plan, conceived by ignorant and sentimental easterners, to conquer barbarians with kindness. They were not aware that the men responsible for its inauguration were keen observers of the Western scene; still less did they comprehend that Western citizens would benefit if the policy were effectively applied.

The closer a Western community lived to hostile Indians, the more averse it was to programs for their welfare. Assimilation was an idea so foreign that most frontier newspapers overlooked it in commenting on the "Peace Policy." An editorial of March 1870 in the *Cheyenne Daily Leader* did not recognize any difference between the new policy and the old. At this time only the Quakers had been invited to appoint administrative personnel, but the program of driving Indians from the great open spaces to reservations, where it was intended that they should be given subsistence, clothed, and prepared for life in Anglo-American society, had been in force since the previous June. Yet the *Leader* declared that "the old policy of feeding the Indians and paying them an annual premium for murder and stealing is still recommended." Its readers would like less of the "Big Father" approach to Indian administration and more support for "the cause of civilization and progress," which meant that the Great Sioux Reservation should be opened to settlement. Perhaps "the cautious and economical policy of the administration" which was trying to avoid an expensive Indian war had some merit, but a fair regard for the "rights" of white population in the West was a more important consideration. The editorial closed with these comments, which represent attitudes on the cutting edge of the frontier :

A good father is not always indulgent. He discriminates and sometimes finds occasion to frown at the wayward children and even to use the rod. . . . If it is necessary let the nation assert its rights and its dignity at the mouth of the cannon. Let snivelling quakers give place to bluff soldiers. Let the hell-hounds of the wilderness for once feel the power of the people whom they defy. The blood of thousands of our murdered fellow-countrymen cries to heaven for vengeance. And how do we avenge them? By an annual tribute of toys and trinkets. By annual subsidies of food, clothing and ammunition. Would that the descendants of the Puritans, who are most officious in promoting the continuance of this policy, had to live for a few months under the shadow of its fulfillment. A short experience of the tender mercies of the Sioux or the Comanches would forever dissipate the poetical and humane ideas of Indian policy which they have contracted from reading Longfellow's Hiawatha and contemplating "picture Indians," in their luxurious parlors.⁶

Five years of experience with the "Peace Policy" did nothing to change the attitude of frontier Wyoming toward Indians. The *Wyoming Weekly Leader* reported conditions among the reservation Sioux in this fashion : "The latest reliable news from

---

⁶ Mar. 9, 1870,

the Indian agencies is . . . that Red Cloud, Red Dog and other noted red men are suffering from dyspepsia and other digestive disasters induced by want of exercise and 'slathers' of Kansas City bacon. Three cheers for that bacon!"

The West had a Christian heritage just as did the East, and frontier citizens recognized a need to reconcile their cause with Scripture just as Protestant reformers looked upon the Bible as the foundation of their movement. When the editor of the *Arizona Citizen* learned that Christianization of Indians was included in the government's program, he had a field day with the Old Testament. "Spare the rod and spoil the child," his article began, was a proverb of Holy Writ. No concept was more rigidly adhered to by divine teachers than the necessity of severe discipline. "According to inspired writings, God in his just wrath destroyed whole nations of wicked people," and "his meek and humble adorers have never entered a single protest against the policy, or even censured it as harsh or barbarous." Christian people had recently affirmed on bended knees that the country had been purified and elevated by the sacrifice of innumerable lives in a civil war which upheld the supremacy of law and preserved national unity. "While President Grant and millions of sincere but . . . misguided philanthropists declare that the Indian must be christianized by kindness, moral suasion, food, and clothing, given him in idleness in everything but the labor of murdering, scalping, and robbing law-abiding citizens, we respectfully suggest, if his christianization be the chief object of these good people, that there are different and well-established methods of attaining this noble end, and these methods have never been held barbarous by the Christian Church." Indeed, the principle that wrongdoers should be punished in this world if possible, and would certainly be punished in the next, was the most prominent teaching of all

---

' Oct. 30, 1875.

Christian sects. Who would deny that murder was the worst of all crimes and assassination the least excusable form of it? Yet the Indian preferred the latter style and was "rewarded with milk and honey, lands and beeves, raiment and idleness . . ." If the work of Christianizing Apaches were prefaced with temporary curtailment of all this beneficence and initiated with a generous amount of lead, perhaps there could be some hope of success. Certainly there was ample Christian authority to recommend such an approach to the Indian problem.[8]

In 1871 Arizona citizens were of the opinion that under the separate direction of the Departments of Interior and War there were two policies in force—the idealistic policy of the Board of Indian Commissioners, and the realistic policy of the Army. Should the Board succeed in its aims, they believed themselves doomed, and therefore petitioned President Grant to support the vigorous war policy of General George Crook. At this time, the President had instructed the Departments of Interior and War to cooperate in gathering the wild tribes of the Southwest upon a reservation at Canada Alamosa in New Mexico Territory. Vincent Colyer, the secretary of the Board of Indian Commissioners, was sent to the collection point with the promise of military assistance, but because local citizens threatened to massacre the Apaches who gathered there, other sites, including Camp Grant in Arizona Territory, were selected. Before Colyer arrived at Camp Grant, the War Department instructed the commander of the post to call in all friendly Indians, and representatives of three bands responded. On hearing of these proceedings, the citizens of Tucson prepared to attack the Indians by organizing an expedition, which marched in the direction of the proposed reserve; but they were dismayed to find the representatives of Interior and War demonstrating an unusual singleness of purpose. Colyer had

---

[8] Apr. 22, 1871.

reached the scene and had persuaded Captain William Nelson to defend a ten-mile radius around Camp Grant; the Tucson volunteers turned back upon learning that artillery was trained on the mouth of a canyon through which they must pass. The experience, however, did not enlighten them. In November, when General John M. Schofield, commander of the Pacific military division, ordered the troops to make war on all Indians off reservations, Southwestern newspapers teemed with reports of Colyer's being "shelved" and "ousted." That Schofield's order made the "Peace Policy" official in Arizona Territory, and that the implementation of it required a combination of military force and humanitarian treatment, were missed by frontier editors.[9]

In some instances the Interior Department did not understand Western people any better than they understood the "Peace Policy." After a term as Commissioner of Indian Affairs, Francis Walker, a native of Boston and generally a shrewd observer, eloquently described the problems of frontier Arizona, but grossly misjudged the Western attitude toward Indians.

It is the almost universal belief throughout the country, that the people of this Territory have a deadly hostility to the Indians, and meditate nothing but mischief towards them; and it certainly must be admitted that press and people alike indulge in expressions which . . . create an impression that the citizens . . . hate an Indian as an Indian, and have no humane sentiments whatever towards the race. . . . When the press of Arizona crys out against the Indian policy of the government, and denounces Eastern philanthropy, they have in mind the warlike and depredating bands, and they are

---

[9] Grant to Sec. of Interior Delano, July 13, 1871 ; Adj. Gen. of the Army, E. D. Townsend, to Comdg. Gen., Dept. of Mo., July 18, 1871 ; Nelson to Asst. Adj. Gen., Dept. of Ariz., Sept. 15, 1871 ; Ariz. Supt. H. Bendell at San Francisco to Colyer, Oct. 24, 1871 ; Gila River agent J. H. Stout to Colyer, Dec. 6, 1871 (mostly copies), Bd. Ind. Com., Ltrs. Rec'd. General Order No. 10, Nov. 21, 1871, War Records.

exasperated by what they deem . . . the weakness and indecision of the executive in failing to protect the frontier. Indians, to them, mean Apaches, and their violence on the Indian question arises from the belief that the administration of Indian affairs has been committed to the sentimentalists, who have no appreciation of the terrible stress which these Indian outrages bring upon the remote settlements. But were the question one of helping . . . a tribe of Indians who are peaceful . . . there is no reason to suppose that the inhabitants of Tucson, or Prescott would be behind an Eastern congregation in readiness for the work.[10]

This was nonsense; the West had no compassion for peaceable Indians. Else why were the citizens of northwestern Minnesota so badly disposed toward the White Earth Chippewa?[11] At best Indians were regarded as a nuisance, as members of a primitive race, and as a hindrance to progress. Generation would succeed generation before many westerners would admit that an injustice had been done the red man. Not until the mid-twentieth century did nostalgia bring thousands of them to museums on Sunday afternoons to gain some appreciation of Indian culture as portrayed by Karl Bodmer, George Catlin, and Alfred Jacob Miller.[12]

---

[10] Francis A. Walker, "The Indian Question," *North American Review*, CXVI (1873), 338.

[11] J. J. Enmegahbowh at White Earth to H. B. Whipple, June 6, 1872, Whipple Papers.

[12] Concerning frontier attitude toward the semiarid West, it is worthwhile to compare the early part of this Chapter with Henry Nash Smith's discussion of the myth of the garden in *Virgin Land* (London, 1950), 123-32 and 174-83.

VI

The Military Position

MANY OF THE ideas which were incorporated into the "Peace Policy" originated with military personnel. The suggestions of General Sully from his camp opposite Farm Island on the Missouri River in 1864, and those of General Sherman in 1866 and 1868, have already been noted. It was Sully who urged the government to gather peaceable Indians near military posts and invite missionaries to educate their children. Although Sully's proposal was original with him, Sherman's plan for two large reservations, one north of the Platte and the other south of the Arkansas, to which all roaming Indians of the plains must go or perish by force of arms, was an elaboration of a stratagem used by General James H. Carleton to subdue the Navajo between 1863 and 1865.[1]

Without the cooperation of the Army the "Peace Policy" was unworkable. Those who favored the employment of Peace Commissioners to assemble the hostile tribes were unrealistic. Commissioner Nathaniel G. Taylor admitted in his report for the Peace Commission in 1868 that the wilder Indians would not willingly confine themselves to reservations, but contended that they would eventually be starved into submission. The frontier could not await such a result. Indeed, it was the frontier that hurried the depletion of the game and ended the possibility of life by the chase in a much shorter period than the twenty-five years within which the Peace Commissioners assumed that it might be possible to assimilate the Indians. Furthermore, frontier population would not tolerate the working out of such

---

[1] Edward E. Dale, *The Indians of the Southwest* (Norman, Okla., 1949), 54.

a scheme. Starvation maddened the natives; their begging, thieving, and murdering became unbearable; nothing less than speedy removal and confinement of Indians upon reservations was satisfactory to the advancing settlers. Only the Army possessed the means of accomplishing this because, of necessity, the means was military force. Still, it was not only Commissioner Taylor who was unrealistic. General Sherman admitted in 1878 that military as well as civilian members of the Peace Commission did not foresee the rapid depletion of game. There were millions of buffalo on the plains in 1868, he remarked, but "not a single one is now seen." The treaties had been written on the assumption "that the government would only have to furnish partial food for the Indian, and that he could procure half or a quarter of the necessary meat by hunting." The Indian Bureau was often forced to rely upon the War Department to feed Indians who came in to the agencies. Deficient or late appropriations and delinquent contractors produced a long series of emergencies which the Army was asked to meet. The Army could not always furnish the needed provisions because the post commissariats were not stocked to supply other than military personnel; however, the temporary aid which was given the Interior Department probably averted death by starvation, and perhaps an Indian uprising, on numerous occasions. In other respects, the Army was important to the application of the "Peace Policy." Sometimes soldiers were required to keep order among Indians gathered on reservations, and again they were called upon to expel intruders. Not least important was their inspection of annuity goods. In accord with another of General Sully's suggestions, several treaties concluded in 1868 and 1869 provided that a military officer should attend annuity payments and report on the quality and quantity of goods delivered, for the purpose of determining whether contracts had been fulfilled. Military inspectors were not employed until

1876; but thereafter the practice of fraud became more difficult.[2]

Military views of what would constitute a wise Indian policy were extremely varied. Colonels George Custer and John Gibbon were unsympathetic with the advocates of assimilation; they considered Indians a vanishing race whose hurried extermination by force of arms was warranted. To such officers in quest of rank, an Indian trail was the road to success. Their view was countered, however, by that of General John Pope, commander of the Missouri military department, who in 1876 proposed the most complex of schemes for the acculturation of Indians. Pope regarded the plan to teach farming to all the tribes as ill-founded because their habits, ideas, and modes of life differed. He compared the nomads of the plains with the semi-civilized tribes of Indian Territory; the Apaches of the Southwest, wretched and thieving vagabonds, with "the Navajoes of New Mexico . . ., occupying fixed homes, cultivating the soil, owning large herds of sheep, and being very skillful in certain kinds of woolen manufactures." Since the tribes were diverse in culture, a successful program would require careful study to determine the kind of occupation best suited to their advancement. Location, too, was an important consideration, having had much to do with the evolution of culture. On this basis the Cheyenne, Comanche, Kiowa, and Sioux were no more adaptable to plowing and reaping than an Arab or a Tartar would have been. Stock-raising, however, suited their situation perfectly. Profits from the sale of beef, hides, mutton, and wool would constitute a powerful incentive to abandon

---

[2] Peace Commission Rpt., House Exec. Doc. No. 1, 40th Cong., 3rd Sess., Vol. 2, 504-505 ; Ann. Rpt. of Gen. of the Army, House Exec. Doc. No. 1, 45th Cong., 3rd Sess., Vol. 2, 4-6 ; Copy of Sully at Milwaukee to Asst. Adj. Gen., Dept. of N. W., Nov. 22, 1864, Bd. Ind. Com., Ltrs. Rec'd. ; Sec. of Interior Chandler to Com. Ind. Aff., Feb. 14, 1876, Bur. Ind. Aff., Ltrs. Rec'd.

depredatory and warlike ways.[3]

It is questionable whether nomadic Indians could have become successful ranchers in a period when grass had begun to challenge the economic supremacy of cotton. The cattle boom was already on; within a decade, white grazers would overstock the ranges; Eastern and foreign capitalists would invest heavily in the business; ranching would become a highly competitive enterprise. Still Pope's recommendation was better than the plan to teach all Indians agriculture, and it had the additional merit of coming before the northern reservations were drastically reduced, in the late eighties, by the return of millions of acres to the public domain.[4]

Pope was critical of the government for expecting the Army to keep Indians on reservations without rations sufficient for their maintenance; it was difficult to force the natives to starve peaceably. The General thought Congress should appropriate more money, and that the high cost of transporting supplies to remote agencies should be pared down by locating Indians at convenient places "within or behind the settlements." Of course, these suggestions did not take into account the influence of public opinion upon federal policy—something which the military mind did not comprehend.

For some high-ranking officers, Darwinian theory had a strong appeal. In 1866 General James H. Carleton, commander of the military department of New Mexico, explained the rapid decrease of Indian population in these terms: "The causes which the Almighty originates, when in their appointed time he wills that one race of men—as in races of lower animals—shall disappear off the face of the earth and give place to another

---

[3] Gibbon at Ft. Shaw, Mont. Terr., to H. B. Whipple, Nov. 15, 1876, Whipple Papers; Copy of Pope to Asst. Adj. Gen. R. C. Drum, Mil. Div. of Mo., Chicago, June 8, 1877, Bur. Ind. Aff., Ltrs. Rec'd.

[4] Ernest S. Osgood, *The Day of the Cattleman* (Minneapolis, 1954), 83 and 94-113,

race, and so on, in the great cycle traced out by Himself, which may be seen, but has reasons too deep to be fathomed by us. The races of the mammoths and mastodons, and the great sloths, came and passed away: the red man of America is passing away!" And one detects the influence of Lewis H. Morgan's *Ancient Society* (1877) upon the opinions of General William T. Sherman and Colonel Nelson A. Miles. Sherman wrote in his report for 1878: "To convert the Indians into a pastoral race is the first step in their upward progress toward civilization; that of the agriculturist must be the next stage, though slower of realization; but in this direction is the sole hope of rescuing any part of the 'nomade' Indians from utter annihilation." The next year Miles expressed the same thesis in an article for the *North American Review:* "The change must be gradual, continuous, and in accordance with Nature's laws. The history of nearly every race that has advanced from barbarism to civilization has been through the stages of the hunter, the herdsman, the agriculturist, and finally reaching those of commerce, mechanics, and the higher arts." Survival of the fittest and progress through evolution both implied that Indians were inferior beings, and therefore justified their extermination or confinement on reservations in order to make way for a "superior civilized race." Had those officers chosen to regard as equals the natives against whom their columns advanced, the performance of duty would have been more difficult.[5]

The attitude of military officers toward Indians who remained on reservations and exhibited good behavior was quite different from their attitude toward the hostile bands. For

---

[5] Rpt. of Jt. Spec. Com. of Cong. on Condition of Ind. Tribes, Senate Rpt. No. 156, 39th Cong., 2nd Sess., 4 ; Ann. Rpt. of Gen. of the Army, House Exec. Doc. No. 1, 45th Cong., 3rd Sess., Vol. 2, 4-6 ; Nelson A. Miles, "The Indian Problem," *North American Review,* CXXVIII (1879), 309.

example, Colonel D. S. Stanley, the commander of Fort Sully in Dakota Territory, was well disposed toward the friendly Sioux. He was genuinely interested in their welfare, wanted them assimilated, and went so far as to advise the Indian Bureau to issue a liberal supply of trade rifles and ammunition as a hedge against their starvation. Conversely, the hostiles angered and frustrated Stanley; he scorned the idea that missionaries could placate them; he was convinced that the only remedy for their recalcitrance was subjugation. Stanley had little hope that a military force operating from the Missouri River or from the Union Pacific and Northern Pacific railroads could hunt down and punish these implacable Sioux unless it had the assistance of a very large number of Indian auxiliaries; but he supposed that philanthropists would defeat such a plan. As it was, the mountainous region lying between the headwaters of the Great Cheyenne and Yellowstone rivers was of no use to the friendly Sioux, who did not dare enter it because they feared death at the hands of their relatives for defecting to the whites. There a murderous Indian felt secure and laughed at the authority of the United States. As Stanley saw it, the only way to handle this situation was to open to settlement the Sioux hunting grounds, which lay in the western part of their so-called permanent reserve, and send in with the immigrants a military force large enough to offer protection. The government did not follow this advice, but matters worked out pretty much in accordance with the Colonel's wishes when the Black Hills were invaded by miners in 1874, and the troops were ordered to "clean out" the Indians two years later.[6]

The military were generally agreed that the assimilation of wild tribes was unthinkable until they had first been subdued. As General Sheridan remarked, an Indian, like a wild horse, needed breaking to make him useful. Sheridan was convinced

---

[6] Stanley to Com. Ind. Aff. Parker, Feb. 20, 1870 ; Stanley to Sec. of Interior Delano, Jan. 20, 1873, Bur. Ind. Aff., Ltrs. Rec'd.

that all the young men of the nomadic bands were prone to steal and that they must first be punished if the government expected them to settle down. He agreed with General Sully that it was an "absolute necessity" for the government "to promptly punish their aggressions on our people, as the only way to put a stop to them. With the wild uncultivated savage, no half measure will answer: you must subdue them before you can compromise with them, and it is in the end charity to them to do so. The sooner these wild tribes are made to feel that they are dependent on the Government for their support, the sooner they will be susceptible of being civilized."

Neither of these officers thought in terms of an evolutionary process. Sheridan believed that after the initial Indian war, which was inevitable, an adequate feeding and educational program would avoid subsequent outbreaks, and make the tribes self-supporting in a relatively short period of time. Progress would vary according to the environment in which assimilation was attempted, and according to cultural diversity. Reservations should be located near military posts and the Army entrusted with the enforcement of discipline; whiskey traders, especially, must be kept out. Assimilation would require the employment of qualified personnel—common sense, courage, determination, patience, good morals, and ability to learn Indian languages were the characteristics which Sheridan recommended. Frequent removal of agents was undesirable because successful administration of Indian affairs depended upon experience; tenure of office would improve the service considerably. Most military officers regarded the subjugation of the tribes as a prerequisite to the expansion of Anglo-American culture and thought no further, but Sheridan and

---

Sheridan to Adj. Gen. of the Army, E. D. Townsend, July 12, 1869, War Records; Sully at Camp Emory, Miss., to Sec. of Bd. Ind. Com., J. K. Cree, Aug. 4, 1872, Bd. Ind. Com., Ltrs. Rec'd.

Episcopal Bishop Henry B. Whipple
(Minnesota Historical Society)

A Caddo village, Indian Territory, 1870's.

Map from "The Christian Weekly," Dec. 12, 1874, depicting
the assignment of reservations to religious bodies.
(Quaker Collection, Haverford College)

Students at the Cherry Creek mission of the Dakota Native Missionary Society, Cheyenne River Reservation. (Smithsonian Institution)

A company of Indian police, Dakota Territory. (Smithsonian Institution)

A day school, Indian Territory, 1870's.
(Quaker Collection, Haverford College)

Standing Bear, Ponca Chief.
(Smithsonian Institution)

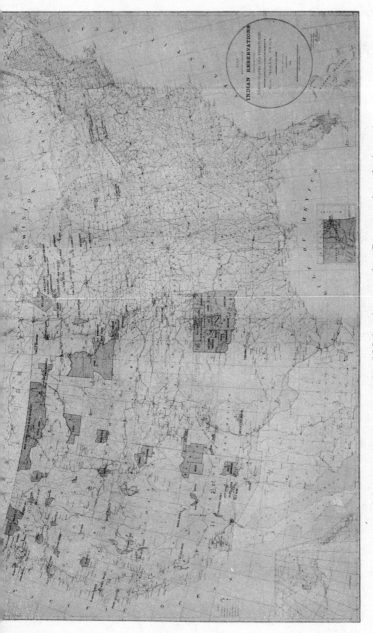

Map of reservations in 1884 prior to the Congressional Act of 1886 under which millions of acres were relinquished by northern tribes. (Library of Congress)

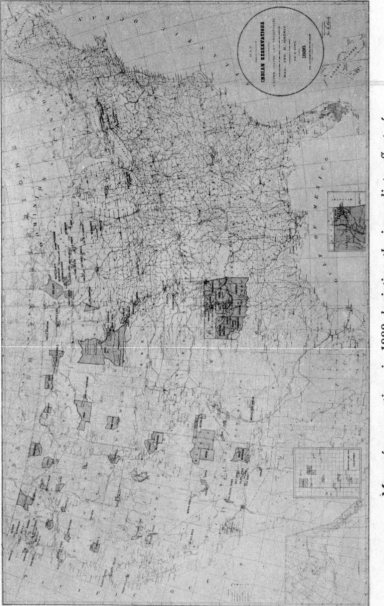

Map of reservations in 1888 depicting the immediate effect of the Congressional Act of 1886.
(Library of Congress)

Sully were concerned that the Indians should become citizens of the United States.[8]

Sheridan's views were important because during the period of the "Peace Policy" he commanded two-thirds the effective force of the whole Army. His jurisdiction extended from Canada to Mexico, and from the Mississippi River westward to, and including, the Rocky Mountain chain. This was the Missouri military division. In his report for 1878 there appeared an objective summary of events which had transpired during the decade just past. With a few exceptions Indians had occupied the entire plains region. Nature had provided everything necessary to sustain life, and whatever else was wanted might be had through barter with white traders. The only professions of the men, who disdained work, were hunting and war. This way of life was suddenly interrupted by the intrusion of white settlers, whose advance the Army was unable to prevent. The whole military force scattered over the plains region never numbered more than fourteen thousand men. "The government made treaties, gave presents, made promises, none of which were honestly fulfilled, and, like all original treaties with Indians in this country, they were the first steps in the process of developing hostilities." In their simplicity the Indians made blind bargains; then saw their lands wrested from their possession, their buffalo, elk, deer, and antelope rapidly diminish. Angered by the violation of treaty rights, the tribes made war, killing men, women, and children, intruders upon their soil, "no difference being made between the innocent or guilty, the armed or unarmed." Years of struggle and the hammering of an inadequate military force compelled the hostiles south of the Union Pacific Railroad to go upon reservations in the Indian Territory. The Army made an effort to prevent the breaking up of the Great Sioux Reservation and to protect their

[8] Ann. Rpt., House Exec. Doc. No. 1, 45th Cong., 3rd Sess., Vol. 2, 37-38.

adjacent hunting grounds in Montana and Wyoming Territories. But "the Black Hills contained gold, the valleys of the South Cheyenne, Belle Fourche, and the Yellowstone, and along the eastern slope of the Bighorn Mountains, invited the agriculturist, while the upper tableland country presented the finest grazing ranges in the world." For hundreds of years the buffalo had fattened upon them. It was too much for the immigrant to resist. War with the Sioux followed, and when it ended these Indians found themselves restricted to reservations "embracing the poorest land of all this extensive region . . . and with no compensation beyond the promise of religious instruction, schools, supplies of food and clothing, and an opportunity of learning the ways in which the white man cultivated the ground." For the most part these promises had not been kept. "In other words, we took away their country and their means of support, broke up their mode of living, . . . introduced disease and decay among them, and it was for this and against this they made war. Could any one expect less?"[9]

Notably, Sheridan was more capable of an objective analysis of Indian affairs after the Sioux had been defeated. Just two years earlier he had written that the Black Hills invasion had nothing to do with their hostility. "They wanted to fight, and have been preparing for it for years back. It is their profession, their glory, and the only thing that stirs them up from absolute idleness." This was penned less than a month after the Custer massacre. Sheridan's task was ahead of him; an officer could not sympathize with a people against whom he was about to conduct a ruthless campaign. Rather, he took the view that war was a prerequisite of assimilation and that since this might be the last one, the military had better do a good job of it.[10]

Although Sheridan agreed with the strategy and the object-

---

[9] *Ibid.,* 34-36.

[10] Copy of Sheridan at Chicago to Sherman, July 18, 1876, Bur. Ind. Aff., Ltrs. Rec'd.

ives of the "Peace Policy" and pledged the fullest cooperation of the military, he was not satisfied with its implementation, from the standpoint either of the Army, of the white community, or of the Indians. Insufficient appropriations to feed starving Indians were responsible for spoliation of the white community, accompanied by dreadful cruelties. The game was depleted; any race would fight rather than starve. Therefore the first remedial step was to provide a regular and increased supply of rations and follow it "with a strong and stable government, backed up by a sufficient number of soldiers to enforce a spirit of obedience and to keep these restless savages within the limits of their reservations."[11]

Another of Sheridan's criticisms was that many of the Indians brought within reservations, where they were out of the Army's jurisdiction, had not been adequately subdued. The reservations were havens of safety from which they made forays upon the settlements and to which they returned before the military could overtake them. For this the Kiowa and Comanche near Fort Sill were particularly notorious, prompting a request from the governor of Texas in 1873 that a regiment of volunteers be raised to protect the northern frontier of his state. Rather than permit the use of volunteers, Sheridan asked for authority to strike the marauding bands within their reserve. Since this would have involved a compromise of the "Peace Policy," such authority was not granted, but during 1874 and 1875, with the cooperation of the Indian Bureau, the plains tribes on reservations in the Indian Territory were disarmed and dismounted. The procedure was so successful that Sheridan decided to apply it to the Sioux after the uprising of 1876. Even the friendlies were deprived of firearms and ponies.[12]

---

[11] Ann. Rpts., House Exec. Docs. No. 1, 42nd Cong., 3rd Sess., Vol. 2, 35-36, and No. 1, 45th Cong., 3rd Sess., Vol. 2, 34 and 37.

[12] Ann. Rpt. of Gen. Pope, House Exec. Doc. No. 1, 41st Cong., 3rd Sess., Vol. 2, 8-9; Copy of Sheridan to Sherman, Nov. 12, 1873, Sec.

Generally, the military were opposed to the issue of arms and ammunition to peacable Indians, on the theory that such supplies would eventually get into the hands of the hostiles. This was especially so during periods and in areas of active hostility. But there were exceptions. Some officers recognized that until the government increased the supply of rations the Indians must hunt, and depletion of game made it impossible to secure an adequate diet without firearms. Even before the game was depleted it was necessary for plains Indians to keep moving in order to subsist, and their movement in scattered bands was precisely what the military wished to prevent. During the Sioux troubles of 1876 and 1877, the sale of arms and ammunition was prohibited at their agencies, causing consternation among the friendlies at Cheyenne River, who were thus deprived of game. To prevent these Indians from becoming outlaws, General Alfred Terry, commander of the Dakota military department, allowed them to organize hunting parties of moderate size, which were accompanied by a detachment of enlisted scouts under the supervision of a military officer. Obsolete army rifles and a limited supply of ammunition were given each Indian for the duration of such hunting expeditions.[13]

It was the "Peace Policy" as it related to the wild tribes of which military officers were most critical. General George Crook, commander of the Arizona military department, delayed implementation of it until April 1873 for the reason that his effective force was inadequate to do more than pursue Indians who were killing citizens and committing depredations. Cam-

---

Interior, Ltrs. Rec'd.; Copy of Sheridan to Sherman, July 18, 1876, Bur. Ind. Aff., Ltrs. Rec'd.

[13] Sec. of War Belknap to Sec. of Interior, Apr. 8, 1874; agent H. W. Bingham at Cheyenne River to Com. Ind. Aff. J. Q. Smith, Jan. 26, 1876; Sec. of Interior to Com. Ind. Aff., Dec. 11, 1877, encl. copy of War Records 7800 A. G. O. 1877, Bur. Ind. Aff., Ltrs. Rec'd. Smith to Bingham, Feb. 8, 1876; Smith to agents Mitchel, Cravens, Burke, et al., Aug. 22, 1876, Bur. Ind. Aff., Ltrs. Sent.

paigns against these were usually unsuccessful because rough terrain and miles of lava beds made tracking difficult. Also, Crook was aware that reservation Indians sometimes went on forays, and was unwilling to allow them immunity from chastisement. Making soldiers subject to the jurisdiction of civilian agents when asked upon reservations to deal with troublemakers was even more distasteful. Through delay the General obtained permission from the Interior Department to station troops upon reserves without surrendering his right to command them. Indian scouts used in campaigns against the roaming bands were to serve as a police force and to constitute a nucleus for the establishment of civil government. Troop commanders and agents were to share in the preparation of Indians for self-government and citizenship, although in fact military authority was preponderant. Understandably, the Board of Foreign Missions of the Reformed Church complained in 1874 of never having had control of the reservations assigned to them in Arizona Territory."

From the military standpoint the "Peace Policy" would have been better administered if it had been handled everywhere as it was under Crook; but even that would not have satisfied a large number of high-ranking officers who favored the transfer of the Indian Bureau to the War Department. There were numerous reasons for this preference. In the first place, there were few military men who had much faith in the efficacy of moral suasion as a means of eradicating primitive inclinations. General Sherman had none whatsoever. As he saw it, the assimilation of the plains tribes could not be accomplished "by means of the present peace agents, because persuasion is wasted on an

" Ann. Rpt., House Exec. Doc. No. 1, 42nd Cong., 3rd Sess., Vol. 2, 78 ; Crook to Schofield, Apr. 12, 1873, encl. General Orders Nos. 12, 13, 14, War Records ; Acting Com. Ind. Aff. H. R. Clum to Supt. Enoch Hoag at Lawrence, Kan., Nov. 24, 1871, Bur. Ind. Aff., Ltrs. Sent ; Rev. J. M. Ferris to Com. Ind. Aff. E. P. Smith, Oct. 17, 1874, Bur. Ind. Aff., Ltrs. Rec'd.

Indian. There must not only be a show of force, but actual *subjection* and *force* used to compel him to guard and protect his growing herd of cattle or sheep, as otherwise he will, in his hunger and improvidence, kill and eat the very cows and ewes issued by the government for the purpose of raising a herd. In like manner, force will be necessary to compel the nomade to plow or hoe his ground, plant his seed, and guard it till harvest." There can be no doubt who the General of the Army thought should administer Indian affairs. General John M. Schofield, commander of the Pacific military division, also wanted Indian management transferred to the War Department. While recognizing that some of the duties of an Indian agent would be distasteful to military personnel, he was convinced that the move was a matter of necessity because events had "demonstrated the utter inability of a civil department . . . to maintain . . . control over uncivilized Indians." If the Army had unlimited authority to deal with hostiles wherever they were found, Indian wars in which soldiers were required to battle "savages" might be prevented.[15]

However sincere Schofield may have been in his argument, there was a more important reason for the military effort to seize complete control of Indian affairs, for if, as General Sheridan predicted, the Sioux war were to be the last one, on what other basis could the Army justify maintaining its current level of strength after peace had been established? Except in time of international crisis and civil war, the Army had been occupied with fighting Indians for the past hundred years. It was the nature of high-ranking officers to desire a large force under their command, and following every period of conflict

---

[15] Sec. of War to Sec. of Interior, Nov. 1, 1873, encl. copy of Maj. N. B. Sweitzer, Comdr. Ft. Ellis, Mont. Terr., to Asst. Adj. Gen., Dept of Dak., St. Paul, Sept. 9, 1873, Sec Interior, Ltrs. Rec'd.; Ann. Rpts., House Exec. Doc. No. 1, 44th Cong., 1st Sess., Vol. 1, 122 and No. 1, 45th Cong., 3rd Sess., Vol. 2, 5-6.

the placement of cadre was a difficult problem.

A clear indication of military concern about ceasing to have any justifiable function was the reaction of officers in 1878 to the Indian police bill. This measure provided for the organization on reservations of constabulary forces composed of trustworthy Indians, under the supervision of Indian agents. While the bill was before Congress, Lieut. Col. W. P. Carlin, commander of Fort Yates near Standing Rock agency, requested the enlistment of additional Indian scouts to hunt down roaming hostiles near the Black Hills, and stated that for this purpose they were "the cheapest and altogether the best soldiers" available. A reporter for the *New York Herald* misquoted Carlin to the effect that Indian police would be more efficient than white soldiers in maintaining discipline, and gave the opinion of Commissioner of Indian Affairs E. A. Hayt that if the bill passed it would be possible "to dispense in large part, if not entirely, with the use of the Army at Indian reservations." Nearly apoplectic with rage, the Colonel wrote a heated letter to the Assistant Adjutant General explaining that he could "conceive of no more pernicious measure so far as the welfare of the Indians and the integrity of the Government" were concerned, than an organized police force of Indians which was not a part of the United States Army. It was a heavy blow to the military when, in the same year, the Indian police bill became law.[16]

One of the major obstacles to the success of the "Peace Policy" was the inability of military and civilian personnel to work in harmony under the separate direction of two departments. Discord and bitterness increased as the contest for control of Indian administration reached a climax in 1878. By that time the job of the Army was nearly finished, and its

---

[16] Copies of Carlin to Asst. Adj. Gen., Dept. of Dak., Feb. 19, 1878 ; Carlin to same, Mar. 23, 1878, Bur. Ind. Aff., Ltrs. Rec'd. ; *New York Herald,* Mar. 14, 1878 ; 20 U.S. Stat., 86.

officers were much in need of an excuse to stay in the business. The immediate cause of a complete breach of relations between the departments of War and Interior was the determination of the Indian Bureau to remove the Kiowa and Comanche from their reservation near Fort Sill to the Wichita agency. This action was prompted by advice from various Quaker officials, including Superintendent Enoch Hoag, and by the recommendation of the Board of Indian Commissioners. Among reasons given for the transfer was the demoralizing influence of soldiers at Fort Sill. As we shall see again, this was an extremely sore point in military circles; the Army's reaction was denial of an escort, and unsupportable charges that Indian appropriations would be sufficient except that they were squandered by the Interior Department. General Sherman argued with great skill that an Indian Bureau under the Secretary of War would be much more efficient than one under the Secretary of the Interior. If the War Department had control of Indian affairs, civilian agents could be employed for the peaceful tribes and military agents for the warlike. Religious denominations could continue the assimilation effort, while the troops could keep order and prevent white encroachment upon the reservations. But then the General disclosed the motive behind his proposal: "We do not wish to transfer our Army to civilian management," he said. "We would rather do the work ourselves with the Army." Most of the Indians had been driven upon reservations where the Interior Department was sovereign. It seemed to high military officials that the jurisdiction of the War Department must extend upon the reservations in order to maintain a strong and independent Army."

---

[17] *New York Times,* Nov. 23, Dec. 1 and 3, 1878. Much official correspondence is quoted. Sherman's statement was made to Senator Saunders, chairman of the joint committee of Congress which was considering the transfer of the Indian Bureau to the War Department.

VII

The "Peace Policy" Evaluated

BEYOND THE PURPOSE of clearing the Western lands for white settlement, it was the aim of the "Peace Policy" to prepare Indians for life in the white man's society. The disappearance of the game at a rate much more rapid than had been expected, and the acceleration of frontier movement during the seventies, compounded the urgency of teaching Indians to support themselves as well as of supplying sufficient rations while they were learning the agricultural, pastoral, and industrial arts. But Congress was not willing to appropriate the money necessary to meet the emergency, and senators and representatives from the West fought lobbying philanthropists inch by inch with the result that supplies usually arrived too little and too late. From nearly every quarter of the West came complaints that the Indians were starving, that agricultural equipment was insufficient or worn out, that school funds were depleted, that agencies were in debt, and that employees were unpaid.[1]

Congress was preoccupied with financial retrenchment, and took the position at the beginning of Grant's administration that in the cases of tribes with which the United States had treaties, no estimates for appropriations would be approved unless they were specifically authorized by treaty. A civilization fund of $100,000 voted in July 1870 was restricted to the benefit of those who did not have treaties with the United States. Since treaties did not provide for all of the necessities, Indian personnel sent out by the churches were handicapped from the start. Enoch Hoag, in charge of the central superintendency,

---

[1] William Welsh at Washington to H. B. Whipple, Feb. 23, 1871, Whipple Papers.

reported that appropriations were made to pay farmers, but were not made to purchase teams or to buy corn to feed work animals; that money was available to pay a blacksmith but not to buy fuel for the forge; and that while a fund had been provided for school buildings and teachers' salaries, there was nothing for the purchase of books or for the subsistence of Indian pupils at boarding schools. In the northern superintendency, the Hicksite Friends experienced similar difficulties and compensated for the deficiency in part through contributions from among their members, who donated more than $21,000 for this purpose in 1869 and 1870.[2]

Influential lobbyists like William Welsh did procure some appropriations not authorized by treaties, but there was never enough money to carry out the program envisaged by the Board of Indian Commissioners. In addition to subsistence, this would have involved an expenditure large enough to educate the younger generation and to provide individual allotments where reservation land was suitable for agriculture. The determination of Congress to appropriate as little as possible, even to the point of defaulting on treaty obligations, eroded the feeding system which lay at the foundation of the "Peace Policy" itself. As more and more Indians were concentrated on reservations, as reservations were made smaller, and as game became scarce, dependence upon governmental charity grew. But most congressmen had no ear for complaints about scanty rations and starving red children, to say nothing of petitions for industrial boarding schools, or requests for funds to survey and improve arable land on which Indians might support them-

---

[2] Com. Ind. Aff. E. S. Parker to Supt. Samuel M. Janney at Omaha, Nebraska, Jan. 26, 1870 ; Com. Ind. Aff. F. A. Walker to Rev. H. Dyer at New York City, Dec. 26, 1871, Bur. Ind. Aff., Ltrs. Sent. Supt. Enoch Hoag at Lawrence, Kansas, to Parker, Apr. 9, 1870, encl. Thomas Wistar and James Rhoads, Friends' Exec. Com., to Hoag, Apr. 8, 1870 ; Janney to Parker, Feb. 2, 1870, Bur. Ind. Aff., Ltrs. Rec'd. Benjamin Hallowell to Vincent Colyer, Jan. 10, 1872, Bd. Ind. Com., Ltrs. Rec'd.

selves. This was particularly true of Western congressmen who were intent upon pleasing their constituencies. Agents managed to meet some of their most pressing needs by persuading traders to deliver supplies on the promise of future appropriations, but in 1875 Congress ruled against the practice and agents were instructed that noncompliance would be cause for their removal. Up to that time Indian appropriations had averaged only $6,362,114 per annum.[3]

Because the Sioux uprising had an averse effect upon public opinion, which in turn influenced Congress, 1876 through 1878 were the leanest of the "Peace Policy" years. A representative of the Board of Indian Commissioners who inspected the Kiowa and Comanche agency in the Indian Territory reported that "there was a very general complaint from the Indians of the scantiness of their rations. Almost every conversation with them terminated with a reference to their hungry children, and a request that I would ask 'Washington' for more." The Cheyenne and Arapaho also felt the pinch and some of them jumped reservation, putting the military to much trouble before they were returned. Although military officers sometimes exploited the starvation of Indians by arguing publicly that the shortage of supplies was owing to inefficiency which might be remedied by transferring the Indian Bureau to the War Department, the General of the Army was capable of viewing the situation objectively. In reply to a request that the Army help feed the Assiniboin and Gros Ventre in the spring of 1878, Sherman remarked: "The Troops are helpless to assist starving Indians, the Indian Bureau is I suppose equally helpless, and I know not what to advise." The point was that neither the War Department nor the Department of the Interior could give subsistence to Indians unless Congress voted sufficient appropria-

---

[3] Sec. of Interior Delano to Whipple, Feb. 21, 1873, Whipple Papers; Com. Ind. Aff. J. Q. Smith to agent J. L. Broaddus at Hoopa Valley, Calif., Feb. 7, 1876, Bur. Ind. Aff., Ltrs. Sent.

tions; and elected representatives, always sensitive to public opinion because of concern for their official longevity, were unwilling to act in the red men's interest during the showdown with the Sioux.[4]

This bowing to public sentiment, a characteristic of any democratic government, was detrimental to the "Peace Policy," and demonstrated the dependence of reform upon legislative support. Jacob D. Cox, Secretary of the Interior during Grant's first administration, recognized the hopelessness of separate efforts by the executive branch in an article for the *International Review* at the end of the seventies:

The question of whether the control of Indian affairs shall remain in the Interior Department or be transferred to the army, is of little practical moment so long as our legislation is such that both military and civil officers are foredoomed to disappointment in any earnest efforts to solve the problem. When the exigencies of a political party may cut down the appropriations to a point where it is known that starvation at many agencies must ensue; when carelessness and indifference postpone even the intended appropriations, till tribes that would be friendly are driven to outbreak by the hunger of their women, and children . . . it is plain that the reform must begin in our legislative bodies, and that they must learn to realize that life and death, peace and war, are at stake when appropriation bills are delayed, before we can hope for much from the efforts even of the best meaning officers on the frontier, whether they are soldiers or Quakers.[5]

The prevention of illicit intercourse between white persons and Indians on reservations was made difficult by a paucity of legal information at the agencies and by the lack of an effective

---

[4] Copy of Rpt. by Wm. M. Leeds, Feb. 5, 1877; copy of telegrams from George Crook to Philip Sheridan, Oct. 26, 1878; Sec. of War Geo. McCrary to Sec. of Interior, June 26, 1878, encl. copy of Lt. Col. John R. Brooke to Asst. Adj. Gen., Dept. of Dak., June 11, 1878, with Sherman's endorsement, Bur. Ind. Aff., Ltrs. Rec'd. Com. Ind. Aff. E. A. Hayt to Sec. of Interior, Oct. 18, 1877, Bur. Ind. Aff., Rpt. Book.

[5] "The Indian Question," VI (1879), 632.

police system. Round Valley in California was overrun in 1873 by lawless men, and agent J. L. Burchard had neither law books nor means of enforcing his authority. The same year, trouble at Fort Berthold, Dakota Territory, arising from the mischievousness of "a low, lying gambler" and squaw man named James Boyle exemplified the problem of dealing with individual intruders. Boyle amused himself by defying agent S. B. Sperry's orders, and encouraged others to do likewise. Calling on the Army did not help because troop commanders considered their duty ended when parties were conducted outside reservations; Boyle enjoyed the notoriety associated with such escorting and returned to brag about it. Even the extra-legal formation of an Indian police company was empty of permanent results because the Indians disbanded after driving Boyle away. This scoundrel was determined "to come whenever he pleased and to stay as long as he might choose"; only a permanent constabulary force stationed on the reservation could control and discipline his kind.[6]

Such intruders sabotaged the "Peace Policy," but rebellious Indians also frustrated efforts toward assimilation until Congress created a permanent Indian police force in 1878. Agent Jared W. Daniels, who had taught the Sisseton Sioux to labor at Lake Traverse, confronted a different problem among the Oglala "Bad Faces" upon being transferred to Red Cloud agency in 1871. Within a year, the intervention of troops was necessary to prevent these Sioux from making an attack upon the agency building wherein the agent and his staff had barricaded themselves. Daniels was left no other choice than to resign with the comment that "Indian Agents must be protected in the discharge of their duties when among a people so little disposed to reciprocate the generous care bestowed upon them by the government." Only one far removed from the situation

---

[6] Burchard to Com. Ind. Aff. E. P. Smith, Oct. 7, 1873, and April 30, 1874 ; Sperry to Smith, Aug. 7, 1874, Bur. Ind. Aff., Ltrs. Rec'd.

could remark, as did Commissioner of Indian Affairs Francis Walker, that Daniels lacked the nerve and comprehension needed to cope with turbulent and insolent Indians. Without a means of enforcing authority, no agent could cope with them; many tried to serve at Red Cloud and failed. In 1878 James Irwin also resigned, "discouraged with the whole Sioux out-fit," and believing they would never assimilate until cured of arrogance by further subjugation.[7]

Like other Indian legislation of the post-Civil War era, the police bill reflected Congressional parsimony. Funds provided for the payment of police personnel were so meager that Indians who from time to time had served as scouts under the auspices of the War Department were discouraged from joining the force; Indian policemen were to receive five dollars per month, whereas scouts were accustomed to receive twenty-three dollars for the same pay period. The low pay made the maintenance of a full quota of suitable constables difficult, but this obstacle was partially overcome by the desire of young tribesmen to be warriors on the side of power and authority. After some delay in supplying them with arms and uniforms, these native squads became indispensable to the maintenance of order on the reservations; forty agencies had Indian constables by 1880, when the total force consisted of 162 officers and 643 privates. Wherever organized, the police performed numerous duties: they acted as guards during annuity payments, protected property no matter to whom it belonged, curtailed timber depredations, hindered the smuggling of whiskey, served as escorts and messengers, accompanied truant pupils to school, and informed the agents promptly of the presence of strangers,

---

[7] Copy of Walker to Sec. of Interior, Nov. 26, 1872; Daniels at Red Cloud to Whipple, Apr. 18, 1873, Whipple Papers; copy of telegram from Gen. John E. Smith at Omaha, Neb., to Col. James B. Fry at Chicago, Oct. 24, 1872; Irwin at Red Cloud to Hayt, Feb. 20, 1878, Bur. Ind. Aff., Ltrs. Rec'd.

whether white or Indian. Since they were vigilant and observant by nature, no clandestine councils escaped their notice; the influence of squaw men was diminished and the power of war chiefs was weakened because the secretive planning of raids became more difficult. The establishment of the Indian police system was, however, of little benefit to the "Peace Policy," which declined following Grant's incumbency.[5]

While the creation of an Indian police force did make it possible for agents to meet the day-to-day exigencies of Indian administration more effectively, their accomplishments were limited by the deficiencies of federal Indian law. For example, the clauses of the Intercourse Acts of 1834 and 1856, which dealt with the punishment of intruders, provided for a fine of one thousand dollars on the second offense but did not provide for imprisonment. Since intruders were generally of a class having no property subject to legal execution, and since the penalty could only be collected by an action of debt, the result was invariably a barren judgment which left delinquents free to renew their annoyances. Of course, the police were not expected to meet the onslaught of mass expeditions such as those organized by the notorious David L. Payne to secure land in Oklahoma. Only the Army was equipped to do that; but the military could be no more effective in bringing offenders to justice than were the Indian police so long as laws governing these activities remained inadequate. A thousand-dollar fine for a second offense, with the further knowledge that conviction was unlikely in Western courts, was little deterrent to trespassers who seemingly had everything to gain and very little to lose. Because of the failure of Congress to strengthen the

---

[5] 20 U.S. Stat., 86; agent V. T. McGillycuddy at Pine Ridge, Dak. Terr., to Hayt, Nov. 17, 1879, Bur. Ind. Aff., Ltrs. Rec'd.; Ann. Rpts. of Com. Ind. Aff., House Exec. Docs. No. 1, 46th Cong., 2nd Sess., Vol. 9, 76-77, and No. 1, 46th Cong., 3rd Sess., Vol. 9, 88-89.

intercourse laws, the problem of the intruder on Indian lands remained unsolved.[9]

|As puzzling to Indian agents as any other difficulty which they encountered was the matter of settling differences which arose among the Indians themselves|The murder of one Indian by another within the boundaries of reservations was not subject to any statute, either state or national, and even when such offenses were committed outside of reservations, in which case the state law might be applied, judges often refused to prosecute.|In 1874, agent John B. Monteith reported that two drunken Nez Percé, while proceeding from Lewiston, Idaho Territory, to the Lapwai agency, had gotten into an altercation and that one had killed the other. Satisfied as to the identity of the guilty party, the agent called the matter to the attention of the deputy United States Attorney; but before any action could be taken, a half-breed named Joe Craig met the murderer in a Lewiston saloon, enticed him outside of town, and slit his throat from ear to ear. The agent had Craig arrested and taken before the United States Commissioner, who was also a county judge, but that official declined jurisdiction in either capacity. Aware that some of his wards were threatening to kill Craig, and not having copies of any United States statutes dated later than 1857, Monteith inquired of the Indian Bureau whether there were any laws bearing on such cases and stated that the peaceable Indians wished to have matters of this nature disposed of in the white man's courts. The Commissioner of Indian Affairs offered an opinion that territorial and state courts had jurisdiction over such offenses when committed outside of reservations, but concluded that nothing could be done in the current instance since these tribunals had refused to take cognizance of it. There seems to have been disparity among the

---

[9] *Laws of the U.S.,* IX (New York, Gould & Banks, 1839), 130-31 ; 11 U.S. Stat., 80 ; Com. Ind. Aff. H. Price to Sec. of Interior, Mar. 13, 1882, Bur. Ind. Aff., Rpt. Book.

states in the matter of prosecuting the offenses of Indians committed off reservations, and it was not until 1896 that the United States Supreme Court upheld state jurisdiction over such cases.[10]

The vexatious circumstances resulting from the failure of Congress to provide a legal system on reservations, as was recommended by the Peace Commission of 1868, were described in 1877 by Bishop William Hare of the Episcopal church in Nebraska. He wrote:

Civilization has loosened, in some cases broken, the bonds which regulate and hold together Indian society in its wild state, and has failed to give the people law and officers of justice in their place. This evil still continues unabated. Women are brutally beaten and outraged; men are murdered in cold blood; the Indians who are friendly to the schools and churches are intimidated and preyed upon by the evil-disposed; children are molested on their way to school, and schools are dispersed by bands of vagabonds; but there is no redress. This accursed condition . . . should make every man who sits in the national halls of legislation blush. And, wish well to the Indians as we may, and do for them what we will, the efforts of civil agents, teachers, and missionaries are like the struggles of drowning men weighted with lead, as long as by the absence of law Indian society is left without a base.[11]

On grounds of expediency, a few agents were bold enough to establish extra-legal systems of Indian government. R. H. Milroy, who became Yakima agent in 1876, was compelled to rid himself of the nuisance of settling minor disputes which arose among the natives in order to have time for more important matters. Therefore, he divided the reservation into five judicial districts, appointed a like number of judges, and announced an election day, at which time the Indians should

---

[10] Monteith to Com. Ind. Aff. E. P. Smith, July 20, 1874, Bur. Ind. Aff., Ltrs. Rec'd. ; Smith to Monteith, Oct. 5, 1874, Bur. Ind. Aff., Ltrs. Sent ; Cohen, *Handbook,* 146.

[11] Quoted in Ann. Rpt. of Com. Ind. Aff., House Exec. Doc. No. 1, 45th Cong., 3rd Sess., Vol. 8, 398.

choose their own magistrates. The candidates were represented by colored slips of paper which the voters deposited in regular ballot boxes. Milroy reported after several years' experience that these Indian judges had tried cases successfully. Mistakes had been rectified by allowing defendants the right of appealing to a panel consisting of all five judges, and if necessary to the agent himself, who acted as a kind of supreme court. Since there were no lawyers, the accused examined witnesses and presented their own defense. A poll tax was levied for the payment of Indian judges. Until the Indian police force was created by act of Congress in 1878, Milroy appointed Indian sheriffs on his own authority, but made the error of trying to extend their jurisdiction beyond the reservation. For this, the agent was threatened with prosecution by Frank Clark, the leading Democratic lawyer in Washington Territory, who advised the Puyallup Indians that they had the same right as white men to bet on horse races and engage in other forms of gambling while off their reservation. Clark's meddling was an example of white contact undermining the capacity of Indian tribes for self-government, even when such government was established on the English model.[12]

Influences from within and without reservations which deterred administrators of the "Peace Policy" in preparing Indians for assimilation were many and varied. Traders encouraged the continuance of life by the chase because there was profit in exchanging manufactured goods for peltry; from the same motive, Indian rings promoted the payment of annuities in cash and were unconcerned that the practice promoted an "easy come, easy go" economic philosophy, that it discouraged an appreciation of monetary values, and that it prevented the development of an incentive to labor. The Army,

---

[12] Ann. Rpt. of Bd. Ind. Com., House Exec. Doc. No. 1, 48th Cong., 2nd Sess., Vol. 12, 725 ; Milroy to Com. Ind. Aff. J. Q. Smith, Sept. 12, 1876, Bur. Ind. Aff., Ltrs. Rec'd.

which as an organization rendered many services, made prostitutes of Indian squaws for the gratification of soldiers, who were removed from the moral restraints of white society and the company of white women. Reports of this practice were substantiated by the foremost citizens of Washington Territory, including the governor, the president of the territorial council, and the most prominent officials in the land office. The effect was seen in a report by agent W. F. Arny from Arizona Territory in 1875 that Navajo women who visited Fort Wingate when the paymaster was due often returned to the agency afflicted with venereal diseases. Of course, such communications provoked the ranking military officers, some of whom resented any implication that their men were guilty of immoral conduct. General John Pope responded on this occasion with a humorously preposterous statement: "We must maintain the general chastity of the soldiers, until Mr. Arny furnishes satisfactory proof to the contrary, and especially I must doubt . . . whether he is right as to who are the actual sufferers by the wickedness to which he refers."[13]

Criticism by Indian Bureau officials of licentious relations between Army personnel and Indian women added to the growing dissension between the Departments of War and

[13] Sec. of War to Sec. of Interior, Nov. 1, 1873, encl. Maj. N. B. Sweitzer, Comdr. Ft. Ellis, Mont. Terr., to Asst. Adj. Gen., Dept. of Dak., Sept. 9, 1873, Sec. Interior, Ltrs. Rec'd; C. A. Huntington, Wm. Pickering, et al., officials of Wash. Terr., to Sec. of Interior O. H. Browning, Feb. 22, 1867; Arny at Defiance to E. P. Smith, Mar. 4, 1875, Bur. Ind. Aff., Ltrs. Rec'd. Felix R. Brunot to Thomas K. Cree, Mar. 11, 1872, Bd. Ind. Com., Ltrs. Rec'd.; E. P. Smith to H. B. Whipple, May 23, 1873, Whipple Papers. Pope's statement is from his endorsement of Sec. of Interior to Sec. of War, Dec. 18, 1874, a copy of which was sent to agent Arny by the Com. Ind. Aff., Feb. 4, 1875. The adverse influence of traders on Indians was discussed by Stephen P. Riggs, "The Indian Question," *New Englander*, XV (1857), 255-57. Riggs had represented the Amer. Bd. Com. Foreign Missions among the Sioux for twenty years prior to the publication of this article.

Interior, making their cooperation, which was absolutely essential to the success of the "Peace Policy," even more difficult. A heated controversy occurred, and reached a climax at the same time as the dispute over which department should manage Indian affairs. During a meeting of high officials with President Hayes late in 1877, Commissioner E. A. Hayt expressed the opinion that the presence of troops at agencies demoralized Indians. General Alfred Terry made objection, whereupon Hayt asserted that there was evidence that soldiers had fathered half the children at Standing Rock agency. Terry, who commanded the military department of Dakota, within which the agency lay, was furious. On several occasions he demanded to see the evidence, and Hayt's failure to produce it suggests an overstatement of the case. Nevertheless, Terry was so disturbed by the charge that he ordered an investigation which purported to prove that approximately one quarter of the Indian children under eight years of age at Standing Rock were half-breeds and that their male progenitors were mostly civilians. The mood of the military resulting from this fracas was apparent in the remarks of the General of the Army. Sherman wrote: "If the President is not convinced that Mr. Hayt knows little of what he spoke in Gen. Terry's presence let us take all troops away from Indian Agencies, and post them to protect the white settlers against the depredations of their young and enterprising braves. Soldiers are of course men, and are denied wives or concubines. They have passions which are common to the sex, but military discipline does something to curb this passion, whereas the Agents and employees are restrained by no consideration, moral or physical."[14]

A pernicious tool in the school of indolence and immorality conducted by traders, soldiers, and squaw men was whiskey. To obtain it, an Indian would give up his material possessions,

---

[14] Sec. of War to Sec. of Interior, June 12, 1878, encl. copies of many documents on the subject, Bur. Ind. Aff., Ltrs. Rec'd.

sell his squaw, and depose his chief. The extent of the traffic was almost beyond imagination. So far as can be determined, there was not a single reservation in the whole country which did not experience difficulty with it. The situation, however, was worse west of the Mississippi River because Indians were more numerous there, while law enforcement was more lax. Railway companies found the shipment of liquor an important source of profit and were unconcerned that distribution of it to Indians violated a federal statute. Whiskey went to the reservations by many means of conveyance, even in the letter pouches of mail-carriers.[15]

This nefarious business reached crucial proportions in the years of the "Peace Policy," and resulted from closer contact of Anglo-American society with the tribes. It was not merely coincidence that whiskey peddling across the northern border of Indian Territory became "quite a serious matter" with the advance of the Kansas frontier. The government could not deny citizens their liquor and, of course, local merchants were not inclined to deny their customers the purchase of numerous jugs, or even of a whole barrel, if an ample supply were on hand. But for the establishment of mining communities such as Helena and Virginia City in Montana Territory, the federal government might have closed the Missouri and Yellowstone rivers to traffic in whiskey except for closely guarded shipments to military posts. Whiskey went through until 1877, when it was stopped for a very brief period during the Sioux campaign. Free flow of "firewater" was disastrous for the Indians, as the Crow agent recorded: "Their practice has been to stop near some village or grog shop, and lay around these dens, get all

---

[15] Attorney General Geo. H. Williams to Sec. of Interior Delano, Apr. 10, 1872, encl. copy of U.S. marshal Logan A. Roots at Helena, Ark., to Williams, Apr. 1, 1872; agent John Young at Blackfeet agency, Mont. Terr., to Com. Ind. Aff. E. A. Hayt, Feb. 18, 1878; agent S. S. Lawson at Mission agency, California, to Hayt, July 29, 1879, Bur. Ind. Aff., Ltrs. Rec'd.

the whiskey they can, trading their best robes, blankets, and even the virtue of their squaws for it. The consequence is drunken brawls, thefts and murders."[16]

Administrators of the "Peace Policy" employed every means at their disposal to prevent the trade. During 1873, the Commissioner of Indian Affairs appealed to the commanding officer at Fort Pembina in Dakota Territory for aid at Crookston, Minnesota. Captain Lloyd Wheaton was at a loss to know what action he might take without the cooperation of the civil authorities. United States marshals received no pay for Indian duty unless they actually made arrests, and the danger of retaliatory proceedings left little incentive to the apprehension of whiskey sellers. Grand juries at Crookston commonly refused to find indictments against guilty persons, and even military officers were sometimes put to the expense of defending themselves against suits "brought for their action in suppressing the introduction of liquor into the Indian Country." The U.S. District Attorney at St. Paul declared that the great defect in enforcing the law was the difficulty in procuring witnesses. On his recommendation and under the provisions of an act of Congress appropriating $10,000 "for . . . punishing violation of the intercourse acts," the Indian Bureau appointed a special detective who during 1874 succeeded in bringing numerous Crookston offenders to trial; but the limited fund made the permanent employment of such an official impossible, and his work was of no lasting benefit. In 1881, the Minnesota liquor trade still

---

[16] Com. Ind. Aff. E. P. Smith to Delano, Jan. 23, 1874, encl. copies of ltrs. from Supt. Enoch Hoag and agent John D. Miles, Bur. Ind. Aff., Rpt. Book ; Supt. James Wright at Helena, Mont. Terr., to Smith, June 21, 1873 ; copies of Col. Nelson A. Miles, Comdr. Cantonment at Tongue River, to Hdqrs. of Yellowstone Comd., Apr. 14, 1877 ; Col. W. B. Hazen, Comdr. Ft. Buford, Dak. Terr., to Asst. Adj. Gen., Dept. of Dak., Apr. 30, 1877 ; Asst. Adj. Gen. Geo. D. Ruggles to Hazen, May 10, 1877, Bur. Ind. Aff., Ltrs. Rec'd.

flourished near the White Earth reservation, and with British Indians across the Canadian border line.[17]

The difficulty of enforcing the federal statute which made it an offense to "sell, exchange, give, barter, or dispose of any spirituous liquor or wine to any Indian under the charge" of a superintendent or agent, was universal. General John Pope wrote from the Southwest in 1880 that the U.S. District Attorney at Santa Fe had refused to prosecute men engaged in selling whiskey outside of the Navajo reservation. Captain F. T. Bennett, the acting Navajo agent, added that it was "almost impossible to get the U.S. Marshal to take hold of such cases and very difficult to convict them upon the strongest evidence." Three reasons were given for the ineffectuality of attempts to enforce the intercourse laws as they related to whiskey in New Mexico, and could as well have been applied to the entire West. These were "the inactivity of the civil officers . . ., their inability to obtain positive proof against those engaged in the liquor traffic, [and] the failure of juries to convict even when furnished with sufficient proof."[18]

But there were weaknesses in the law itself which Congress refused to correct. It was necessary to prove, for example, that an Indian who received liquor was under the charge of a superintendent or agent. Difficulties with this clause were particularly onerous near the Canadian border, because the Indians had no respect for international boundaries. Chief Justice Orange Jacobs of Washington Territory reported in 1873 that large

---

[17] E. P. Smith to Wheaton, June 22, 1873, with endorsements of Wheaton and C. K. Davis; detective M. V. Nichols at Detroit, Minn., to Smith, Sept. 22, 1874, Bur. Ind. Aff., Ltrs. Rec'd.; Com. Ind. Aff. to Sec. of Interior, Aug. 5, 1873 and June 9, 1881, Bur. Ind. Aff., Rpt. Book.

[18] 12 U.S. Stat., 339; Pope at Ft. Leavenworth, Kan., to Gen. Sheridan, June 16, 1880, Bur. Ind. Aff., Ltrs. Rec'd.; Com. Ind. Aff. to Sec. of Interior, June 7, 1881, with extracts from ltrs. of Bennett and Gen. Edward Hatch at Santa Fe, Bur. Ind. Aff., Rpt. Book.

numbers of Indians from British Columbia were in the habit of making visits to Puget Sound, where they remained for from one to six months. Their presence practically nullified the liquor law and thereby filled the country with drunken Indians. Whether or not foreign Indians were under the charge of superintendents and agents when in their area of jurisdiction had been argued before Jacobs "a great number of times," but he had always avoided a decision. Endeavoring to close this loophole, Commissioner Edward P. Smith proposed that Congress amend the law by making it a federal offense to "sell, exchange, give, barter, or dispose of any spirituous liquor or wine to any Indian under the charge of any Indian Superintendent or Indian Agent . . ., *or to any Indian not a citizen of the United States within the jurisdiction thereof";* but no such amendment was made.[19]

The most glaring weakness in the law, however, was that it offered very little protection from peddlers who established shops just outside reservations. These peddlers could not be arrested unless caught in the midst of a transaction, and their establishments became so numerous that it was impossible to keep them under surveillance. In the case of the *United States* vs. *Forty-three Gallons of Whiskey,* 1876, Judge David Davis, in delivering the opinion of the Supreme Court, had this to say: "If liquor is injurious to them inside a reservation, it is equally so outside of it; and why cannot Congress forbid its introduction into a place near by, which they would be likely to frequent? It is easy to see that the love of liquor would tempt them to stray beyond their borders to obtain it; and that bad white men, knowing this, would carry on the traffic in adjoining localities, rather than venture upon forbidden ground." The prohibition against liquor, like other provisions of the

---

[19] Copy of Jacobs at Seattle to Atty. Gen. G. H. Williams, Feb. 16, 1873, Sec. Interior, Ltrs. Rec'd; Smith to Sec. of Interior, Jan. 23, 1874, Bur. Ind. Aff., Rpt. Book.

Intercourse Act of 1834 was not enforceable because of the anachronistic nature of the statute.[20]

Against obstacles so great as have been described, agents were asked to labor at the salary of fifteen hundred dollars per annum. That the religious denominations were hard pressed to secure and retain capable men in the service was evident from the rapid succession of personnel. Particularly severe was the financial embarrassment of agents who were accompanied by their families to remote regions. Only the traveling expenses of actual employees were paid by the government; there was no allowance for subsistence, and in some cases no residence was provided. The sense of Christian duty which brought many of these agents to their posts and simultaneously required them to care for their families caused much turmoil of conscience. Could men of talent and good character be expected to subject their families to the hardships and dangers of a wilderness, deprive their children of an education, give a bond for $25,000, and run the risk of having their reputations ruined, for a salary "less than that paid to a third-class clerk in Washington, or to a village postmaster"? No wonder that J. A. Tonner at the Colorado River agency in Arizona Territory thought longingly of San Francisco, and in 1871 repeatedly asked the Board of Missions of the Reformed Church to find a successor. The maintenance of an agent and his family in the Southwest cost more than it did in Kansas and Nebraska or in the Northwest. Still agent Tonner stayed on until 1875—a mark of his patience and sincerity of purpose—while others quickly resigned to find more suitable employment.[21]

---

[20] 93 U.S. Rpts., 195-96. The case originated at Crookston, Minnesota.
[21] Ann. Rpts. of Com. Ind. Aff., House Exec. Docs. No. 1, 43rd Cong., 1st Sess., Vol. 4, 377-78, and No. 1, 44th Con., 2nd Sess., Vol. 4, 382. Tonner to Vincent Colyer, Oct. 12, 1871, Bd. Ind. Com., Ltrs. Rec'd. ; Rev. John Lowrie for Presbyterian Bd. of Foreign Missions to Delano, Nov. 3, 1870, and Oct. 8, 1873, Bur. Ind. Aff., Ltrs. Rec'd.

Throughout the seventies the question of salary was presented to Congress again and again. Hoping to impress that
body with the importance of it, Commissioner J. Q. Smith in
1876 described the function of the agent:

Not only are committed to him the conduct of the agency business
proper, the erection and care of buildings, the supervision of farming
and mechanical operations, the purchase and care of stock, the
proper receipt and distribution of supplies, the management of
schools, the keeping of accurate and complicated financial accounts,
and the furnishing of information and advice as a basis of action
by this office (Indian Bureau), but upon his skill, tact, and ability to
influence and control his Indians, success in the administration of
Indian affairs wholly depends. No man, who is not possessed of
talents of a high order and great variety, can be completely successful
as an Indian agent.[22]

All of this on fifteen hundred dollars a year and without the
comfort of an expense account for the entertainment of visiting
dignitaries! The lawmakers were immovable. Regardless of
detailed recommendations for gradation in pay according to
location and responsibility, Congress did nothing.[23]

With many adverse circumstances threatening their program,
it was unfortunate that some reformers and denominational
representatives placed sectarian interests ahead of the Indians'
welfare. From 1864 until his death in 1878, William Welsh
worked tirelessly, making trips to the Indian country, stirring
up the leaders of the various denominations, and agitating the
cause among congressmen. But Welsh caused much strife
among some of the religious societies. Near the close of 1870, he
wrote to Secretary of the Interior Delano and proposed the
transfer of the Santee agency from the Hicksite Friends to the
Episcopalians. His principal arguments were that the Friends

---

[22] Ann. Rpt., House Exec. Doc. No. 1, 44th Cong., 2nd Sess., Vol. 4,
381-82.
[23] Ann. Rpts. of Com. Ind. Aff., House Exec. Docs. No. 1, 43rd Cong.,
2nd Sess., Vol. 6, 324, and No. 1, 45th Cong., 2nd Sess., Vol. 8, 402.

had no mission among the Santee, that the Episcopal church had been the first to establish one, and that the transfer of the Santee agency would give unity to the work of the Episcopalians among the Sioux. Welsh had set the stage for his letter to Delano by publishing in the *Washington Chronicle* an account of a council held by himself with the Santee, in which they were alleged to have "unanimously asked to have their reservation placed under the care of the Episcopal Church, that the whole Sioux nation might be bound together in one brotherhood." In an effort to placate the American Board of Commissioners for Foreign Missions, who also had a mission among the Santee, Welsh proposed the assignment of the agencies at Lake Traverse and Devil's Lake in Dakota Territory to them. The Santee, having made great progress since their removal to northeastern Nebraska following the Minnesota uprising of 1862, would be a credit to whichever church controlled their agency. The Friends' executive committee ordered an immediate investigation and discovered no truth in Welsh's statement of Santee preference for Episcopalian management, but refused to make their findings public because it seemed "highly important that the friends of the Indians should avoid even an appearance of difference amongst themselves, and especially one of a sectarian character." No change in Santee administration was made. Welsh's aggressiveness, however, caused strained relations between the A.B.C.F.M. and the Episcopal church, which continued as long as the "Peace Policy" was in effect.[24]

Equally odious was his conduct in bringing unsubstantiated

---

[24] *Washington Chronicle*, Dec. 9, 1870. Welsh at Philadelphia to Delano, Dec. 15, 1870 ; Supt. Samuel M. Janney at Omaha to Com. Ind. Aff. E. S. Parker, Dec. 28, 1870, encl. sworn statement to Santee chiefs refuting Welsh's claim that they preferred Episcopalian management ; William Dorsey for Friends' exec. com. to Parker, Jan. 11, 1871, Bur. Ind. Aff., Ltrs. Rec'd. Copy of Alfred Riggs at Santee agency to N. G. Clark, Sec. of A.B.C.F.M., July 6, 1877, Bd. Ind. Com., Ltrs. Rec'd.

charges against Edward P. Smith during the latter's term as Commissioner of Indian Affairs. Smith, a Congregational minister from New York City, served as agent to the Minnesota Chippewa during the early seventies and became chief of the Indian Bureau in 1873. As Chippewa agent, he was confronted with the problem of finding a means of subsistence for the Pillagers at Leech Lake. Their treaty funds were all but gone; their diet had been reduced to fish and berries by the rapid depletion of game; they knew nothing of agriculture, and possessed neither teams nor farm implements. In want of a better solution, it occurred to Smith that the sale of Leech Lake pine timber would afford the Pillagers, and other destitute Indians, temporary relief. Because of previous experience with meddling speculators, the agent saw no possibility of securing agreement among the seven widely scattered bands which had an interest in Leech Lake pine. Therefore he decided to proceed on the newly-promulgated theory of wardship, and concluded a contract with A. H. Wilder of St. Paul at $1.15 per thousand feet of stumpage for all merchantable pine timber within three miles of driving streams. The Indians were to receive at least $20,000 each year, whether or not that much timber was cut. Shortly thereafter Smith was made Commissioner of Indian Affairs, and explanation to the Pillagers of what had been done was left to his successor. Ostensibly, the Indians objected to the price, but it was doubtful whether they were capable of independent judgment. The *Saint Paul Dispatch* accused Smith of having personal interests in view, and this calumny aroused the suspicion of Welsh, who soon had a rumor going that the Indian Bureau was corrupt. After repeated requests by Commissioner Smith, Secretary Delano ordered a thorough investigation. Welsh submitted allegations charging Smith with fraud, but declined to support them before the investigating commission. Although Smith was exonerated, Welsh's unproved charges left his administration under a cloud, and assisted

Western congressmen who wished to end the "Peace Policy".[25]

While there was internecine warfare in some quarters of the Protestant household, there was cooperation in others. It was imperative that there should have been, because congressmen from the Western states and territories prevented the confirmation of religious appointees whenever they could. Two Quaker candidates were rejected by the Senate in 1876 because they were not residents of Nebraska, where they were meant to serve. The politicians were anxious to re-establish the spoils system, and found an opportunity when Rutherford Hayes succeeded Grant. Hayes' selection of Carl Schurz as Secretary of the Interior was a heavy blow to denominational influence. While Schurz admitted in 1877 that "the present system which permits religious societies to nominate candidates for Indian agencies is, in some respects, undoubtedly an improvement upon the former practice of making appointments in the Indian service on political grounds," he declared that it was "by no means perfect" and that a needed "element of stability" might be achieved by "an arrangement enabling the department to assign an officer upon his entrance into the service to a place of minor importance and then to promote him in grade of duty and pay according to merit." His commendable fight for civil-service reform culminated with the Pendleton Act of 1882, but by that time the politicians had regained control of appointments to the Indian service. John L. Burchard, the Methodist

---

[25] Smith to Delano, Oct. 24 and Nov. 15, 1873, Bur. Ind. Aff., Rpt. Book ; Rpt. of Com. to Investigate Charges against E. P. Smith, Dept. of Interior Pamphlet (Washington, Feb. 2, 1874). There is much helpful correspondence in the Whipple Papers dated August through December 1873. After he resigned as chairman of the Bd. Ind. Com. in 1870 because of a dispute with the Indian Bureau over authority, Welsh also made damaging statements against Commissioner E. S. Parker. Because the Supreme Court denied that Indians might sell their timber in 1873, the Attorney General revoked the Wilder Contract in 1875: U.S. *vs.* Cook, 19 U.S. Rpts., 591 ; Smith to Sec. of Interior, June 17, 1875, Bur. Ind. Aff., Rpt. Book.

agent at Round Valley, California, was denounced and relieved, and his successor was appointed, without consultation with the Methodist Mission Board. By 1880, strained relations with the government had caused the Methodists to withdraw from further participation in the "Peace Policy." The pattern was the same with the Societies of Friends. Differences with Secretary Schurz and Commissioner E. A. Hayt were accompanied by an increase of political influence on Indian appointments. One by one, the Quakers were deprived of their agencies, and although a few of them remained in office, in May 1879 the Orthodox group renounced any further responsibility for Indian management. After 1880 only two agencies, the Great Nemaha and the Santee, were left in charge of Hicksite agents, and these were given up in 1882 and 1885. The most rapid change throughout the service had occurred in 1878, when new agents were appointed to thirty-five of the seventy-four agencies.[26]

Schurz' estimation of religious appointments to the Indian service as an improvement over the old system, but by no means perfect, was a fair one; there can be no doubt that Indian administration lacked continuity and stability. The rapid turnover of personnel alone would support the Secretary's appraisal. But church officials had recognized the shortcomings of the "Peace Policy" all along. Commissioner Edward P. Smith wrote in 1873 that there had "been several failures during the year, from want of adaptation to the service, or from want of integrity," and the Board of Indian Commissioners reported

---

[26] Wm. Stickney, Sec. of Bd. Ind. Com., to Pres. Grant, Mar. 30, 1876, Bd. Ind. Com., Ltrs. Sent; John M. Reid for Methodist Mission Bd. to Com. Ind. Aff., Mar. 4, 1878 and July 2, 1880, Bur. Ind. Aff., Ltrs. Rec'd. A. C. Barstow of Bd. Ind. Com. to Senator Dawes, Feb. 13, 1881, Dawes Papers. Schurz' Ann. Rpt., House Exec. Doc. No. 1, 45th Cong., 2nd Sess., Vol. 8, xiv; Hayt's Ann. Rpt., House Exec. Doc. No. 1, 45th Cong., 3rd Sess., Vol. 9, 439 and 442. Kelsey, *Friends and the Indians,* 184-87.

two years later: "Some of these larger Agencies require talents in the Agent of a higher class than can easily be commanded by the small salaries affixed by law. It would not seem strange, therefore, if now and then one should prove incompetent; or considering the infirmities of our nature, and the unscrupulous character of some of the contractors and traders with whom they are brought in contact, now and then one should become corrupt; but we feel confident, that in this department, the government was never so honestly served, as at the present time." There was not perfection, but there was improvement because agents sent out by the churches were committed to the Indians' welfare. Such personnel were a minority before the "Peace Policy" was begun.[27]

There is no more tangible evidence of the good will with which Protestant groups sought to reform Indian administration than the services performed, without pay, by their representatives on the Board of Indian Commissioners. Besides advising the Interior Department on means to assimilate the tribes, these philanthropists tried to eliminate both waste and fraud from the business of providing Indians with subsistence. Prior to the Board's organization, it had been customary to receive bids for annuity goods and other supplies in classes. Under this system, contractors were obliged to submit a single bid for all of the articles in a particular category. Because certain contractors had connections within the Bureau of Indian Affairs, contracts were awarded year after year to the same business houses, and were regarded as monopolies. To correct this abuse, the Board abolished the old arrangement and restored competition by requiring that bids be made for each article separately. No contracts were awarded without the Board's approval, following careful inquiry concerning the

---

[27] Smith's Ann. Rpt., House Exec. Doc. No. 1, 43rd Cong., 1st Sess., Vol. 4, 377; Address of the Bd. Ind. Com. "To the Christian Public," July 29, 1875, Bd. Ind. Com., Ltrs. Rec'd.

quality, price, and deliverability of the goods. Visitations of the members at agencies provided an opportunity to ascertain whether the Indians were receiving what the contractors agreed to supply. Thus, through the application of free enterprise and through inspection, the Board worked toward economy and honesty in this important phase of Indian administration. Because the Indian service was notorious for fraud when Grant became President, it was impossible for ten men to effect a total reform. However, with the exception of the period following the resignation of the first Board early in 1874, "when a loose system of purchase and inspection again prevailed, and loud and earnest complaints were made . . . on the inferior quality of all goods purchased" for that year, there was steady improvement.[28]

An idea of what the contractors were getting away with during Grant's first term may be had through a report by Samuel Walker, the Board's chief clerk, on the delivery of supplies at the Red Cloud and Whetstone agencies in 1873. He found the bacon "very good" but declared that the coffee, the sugar, and especially the flour "looked inferior." Even so, this flour was better than the "nondescript article" which was delivered the previous year. At both agencies the manner of doing business was very loose. No scales for weighing in gross were provided, and contractors usually obtained receipts for what appeared on their bills of lading; no record was kept of the amount of goods actually distributed to the Indians. Fraud was obvious in beef contracts. At Whetstone the examiner learned that the average net weight of cattle was determined by slaughtering a few selected animals, and the butcher was known to have weighed the end-gate of a wagon with each of the four quarters of a beef. At Red Cloud "there was clearly collusion" between agent J. J. Saville and L. H. Bosler "to

---

[28] Ann. Rpts. of Com. Ind. Aff., House Exec. Docs. No. 1, 45th Cong., 2nd Sess., Vol. 8, 405, and No. 1, 45th Cong., 3rd Sess., Vol. 9, 474.

obtain payment from the Government for beef not delivered."
No statement of the beef account with the contractor was kept
at the agency. Bosler received payment on the basis of receipts
which he made out himself. Excessive collection was
furthered by grossly overestimating the number of lodges
present at issue time. Saville's story that he could not
count his Indians as ordered by the Interior Department in the
autumn of 1873 because they entertained superstitions about
being numbered, and fired on him in protest, is questionable in
view of the fact that General Sheridan reported the following
spring that Red Cloud's and Spotted Tail's people were in the
habit of visiting one another's agencies at issue time. It is highly
probable that this was the Indians' way of seeking to overcome
the shortage of rations for which dishonest personnel were
somewhat responsible. The taking of a census would ruin the
arrangement, as Sheridan pointed out. Bosler was the most
infamous thief in the business, and his operations at Red Cloud
with the concurrence of Saville undoubtedly made the situation
at that agency worse than elsewhere.[29]

Gradually, techniques were developed for curbing fraud. A
favorite trick of cattle-dealers was to stampede the herd after
receiving payment, thereby stealing it back. To overcome this,
the Sioux agents received orders from the Indian Bureau late in
1873 that all animals delivered must be branded so that they
could be identified later if found in a contractor's herd. The
Indian Inspector Bill of 1873 placed five examiners in the field
with authority to correct abuses by suspending unfit employees
and by exercising the powers of law-enforcement officers. The
system of inspection was perfected further in 1876, when
military officers at near-by posts began attending the delivery
of goods at the agencies. The reports show that, with the

---

[29] Copies of Walker's Rpt. to Felix R. Brunot, Chm. of Bd. Ind. Com.,
Dec. 6, 1873 ; and of Sheridan to Sherman, Mar. 3, 1874, Bur. Ind. Aff.,
Ltrs. Rec'd. The agencies were thirty-five miles apart.

exception of cattle, most of the supplies received between 1877
and 1879 were commensurate with the terms of contracts and
that poor beef was either rejected or bought at discount. By
this time, platform scales had been installed at most of the
agencies, leaving little opportunity to defraud by misrepresentation of weight. In 1880 Carl Schurz commended the change
which had been effected in the following words: "Complaints
that the Indians do not obtain the goods appropriated by
Congress, or obtain them only in inferior quality, are disappearing. Cases of peculation and gross misconduct on the part of
Indian agents have become exceedingly rare, so much so that
even the reports of military officers who have been the most
watchful, ever ready and willing critics of the Indian service
while in the hands of civilians, have become almost entirely
silent upon this subject. . . ." During Hayes' administration there
was greater insistence that agents be prompt in the rendering of
accounts. Fraud was reduced to a minimum, not so much
because Indan agents were more honest as because it had
become more difficult to commit.[30]

The question of how much the "Peace Policy" accomplished
toward the assimilation of Indians is uncertain, but it seems

---

[30] E. P. Smith to agent H. W. Bingham at Cheyenne River, Dak. Terr.,
Nov. 28, 1873, Bur. Ind. Aff., Ltrs. Sent. Sec. of Interior to Com. Ind.
Aff., Feb. 14, Oct. 4 and 13, 1876, Aug. 21, 1877 ; T. J. Wint at Ft. Sill,
Ind. Terr., to Com. Ind. Aff. J. Q. Smith, Oct. 4, 1877 ; Capt. R. E.
Johnson near Crow Creek and Lower Brule agencies to Asst. Adj. Gen.,
Dept. of Dak., Jan. 12 and Sept. 28, 1878 ; 2nd Lt. Wm. Lassiter at
Wichita agency to Post Adj., Ft. Sill, Feb. 12, 1878 ; 1st Lt. G. E.
Overton near San Carlos agency to Post Adj., Camp Thomas, Ariz.
Terr., May 24, 1879 ; Comptroller of U.S. Treasury W. W. Uptoro to
Com. Ind. Aff., Feb. 28, 1880 (mostly copies), Bur. Ind. Aff., Ltrs.
Rec'd. Schurz' Ann. Rpt., House Exec. Doc. No. 1, 46th Cong., 3rd
Sess., Vol. 9, 17. Loring B. Priest, *Uncle Sam's Stepchildren,* 66, states
that "no positive action was taken to check" fraud in the Indian service
until "Hayes announced the appointment of Carl Schurz as Secretary
of the Interior in 1877." The evidence refutes Priest ; Schurz' contribution was greater efficiency in administration.

doubtful whether anything in that direction was achieved at most agencies. In 1878, after studying the situation at San Carlos in Arizona Territory for at least a month, Inspector E. C. Watkins gave the following account:

These Indians are ripe for civilization. They only need a school, farming utensils, and proper instruction, to make rapid advancement. Idleness is the greatest bane among them now. They are fed, and kept on the reservation; only allowed to hunt, to a limited extent. Comparatively few . . ., under such circumstances, will find sufficient, or suitable employment. Gambling is the most prevalent vice. But so much leisure leads to differences among themselves; and sometimes to schemes for making tiswin (a crude whiskey), and even raids, outside the reserve . . . The first thing to be done this summer is to . . . *start a school.* Then buy wagons, harness , and farming tools, and seed for issue early next Spring. . . . The seed, and other supplies purchased under contract are of no use this season as they have not yet been delivered. The failure to get seed for Spring planting is a great misfortune.[31]

Instances of rapid progress were the exception rather than the rule. Although a law was passed in 1874 which required able-bodied male Indians between eighteen and forty-five years of age to perform service in return for provisions, except where the Secretary of the Interior made exemptions, agents had a difficult time persuading tribesmen to labor. Agent J. L. Broaddus of Hoopa Valley in California despaired at the prospect of Indians harvesting their own farm crops, and was convinced that the wheat would "be threshed before it was cut." In making fencing materials during the winter, the production of his wards had fallen short of the cost of beef and flour to feed them.[32]

As characteristic as this was of the majority of male Indians,

---

[31] Watkins to Hayt, May 25, 1878, Bur. Ind. Aff., Ltrs. Rec'd.
[32] 18 U.S. Stat., 176 ; Broaddus to Com. Ind. Aff., Jan. 22, 1876, Bur. Ind. Aff., Ltrs. Rec'd.

it would be unfair to leave the red race in such a bad light. Many of the Shoshoni were industrious, clearing and cultivating small patches of land in the valleys of eastern Nevada, but pressure from white encroachment prompted their removal to arid land which would produce nothing. Some of the Cheyenne and Arapaho were good freighters, but their supplies were transported by white contractors while Indian teams and wagons stood idle. It was futile to attempt their vocational education under such circumstances, and cruel to promise them the benefits of Anglo-American culture.[33]

Reports from Yakima in Washington Territory, from Santee in Nebraska, from Sisseton in Dakota Territory, and from White Earth in Minnesota were more encouraging. At Yakima, agent James Wilbur not only relied upon the natives to cut firewood, to provide rails for fencing, and to make hay, but taught them carpentry and the manufacture of saddles, harness, and wagons. In addition, his Indians did well as herders, having a surplus of beef for sale in 1878. Agricultural progress at the other three agencies was marked by a surplus of grain the same year.[34]

But most of the tribes were dependent upon Congressional charity when the "Peace Policy" ended. Only a small portion of the lands which they occupied were either grazed or cultivated, and in many instances the appropriations for vocational education were wasted because they were insufficient or misapplied. Certainly it was a mistake to attempt the agricultural instruction of nomadic Indians of mountain and plain; animal husbandry would have suited them much better. A greater

---

[33] Levi Gheen, farmer for Western Shoshoni, at Hamilton, Nev., to E. P. Smith, Mar. 15, 1873, and Oct. 3, 1874 ; Inspector John McNeil at Wichita, Kan., to Hayt, Sept. 9, 1878, Bur. Ind. Aff., Ltrs. Rec'd.

[34] Ann. Rpts. of Com. Ind. Aff., House Exec. Docs. No. 1, 45th Cong., 2nd Sess., Vol. 8, 400, and No. 1, 45th Cong., 3rd Sess., Vol. 9, 441.

mistake from the point of view of their eventual assimilation, however, was to allow Indians to become dependent upon Congressional charity for a life of idleness on reservations. According to Inspector John McNeil, Indians were most tractable immediately after they had been thoroughly subdued and rendered destitute. McNeil made this observation in advising an assimilation program for the Nez Percé following their humiliation in 1877. Considering the progress made by the Santee Sioux at Niobrara in Nebraska and at Lake Traverse in Dakota Territory after harsh treatment in the wake of their Minnesota uprising, it appears that the best opportunity to prepare most Indians for productive citizenship was lost largely through Congressional parsimony.[35]

Those who initiated the "Peace Policy" were aware that the great hope of the red race lay in the education of Indian children. Its administrators learned quickly that the most effective method was through their enrollment in industrial boarding schools. The environment of an Indian village could not be overcome by any other means. Yet in 1878, out of an estimated 33,000 Indian youth of school age, not including the Five Civilized Tribes, there were boarding-school accommodations for only 2,589 whereas Commissioner E. A. Hayt had estimated that 8,000 could be brought into such institutions within a short time if it were not for the fact that money for the employment of teachers, for the erection of school buildings, and for feeding and clothing the scholars had not been appropriated. Under these circumstances, Hayt predicted that progress which might be made in a decade would require a generation. Considering that the small number of Indian children who spent from one to three years in boarding schools were thrown back into the social environment created by those who still lived under

---

[35] McNeil at Ft. Hall, Idaho Terr., to Hayt, Aug. 28, 1879, Bur. Ind. Aff., Ltrs. Rec'd. Ann. Rpt. of Com. Ind. Aff., House Exec. Doc. No. 1, 43rd Cong., 1st Sess., Vol. 4, 376-77,

primitive conditions, the Commissioner's prediction seems much too conservative.[36]

More adequate provision of educational facilities came at the end of the seventies. Most notable was the enrollment of Indian students at Hampton Normal and Agricultural Institute in Virginia, and the establishment of two other boarding schools at Carlisle Barracks in Pennsylvania and at Forest Grove in Oregon. The movement to educate Indians in schools far removed from tribal locations was begun by a Presbyterian Army officer, Captain Richard H. Pratt, who in 1875 was placed in charge of seventy-two Cheyenne, Arapaho, Kiowa, and Comanche prisoners at Fort Marion, Saint Augustine, Florida. In preference to the dullness of simple confinement, Pratt determined to give them industrial training. When the government ordered their return to Indian Territory early in 1878, many wanted to remain in the East, and it was agreed that they might continue their education under private sponsorship. Pratt's work had aroused such enthusiasm among wealthy winter residents near St. Augustine that funds were raised to sponsor twenty-two students, seventeen of whom went to Hampton, a Negro school under the direction of General Samuel C. Armstrong. Armstrong had already proposed the integration of Indians with Negroes at Hampton and requested Pratt's help to procure one hundred and fifty additional students, preferably from among the Nez Percé, who had just been defeated. What machinations caused the Interior Department to substitute thirty-four Sioux cannot be discerned, but in September 1878 Pratt and his wife set out for the Sioux agencies to select an equal number of boys and girls between fourteen and twenty years of age.[37]

---

[36] Ann. Rpt., House Exec. Doc. No. 1, 45th Cong., 3rd Sess., Vol. 9, 457-58. There were day-school accommodations in 1878 for 5,082 Indian students.

[37] Boarding-school accommodations were increased to 3,461 in 1879: Ann. Rpt. of Com. Ind. Aff., House Exec. Doc. No. 1, 46th Cong., 2nd

Not entirely satisfied with the idea of educating Indians and Negroes jointly and being cognizant of Hampton's limited capacity unless additional buildings were erected, Pratt requested permission to open a separate school in the deserted Army barracks at Carlisle, Pennsylvania. The Secretary of the Interior and the Secretary of War agreed, and though the scheme lacked financial support, operations were begun with the arrival in October 1879 of sixty boys and twenty-four girls from Rosebud, Pine Ridge, and other Sioux agencies on the Missouri River. These were followed by students representing all of the tribes in the Indian Territory, excepting the civilized group, bringing total enrollment to 158 by the end of that year. Located in the fertile and salubrious Cumberland Valley and having brick buildings capable of providing accommodations for at least four hundred more children, Carlisle was an excellent choice. The major problem was lack of funds, and this obstacle was overcome in 1882, when Congress appropriated $67,500 for the benefit of the new institution. From that date success was assured.[38]

Although Pratt did not use coercion in selecting Indian students, he argued, as did his fellow Presbyterians, that their

Sess., Vol. 9, 73. Armstrong to Schurz, Oct. 29, 1877, July 5 and Aug. 13, 1878; Armstrong to Adj. Gen. of the Army E. D. Townsend, May 20, 1878; Armstrong to Hayt, Aug. 28, 1878; copy of Schurz to Sec. of War, Aug. 30, 1878; Townsend to Schurz (Spec. Order No. 190), Sept. 2, 1878, Bur. Ind. Aff., Ltrs. Rec'd. Hayt to Armstrong, Aug. 20, 1878; Hayt to Pratt, Sept. 2, 1878, Bur. Ind. Aff., Ltrs. Sent. J. M. Linn, "The Relation of the Church to the Indian Question," *The Presbyterian Review*, I (1880), 681; Priest, *op. cit.,* 142. A good biography of Pratt is Elaine Goodale Eastman, *The Red Man's Moses* (Norman, Okla., 1935).

[38] Ann. Rpt. of Com. Ind. Aff., House Exec. Doc. No. 1, 46th Cong., 2nd Sess., Vol. 9, 73-74; 22 U.S. Stat., 85. Pratt and Armstrong emphasized academic and industrial education but agreed that Christianity should have a prominent part in assimilating Indians: White Bear at Hampton to Bishop Whipple, June 3, 1878; Pratt at Randolph, N.Y., to Whipple, Aug. 1, 1878, Whipple Papers.

presence in the East would insure the good behavior of their elders at home. In 1880 two-thirds of the students at Carlisle were the children of chiefs and headmen. The tribes represented were Sioux, Cheyenne, Arapaho, Kiowa, Comanche, Pawnee, Menomonee, Iowa, Sac and Fox, Lipan, Ponca, Nez Percé, Wichita, Apache, and Pueblo. Pratt envisioned all of these as citizens of Eastern states.[39]

The progress of Indians at Hampton and Carlisle had three immediate effects. It led to the establishment in 1880 of a third school for Indians of the Pacific region at Forest Grove, Oregon, under the direction of Lieutenant M. C. Wilkinson; it helped arouse a strong interest in Indian assimilation among benevolent people by demonstrating that Indian children were "as bright and teachable as average white children of the same ages"; and it produced the most vituperative attack upon advocates of Indian education that Western sponsors of the inferior-race concept could deliver.[40]

The view of the West had prevailed throughout the "Peace Policy" decade largely because public opinion could not be evoked in favor of an undefeated people. The words of Commissioner Francis Walker written in 1873 were prophetic: "So long as the attention of the executive department is occupied by efforts to preserve the peace; so long as Congress is asked yearly to appropriate three millions of dollars to feed and clothe insolent savages; so long as the public mind is exasperated by reports of Indian outrages . . ., so long will it be vain to expect

---

[39] Pratt at Carlisle to Com. Ind. Aff., Feb. 24, 1880, Bur. Ind. Aff., Ltrs. Rec'd.; Pratt to Whipple, Aug. 1, 1878, Whipple Papers; Ann. Rpt. of Com. Ind. Aff., House Exec. Doc. No. 1, 46th Cong., 3rd Sess., Vol. 9, 87; Linn, *op. cit.*, 681.

[40] Ann. Rpts. of Com. Ind. Aff., House Exec. Docs. No. 1, 46th Cong., 2nd Sess., Vol. 9, 73, and No. 1, 46th Cong., 3rd Sess., Vol. 9, 86-87. An account of a blistering verbal assault on Pratt and Wilkinson by Senator Plumb of Kansas is in Pratt to Senator Dawes, Mar. 18, 1882, Dawes Papers.

an adequate treatment of the question of Indian civilization."[41] A change was at hand, and the increase of educational facilities was but one indication of it. As will be shown in the chapter which follows, historical events produced a more favorable climate of public opinion, which made reform legislation possible during the 1880's.

In many respects the "Peace Policy" was a failure. It was least effective insofar as it sought to clear the Indians from the great open spaces in advance of white settlement, and to prepare them for assimilation. The insufficiency of appropriations and the refusal of Congress to legislate needed changes, together with the many other obstacles which have been discussed, made the accomplishment of these objectives impossible. However, much was done for which administrators of the policy are deserving of credit. The system of purchasing supplies was greatly improved. Generally speaking, agency personnel were much more honest and much more interested in the red man's welfare than those individuals who held office during the sixties. Finally, and perhaps most important, techniques were developed which helped rid the Indian service of many fraudulent practices which were rampant when the "Peace Policy" began.

---

[41] "The Indian Question," *North American Review*, CXVI, 357.

VIII

Public Opinion and Historical Events

INDIAN ASSIMILATION WAS not a question of partisan politics, but of sectional attitudes. The West was fervently opposed to all constructive recommendations because association with the tribes had cultivated contempt for and even hatred of the red race. Conversely, the East until about 1880 was rather passive because separation from the frontier, and little appreciation of conditions there, allowed people to entertain romantic notions of Indian life. The passive character of public opinion in the East, broken only by sporadic bursts of sympathy when Indians were massacred, gave the West a controlling influence upon legislation respecting Indian affairs.

There had never been a want of recommendations looking toward assimilation. In 1826 the first head of the Indian Office, Thomas McKenney, suggested the individual allotment of land to youthful Indians as part of an educational program. A proposal for "something, however simple, in the shape of a code of laws, suited to their wants" appeared in Commissioner Elbert Herring's report for 1833. And in 1851 Commissioner Luke Lea pointed out the desirability of incorporating the Indians "into the great body of our citizen population." These suggestions were repeated again and again. Especially did the Interior Department draw attention to a need for changes in the legal status of Indians as Anglo-American civilization began to overrun the Great Plains. Secretary James Harlan wrote in 1865 that "the want of an acceptable and efficient provision for the administration of justice has been sensibly felt in cases arising between members of the tribes, or between Indians and the white men who have been permitted to reside among them." Between 1869 and 1881, the Board of Indian Commissioners

168

repeatedly urged Congress to provide for the individual allotment of land to Indians on reservations, and "to afford them
all reasonable aid in their preparation for citizenship."[1]

But congressmen were unwilling to assume responsibility for
legislation required to accomplish a change of policy. To get
approval of appropriations promised by Indian treaties was
difficult enough, and although some other bills were passed
during the 1860's and 1870's, none altered the objectives of
policy. Among these were an amendment to the Intercourse
Act of 1834, aimed principally at the illicit whiskey traffic;
several provisions for inspection, meant to make agents and
contractors more honest; and the creation of an Indian police
force, an attempt to keep order on the reservations. Such laws
were in harmony with Western desires to isolate Indians, to
keep them quiet, and to prevent forays off the reservations.[2]

If there were to be any changes that involved the displace-
ment of an obsolete system; that looked to principles of equity
and justice as fundamental precepts; that sought the transition
of this Stone-Age people and their integration in Anglo-
American society, then public sentiment needed to become
thoroughly aroused in their favor. Unfortunately for the Indians
and for the few advocates of reform who were willing to plead
their cause whatever the circumstances, events during the 1870's
raised instead a cry for extermination. Even romantic Easterners were sobered.

First there occurred the Modoc War of 1873, which severely
taxed military ingenuity before a small band of Indians under
a war leader named Captain Jack was finally blasted out of the
lava beds of northern California. Being located in the vicinity

---

[1] Ann. Rpts., Senate Exec. Docs. No. 1, 19th Cong., 2nd Sess., Vol. 1,
508 ; 26th Cong., 1st Sess., Vol. 1, 186 ; 32nd Cong., 1st Sess., Vol. 3,
274 ; 39th Cong., 1st Sess., Vol. 2, ix.

[2] Estimates of deficiencies, House Exec. Docs. No. 132, 43rd Cong.,
2nd Sess., Vol. 15, and No. 56, 46th Cong., 3rd Sess., Vol. 18.

of Yreka, where delay in removing them had caused settlers to become desperate, this "barbarian folk, proud and free," defied Commissioner Francis Walker's order that they be settled, "by force if necessary," upon the Klamath reservation in Oregon. The Modocs murdered a few settlers who were on land which they claimed, then fled to the lava beds, where troops overtook them in January. During the battle which ensued, the soldiers commanded by Colonel Frank Wheaton were soundly beaten, and under pressure from the War Department, General William T. Sherman authorized conciliatory measures. President Grant was disposed to give the peace advocates a chance; perhaps they might do better than the military. It was an ill-founded hope, for peace commissioners made no progress and resigned almost as fast as they were appointed.[3]

Meanwhile the troops were reinforced; when March came they outnumbered the Modoc warriors ten to one, and were becoming restless. General Sherman, who had no faith in the peace commissioners, became impatient. He wired General E. R. S. Canby, commander of the Columbia military department, who had gone to the scene to supervise activities: "Should these peaceful measures fail, and should the Modocs . . . again resort to deceit and treachery, I trust that you will make such use of the military force that no other Indian tribe will imitate their example, and that no reservation for them will be necessary except graves among their chosen lava beds." Tension mounted. Finally, Alfred Meacham, the chairman of the peace delegation, decided against his better judgment to accept an

---

[3] J. M. Schofield to W. T. Sherman, Apr. 21, 1873, and James F. Gagley at Canyonville to Sherman, May 2, 1873, War Records. Rpt. on difficulty with Modocs, House Exec. Doc. No. 201, 42nd Cong., 3rd Sess., Vol. 9, 7. J. F. Santee, "Edward R. S. Canby, Modoc War, 1873," *Oregon Historical Quarterly*, XXXIII (1932), 74-75. A detailed and scholarly account is Keith A. Murray, *The Modocs and Their War* (Norman, Okla., 1959). An older and popular treatment is D. P. Payne, *Captain Jack* (Portland, 1938).

invitation of the Modoc chief to a final parley in the Indian council tent which had been erected about one mile in front of their stronghold. With him went the Reverend Eleazar Thomas, a Methodist minister from San Francisco; agent L. C. Dyar, from the Klamath reservation; Frank Riddle and his wife, Winema, as interpreters; and General Canby. Captain Jack and his cohorts had set a trap. In the midst of the proceedings, both Thomas and General Canby were wantonly slaughtered, and the rest narrowly escaped. Meacham was badly wounded. This was April 11, 1873. Not until June 1 did the Army, after having endured severe losses, force the Modocs to surrender.'

News of this savage betrayal stirred the whole country. *The Saint Paul Daily Press* reported, "The feeling of indignation against the Modoc murderers, as attested by conversations with all the leading officials in Washington, reaches a degree of intensity which no Indian treachery has ever heretofore created." At Yreka, California, citizens loudly denounced the Secretary of the Interior and expressed contempt for pacifism with a taunt inscribed upon a large poster: " 'Make Peace if it Takes all Summer. Signed: C. Delano'." The nation demanded a war of annihilation. Civilian officials and their pet "Peace Policy" were denounced, while General Sherman's order for the extermination of the Modocs was applauded everywhere.[5]

A second event which discredited the reformers even more was the Custer massacre. A treaty in 1868 created the Great Sioux Reservation, including all the land within the present limits of South Dakota west of the Missouri River. Besides this permanent abode, it was agreed that the territory north of the North Platte River and east of the Big Horn Mountains would remain unsettled, as hunting grounds for the Sioux Nation.[6]

' Schofield to Sherman, Apr. 12, 1873, War Records; Santee, *op. cit.*, 75-78, quotes Sherman and describes Modoc treachery.

[5] *The Saint Paul Daily Press,* April 15 and 16, 1873; Payne, *op. cit.*, 185,

This "permanent" arrangement was challenged by the adjacent white community when the Big Horn Association was formed at Cheyenne in March 1870. The talk was of an expedition. A delegation was in Washington seeking consent and cooperation from the government. The motives, the frame of mind, and the intentions of the sponsors were portrayed in the *Cheyenne Daily Leader* with clarity and force:

The rich and beautiful valleys of Wyoming are destined for the occupancy and sustenance of the anglo-saxon race. The wealth that for untold ages has lain hidden beneath the snow-capped summits of our mountains has been placed there by Providence to reward the brave spirits whose lot it is to compose the advance-guard of civilization. The Indians must stand aside or be overwhelmed by the ever advancing and ever increasing tide of emigration. The destiny of the aborigines is written in characters not to be mistaken. The same inscrutable Arbiter that decreed the downfall of Rome, has pronounced the doom of extinction upon the redmen of America. The attempt to defer this result by mawking [sic] sentimentalism in favor of savages is unworthy a great people. The government may discourage but it cannot prevent this expedition. It may discountenance but it dare not retard. Big Horn will be explored in spite of all the red tape in Washington. Western men have a style of coming at results by short and direct means. If these Indian treaties have got into such a tangled knot that they cannot be untied, the sword of the pioneer will sever them.[7]

It was reported in April 1872 that white inhabitants in and around Sioux City, Iowa were becoming excited about the reputed value of the Black Hills country for agriculture and mining, and that there would be imminent danger of a Sioux uprising if the existing treaty obligations were violated through "the probable invasion of the same by companies of miners." The plans of the Black Hills Mining and Exploring Association

---

[6] Kappler, *Laws and Treaties,* II, 770-75.

[7] *Cheyenne Daily Leader,* Mar. 3, 1870. The Big Horn Association is discussed in Ernest S. Osgood, *Day of the Cattleman* (Minneapolis, 1954), 72-73.

of Sioux City were thwarted, however, when the Army was ordered to disperse any expedition headed for the Black Hills. Nevertheless, interest in the area grew and when a scientific detachment, which accompanied Custer on an exploratory march in 1874, confirmed rumors that the Hills contained gold, there occurred a great rush, bringing miners from nearly every state in the Union. The Army could not stem the tide, and peace negotiations in 1875 failed to mollify the irate Sioux.[8]

It was not only the trek into the Black Hills by a host of gold-seekers, however, which provoked the Unkpapa and the Oglala bands. Nearly as important, though not as spectacular, was the fanning out of settlers into the rich mountain valleys near Bozeman and Helena in Montana Territory. The Crow agent stated in March 1876 that the easternmost settlements of that territory had been harassed by the Sioux for several years, and that seventeen attacks had been made on white parties in the Yellowstone Valley during the preceding eight months. It was this state of affairs which had caused Governor B. F. Potts, in July 1875, to protest so vigorously: "How long is this policy to last? Are we to have our people killed and their property destroyed and no relief afforded?"[9]

Had the Sioux been content with their raids on parties of immigrants, perhaps the Congregationalist Commissioner of Indian Affairs, Edward P. Smith, would have been more reluctant to act. But this was not the case. Sitting Bull and other hostile chiefs had been making war against the Arikara, Mandan, Gros Ventre, Assiniboin, Blackfeet, Piegan, Crow,

---

[8] F. A. Walker to C. Delano, April 16, 1872, Bur. Ind. Aff., Rpt. Book. Harold Briggs, "The Black Hills Gold Rush," *North Dakota Historical Quarterly*, V (1931), 79, 82-83, and 88. W. M. Wemett, "Custer's Expedition to the Black Hills in 1874," *N. Dak. Hist. Quart.*, VI (1932), 299.

[9] Inspector E. C. Watkins to E. P. Smith, Nov. 9, 1875, and agent Dexter Clapp to J. Q. Smith, Mar. 10, 1876, Sen. Exec. Doc. No. 52, 44th Cong., 1st Sess., 3-5 and 10-11. Potts to Delano, July 9, 1875, Bur. Ind. Aff., Ltrs. Rec'd.

and other friendly tribes who were settled near agencies under the supervision of missionaries. These Indians were critical of the government for its failure to provide protection, and were threatening to return to their barbaric ways. The "Peace Policy" was in jeopardy.[10]

Therefore Smith, under instructions from Secretary Chandler, issued an ultimatum meant for Sitting Bull and the other hostile Sioux, that they must come to agencies prior to January 31, 1876 or "be deemed hostile, and treated accordingly by the military force." No consideration was given the plight of peaceable Indians who, because the government had not provided sufficient rations, were hunting on the Powder River. Theirs was a choice of trying to elude the Army or scrambling across a barren, storm-swept wasteland, in the dead of winter, to agencies incapable of supplying subsistence. A few returned and the rest remained where they were.[11]

Commissioner Smith, who left office shortly after issuing this ultimatum, has been adversely criticized for not allowing the Sioux more time to comply. Yet he acted wholly in keeping with both civil and military counsel. Inspector E. C. Watkins had advised that troops be sent during the winter, and the sooner the better. General Philip Sheridan was consulted, and his reply of January 4 called for action as speedily as possible, "so that the enemy may be taken at the greatest disadvantage" in a winter campaign.[12]

The new Commissioner, J. Q. Smith, agreed completely with his predecessor's action and urged prompt execution of the threat to begin military operations. Thus on February 1 Sec-

---

[10] Watkins to Smith, Nov. 9, 1875, *ibid.*

[11] E. P. Smith to agents Hastings, Howard, Bingham *et al.*, Dec. 6, 1875, and Rpt. of Hastings at Red Cloud agency to J. Q. Smith, Apr. 3, 1876, *ibid.*, 6 and 12. P. E. Byrne, *The Red Man's Last Stand* (London, 1927), 28.

[12] Watkins to Smith, Nov. 9, 1875, and Sheridan to Sherman, Jan. 4, 1876, Sen. Exec. Doc. No. 52, 44th Cong., 1st Sess., 3-5 and 7-8.

retary Chandler turned the hostile Sioux over to the War Department for such action by the Army as might be deemed proper in view of the circumstances. The troops required a month to get under way. General Crook's command marched north from Fort Fetterman in Wyoming Territory under orders to find and subdue the hostiles, but had an unfortunate encounter with a band of Sioux and Northern Cheyenne on March 17 which compelled a withdrawal. Plans were then made to send three columns against the Indian encampment which was located in the Little Big Horn Valley. General Crook from Fort Fetterman, Colonel John Gibbon from Fort Ellis in Montana Territory, and Generals Alfred Terry and George Custer from Fort Abraham Lincoln near Bismarck on the Missouri River, were given charge of the assignment. All might have gone well had it not been that on June 17 Crook engaged a band of Oglala Sioux led by Crazy Horse, and suffered a defeat which prevented him from making a scheduled rendezvous with the other forces on the Yellowstone River. Terry, Custer, and Gibbon met and discussed the plan of operations. Then Custer followed an Indian trail up the Rosebud, while Terry proceeded with Gibbon up the Yellowstone and Big Horn, intending to strike the Indian camp in the valley of the Little Big Horn. The trouble was that Custer got there first, and having made the mistake of dividing his command, proceeded to make the attack while Terry and Gibbon were yet some forty miles away. Nearly every American is familiar with the fatal error through which that ambitious but foolhardy commander sacrificed his entire battalion. Less well understood is the effect that it had upon public opinion and therefore upon the question of Indian reform.[13]

When the news reached the Twin Cities on July 6, ten days

---

[13] Smith to Chandler, Jan. 21, 1876, and Chandler to Sec. of War, Feb. 1, 1876, *ibid.*, 8-9. P. E. Byrne, "The Custer Myth," *N. Dak. Hist. Quart.*, VI (1932), 191-93.

after the catastrophe, it spread like a flash of lightning throughout the area. Custer's men were well known; the Seventh
Cavalry had been stationed at Fort Snelling and was expected
to return there. Not since the dark days of the Civil War had
Minnesotans been so stirred with horror and excitement over
the news of a battle. And the "hardy" pioneers of the western
border, some of them newly arrived from the East, experienced
such shock that they made for the nearest settlements as fast as
their legs or teams could travel. One hundred families had
arrived at Herman, Minnesota by July 13. An inability to
distinguish friendly Indians who were roaming off their reservation from the hostile ones with whom Custer had tangled
seven hundred miles away was apparently the cause of their
panic.[14]

If the first reactions of the adjacent West were horror and
fright, those that followed were quite the opposite. The
Bismarck Weekly Tribune was correct in estimating that
". . . the temper of the Americans, . . . will demand a prosecution of the war in a manner so vigorous that the fiends of the
plains will be glad to surrender their arms. . . ." Some wanted
"the Indians exterminated root and branch, old and young,
male and female," while others were only a little less blood-
thirsty. The editor of the *Tribune* demanded the abolition of
all treaties, agencies, and reservations. The situation called, he
said, for prompt punitive action against the hostiles. Rather
than agencies, the government should establish "Indian posts"
where all the peaceably inclined must go "or die of war and
famine." When hostilities were ended, perhaps these could learn
to live as white people, but meanwhile, "Let that christian
philanthropy which weeps over the death of a lazy, lousy, lying,
stealing red skin, whose hands are still reeking with the blood

---

[14] *Saint Paul and Minneapolis Pioneer-Press and Tribune,* July 7 and
13, 1876.

of defenseless women and children, . . . take a back seat."[15]

A disinterested observer could scarcely have missed the rationalization of the *Saint Paul Pioneer-Press*. There was no reason to criticize the "Peace Policy" insofar as it sought to promote Indian civilization, it stated. Neither was there any objection to the kind and just treatment of Indians, so long as they were willing to conduct themselves in a manner necessary to the peace and security of the frontier! What the paper disapproved was the "wishy-washy humanitarianism" and the "imbecile stupidity" that sought peace with openly hostile bands through bribes, instead of punishing them for their crimes. That the invasion of the Black Hills might have had something to do with the ferocity of the red man's resistance was unthinkable. The Indians did not take up arms to defend their treaty rights, but rather to defend their violation of treaty obligations.[16]

When the *Springfield* (Mass.) *Union* suggested that the Sioux were not the aggressors and lamented their probable extermination, the *Pioneer-Press* countered with a verbal attack on its editors. The people of the West were getting tired of this sort of "maudlin sympathy." The *Union* either was inexcusably ignorant or had maliciously misstated the facts. Would that paper admit the right of the criminal to murder his arresting officer? Minnesotans had not forgotten that it was such false philanthropy which induced President Lincoln to save one hundred and fifty red assassins from the felon's rope in 1862. If the troops, in an exasperated temper, should show no mercy, the reason would be clear, for they had learned through bitter experience that justice in dealing with Indians was a

---

[15] *Ibid.*, July 18, 1876 ; *Bismarck Weekly Tribune*, July 12, 1876.
[16] *Saint Paul and Minneapolis Pioneer-Press and Tribune*, July 13 and 18, 1876.

matter of instant retaliation. Different sectional attitudes were portrayed in these newspapers. The West regarded Indians with contempt and wanted their land; being removed from frontier conditions, the East was romantic and sentimental.[17]

But because of the emotional upheaval which accompanied the fate of Custer's column, Western editors had less regard for fact and reason than those in the East. The *Pioneer-Press* charged that ignorant sentimentalism underlay the "Peace Policy" and had "filled the land with pious wails over the wrongs of the Indians . . . till not only the benevolence of Christian sects but the public sentiment of the whole country has been duped by systematic fraud in the interest of missionary funds." This was a gross misrepresentation of those main currents which inspired the reform movement.[18]

Bishop Whipple, who was opposed to the use of public money by religious bodies no matter for what purpose, and who had never used any for his missions, was hard pressed to defend the "Peace Policy." His long and diplomatic letter to President Grant of July 31, 1876 reflected the gravity of the situation. He would yield to no man in his sympathy for the courageous pioneers of the border, who were always the first victims of savage hate. His heart went out to the gallant soldiers who died without thought of self. Every friend of the Indians owed the President a debt of gratitude for earnestly trying to improve the management of their affairs. The "Peace Policy" had been instituted at a time when the Indians were either openly hostile or sullen and turbulent. Peace had been established by sending out the bravest and best officers, men

---

[17] *Ibid.*, July 12, 1876. The *Pioneer Press* was incorrect about the number of Sioux saved by Presidential intervention; Lincoln approved death sentences for only 39 of 303 Indians condemned to be hanged by the military commission under the direction of General H. H. Sibley: Kenneth Carley, *The Sioux Uprising of 1862*, 64-65.

[18] *Ibid.*, July 18, 1876.

who had grown grey in the service of their country and whose word was as good as their bond. They had been sent "because the Indians would not doubt a soldiers honor." The Sioux treaty was ratified by the Senate, making it the supreme law of the land. It was sanctioned by the people and the press, because it ended a shameful Indian war that had cost thirty millions of dollars, and the lives of ten citizens for every Indian slain. "A violation of its plain provisions was an act of deliberate perjury." The United States had made its own compact with the weaker party and had then broken the agreement. The "Peace Policy" had never been properly understood by the people. They supposed that its purpose was to grant the savages immunity for their wrongs, while law to punish crime was the first thing that the Indians' friends were asking. The President had done all that was in his power. He had provided for the nomination of honest agents and for the honest purchase of Indian supplies. Mistakes had been made, but the situation in these respects was much improved. The Bishop warned against transferring the Indian Bureau to the War Department, and compared such a move with trying to "make a bad bank note good by changing pockets." True reform must involve a change of the whole system, and might well begin with the creation of an independent Department of Indian Affairs. Also, the tribes should be concentrated on large reservations. Make two for those on the Pacific coast; place the Minnesota Indians at White Earth; and settle those of New Mexico and Colorado, and the Sioux, in the Indian Territory. Probably the Sioux would not willingly remove at once, but twenty bands might consent to go. Their subsequent prosperity would encourage others to follow. When an Indian gives up his wild life, provide him with a patent to 160 acres of land and make it inalienable. Provide a system of Indian government. Give Indian agents magisterial powers; let the U.S. marshals appoint the requisite number of civilized Indians as a constabular force; and require district judges to hold one session per year within the bounds of Indian reservations.[19]

This letter got action, but it also placed Whipple in an unenviable position, for he and other peace advocates were appointed to a commission to negotiate with the Sioux. Congress had passed the annual Indian appropriation bill on August 15 with a proviso which constituted the stiffest kind of ultimatum. Nothing more would be appropriated for the subsistence of the Sioux unless they should first relinquish all of the territory granted them as hunting grounds, plus that part of their reservation which lay to the west of the 103rd meridian. They must allow the building of three roads across what remained of the Great Sioux Reserve, agree to receive all supplies in the future at various points on the Missouri River, and undertake in earnest a program intended to make themselves self-supporting.[20]

Other members of the commission were George W. Manypenny, who served as chairman, H. C. Bulis, A. G. Boone, and Newton Edmonds. A. S. Gaylord, the Assistant Attorney General, was made legal adviser and the Reverend S. D. Hinman, a missionary to the Santee Sioux, was appointed interpreter. General H. H. Sibley was also appointed but, because of ill health and a conviction that the government should not send a peace delegation until the Sioux had suffered some major reverses, he declined to serve. In Sibley's place the choice fell upon Whipple's old friend and partner of the Lake Traverse experiment, Dr. Jared W. Daniels.[21]

Instructions sent to members of the delegation by the Commissioner of Indian Affairs stated that President Grant was

---

[19] Copies of Whipple to Grant, July 31, 1876 and of Whipple to W. K. Rogers, Pres. Sec., Aug. 6, 1877, Whipple Papers.

[20] J. Q. Smith to Whipple, Aug. 21, 1876, Whipple Papers; 19 U.S. Stat., 192.

[21] Sibley to Whipple, Aug. 24, 1876, and Smith to Whipple, Aug. 25, 1876, Whipple Papers.

interested in making the Sioux self-supporting, and that this
would require their removal to a region more favorable to
agriculture than Dakota. The delegates should persuade the
Sioux that Indian Territory was exclusively the domicile of
Indians, and that its climate was conducive to prosperity. If
necessary, the tribes might send representatives to the region
before making a final decision. The Indian Bureau was not,
however, willing to let the matter stand or fall on this basis
alone. Commissioner J. Q. Smith added that if the Sioux removed, the government would most probably provide ample
assistance until they should become self-sustaining, whereas if
the government's proposal were rejected, they would receive
supplies along the Missouri River, "in probably scanty and
diminishing quantities."[22]

Such was the message of woe which the champions of peace
and reform brought an afflicted people—not to the hostile
camps, but to the agencies where friendlies trembled with in-
security at the sight of large bodies of troops passing through
the reservation: to Red Cloud, where the Indians said, "We
are glad to see you; you have come to save us from death"; to
Spotted Tail, Standing Rock, Crow Creek, and Santee. The
Sioux were reluctant, but they gave up the land west of the
103rd meridian which Congress had demanded. Removal to
Indian Territory was unacceptable, however, because the
Sioux felt as much sentimental attachment to Dakota as those
who took it from them have since developed—a point which
one of the chiefs was said to have made with great clarity:

If you white men had a country which was very valuable, which
had always belonged to your people, and which the Great Father
had promised should be yours forever, and men of another race
came to take it away by force, what would your people do? Would
they fight?[23]

---

[22] Smith to Sioux Commission, Aug. 24, 1876, Whipple Papers.
[23] Rpt. of Sioux Commission, Senate Exec. Doc. No. 9, 44th Cong.,
2nd Sess., 5-8.

With the exception of the Santee, the tribes on the Missouri River would not even consent to look at lands in a new country, and only those at Red Cloud and Spotted Tail actually sent delegations to the south. Red Cloud refused to go in person but sent representatives, who were reported to have spoken favorably of what they saw. Spotted Tail, himself, went to Indian Territory with no intention of being pleased, but rather to fulfill the letter of his agreement.[24]

The peace advocates had done their work, but did not concur completely in the proceedings. Why did men of conscience and integrity undertake so unsavory a task? Certainly they might have presented any number of excuses for refusing to go. General Sibley's decision was officially due to poor health. Some believed that to decline would not better the condition of the friendly Sioux. Such reasoning was manifest both in the proposals which the commissioners presented to these tribes and in the articles of agreement which the Indians were obliged to sign. One cannot read either without being reminded of Whipple's letter to President Grant, or of what he had said on numerous other occasions. Congress offered a bitter pill, which was made more palatable to the Indians by placing well-intentioned men in charge of its administration.[25]

Moreover, Manypenny hoped that the delegation's work would receive favorable attention by the press. It might be the means, therefore, of keeping the cause which he and Whipple represented before the public. Such expectations faded when the chairman observed that only three major papers had printed abstracts of the Sioux commission's report, while others scarcely mentioned the subject. Throughout the country, newspapers were preoccupied with reporting military preparations

---

[24] J. W. Daniels and A. G. Boone to G. W. Manypenny, Dec. 13, 1876, *ibid.,* 19-20.

[25] Daniels to Whipple, Nov. 16, 1876, Whipple Papers ; Rpt. of Sioux Commission, *op. cit.,* 6, 13, and 22.

to render the northern plains Indians incapable of further resistance.[26]

The Army was antagonistic toward the commission because some military officers were not interested in assimilation and because most of them wanted control of Indian administration —an arrangement to which Manypenny and Whipple were known to be opposed. Furthermore, the Army was not in a mood to distinguish between roaming hostile Sioux and friendly ones at the agencies. Necessity required that all be forcibly disarmed and dismounted; and this the soldiers proceeded to accomplish at the agencies as soon as the commissioners were through with negotiations.[27]

Colonel John Gibbon was extremely averse to assimilation. He regretted that Bishop Whipple had signed the "treaty." A provision requiring these Indians to fly would be as effective as the one requiring them to labor. It was a mistake to bind the United States to keep bad white men and mixed bloods off their reservations, because the Army was too small for the task. He summed up his attitude in these words: "The remnant of this rapidly disappearing race will give us no trouble by going to war if only we will feed and clothe them, and for these purposes the amounts appropriated by Congress are ample."[28]

During hostilities with the Sioux, their agencies were placed under military control, and Lieutenant Colonel W. P. Carlin commanded Standing Rock. His view was that, under the administration of competent and faithful agents, the Sioux could be made self-supporting in a very few years. Once they had been disarmed and dismounted it was of prime importance, however, that the government prevent those on reservations

---

[26] Manypenny to Whipple, Jan. 2, 1877, Whipple Papers.
[27] Inspector William Vandever to Whipple, Oct. 28, 1876, Whipple Papers.
[28] Gibbon at Ft. Shaw, Montana Territory, to Whipple, Nov. 15, 1876, Whipple Papers.

from acquiring weapons or ponies in the future. The Indians should be made to live in log houses built by their own labor, to raise livestock, and to cultivate gardens. In addition, they ought to have a legal system governing crimes committed against one another.[29]

Colonel Carlin's recommendations were associated with a movement, which gained much support during the Sioux troubles of 1876, to transfer the Indian Bureau to the War Department. Despite Bishop Whipple's opposition, General W. S. Hancock managed to enlist the suppport of William Welsh on the basis that many military Indian agents would be members of the Episcopal church. The attempt of the military to seize the Indian Bureau and its agencies persisted for two years. In 1877, General John Pope even blamed the Interior Department for the starving condition of the Cheyenne and Arapaho, when it was plain that depletion of game and Congressional parsimony were responsible for their plight. A bill before the House of Representatives in 1878 caused George Manypenny to carry on a lively correspondence with several congressmen as part of an effort which put the issue to rest. The experience made him bitter toward military personnnel, who he said were "all tarred with the same stick." Among the Sioux commissioners, Bishop Whipple was the one who maintained the most charitable view of the Army.[30]

The years 1876 and 1877 were surely a time of trouble for the advocates of Indian assimilation. Adverse public opinion was felt in all aspects of the question. Appropriations, so vitally needed to make the "Peace Policy" a success, suffered along

---

[29] Carlin to J. Q. Smith, Nov. 19, 1876, Bur. Ind. Aff., Ltrs. Rec'd.

[30] Senator Angus Johnson to Whipple, Apr. 22, 1876 ; John B. Sanborn to Whipple, Apr. 28, 1876 ; Welsh to Whipple, May 13, 1876 ; Manypenny to Whipple, Nov. 7, 1876, Jan. 2, 1877, Apr. 6 and 19, 1878, Whipple Papers. Sec. of War to Sec. of Interior, Oct. 2, 1877, encl. copy of rpt. on Cheyenne and Arapaho with Pope's endorsement, Bur. Ind. Aff., Ltrs. Rec'd.

with the rest. Even the Christian ladies of the Indian Hope Association at Philadelphia were constrained to admit that the red men had given little cause for sympathy, and did not resume efforts for that "persecuted people, whose original grandeur of character" was now hidden from their sight, until the beginning of 1878.[31]

In the meantime, hard-core reformists were unceasingly vigilant and looked forward to more favorable times. The most determined of these was Bishop Whipple, whose concern for the red man's welfare was more than a decade and a half old. His articles in newspapers, his voluminous correspondence with the Commissioner of Indian Affairs and the Chief Executive, and a personal interview, early in 1877, with the President, his Secretaries of Interior and War, and General Sherman mark him as the central figure of the movement.[32]

A climate of public opinion more favorable to reform was in the making as the people spent their anger through military operations which broke the power of the northern plains tribes and turned proud warriors into objects of pity. In a curious way, historical events kindled public interest first in subjugation and then in assimilation. News of Custer's death stirred the whole country to demand relentless war; then, as public indignation subsided, a different kind of tragedy was made known which pricked the conscience of Eastern citizenry and furthered the cause of reform. It concerned the removal of the Ponca tribe from their Dakota reserve to Indian Territory, and the attempt of a Ponca chief to return north.

---

[31] Ann. Rpt. of Com. Ind. Aff., House Exec. Doc. No. 1, 44th Cong., 2nd Sess., Vol. 4, 382-83 ; J. Q. Smith to Whipple, Jan. 26, 1877, Whipple Papers ; Mrs. John Lucas to Rutherford B. Hayes, Feb. 5, 1878, Bur. Ind. Aff., Ltrs. Rec'd.

[32] Whipple to W. K. Rogers, Pres. Sec., May 19, 1877, and Whipple to Hayes, Sept. 28, 1877, Bur. Ind. Aff., Ltrs. Rec'd. Copy of Whipple to Grant, July 31, 1876 ; J. Q. Smith to Whipple, Jan. 26, 1877 ; Manypenny to Whipple, Feb. 23, 1877, Whipple Papers.

When the Great Sioux Reservation was established in 1868, land granted to the Ponca by treaties in 1858 and 1865 was mistakenly included within it, and caused difficulty between the tribes. The Ponca were peaceable Indians who were accustomed to agriculture, and some of them by red men's standards were considered prosperous. Because the Sioux claimed their land, the Ponca were compelled to consider moving to the Omaha agency in Nebraska. Both the Omaha and the Indian Bureau were agreeable, but for one reason or another the arrangements were not completed. Thus the Ponca were still in their troubled position when the peace advocates were sent to the Sioux in 1876.[33]

The Congressional proviso of August 15, which demanded concessions from the Sioux as a condition of further aid, also called for removal of the Ponca, *with their consent,* to Indian Territory. Appropriations amounting to $40,000 were made for this purpose. Manypenny's commission was advised to consider placing some Sioux on the old Ponca reserve if the more powerful tribe refused to emigrate southward. The peace delegation concurred in this recommendation, and suggested that Spotted Tail receive the Ponca lands, should he elect to locate on the Missouri River. Apparently Manypenny and Whipple assumed that the Ponca would willingly remove to the Indian Territory, else they could not have agreed to the surrender of the reserve at Niobrara. Surely the possibility of forcible removal was no part of their thinking; yet unjust proceedings resulted from their uncritical acquiescence in governmental design.[34]

---

[33] Rpt. on Ponca Removal, Senate Rpt. No. 670, 46th Cong., 2nd Sess., Vol. 6, v-vi and xxii; E. A. Hayt to Carl Schurz, Feb. 3, 1879, House Rpt. No. 107, 45th Cong., 3rd Sess., Vol. 2.

[34] 19 U.S. Stat., 192 and 287; Com. J. Q. Smith to Sioux Commission, Aug. 24, 1876, Whipple Papers; Rpt. of Sioux Commission, Senate Exec. Doc. No. 9, 44th Cong., 2nd Sess., 9.

The report of Manypenny's commission was dated December 18, 1876. Approximately one month later, Inspector Edward C. Kemble arrived at the Ponca agency under orders to carry out the government's plan. After holding several councils, he telegraphed the Commissioner of Indian Affairs that the Ponca would not give up their reservation without first sending ten representatives to investigate Indian Territory. To this the government agreed, with the understanding that the Ponca delegation would proceed to Washington for completion of negotiations if the Indians were satisfied with Oklahoma lands. Like Spotted Tail, however, the Ponca chiefs did not make their journey south with the intention of being pleased. Rather, they agreed among themselves while en route not to find any suitable location. After viewing the reserves of the Osage and the Kaw, they demanded that Kemble take them either to Washington or back to their reservation. According to Kemble's own account, the Inspector wished to proceed to a depot and telegraph for additional instructions, but the chiefs would not hear of it, and eight of them slipped away by night for the homeward journey to Niobrara.[35] Having returned as far as the Omaha agency, they sent the following wire to President Grant:

Did you authorize the man you sent to take us down to the Indian Territory to select a place for our future home, to leave us there to find our way back as best we could if we did not agree to go down there? This he told us, and left us without a pass, interpreter, or money, because we would not select one of three places, telling us if we did not go there peaceably, we would be driven by soldiers at the point of the bayonet from our present homes. We were so left, and have been thirty days getting back as far as the Omahas—hungry, tired, shoeless, footsore, and sad at heart. Please answer us at once, for we are in trouble.[36]

From Independence, Kansas, Kemble inquired whether the

---

[35] Rpt. on Ponca Removal, *op. cit.,* ix, xxiv, and 18.
[36] *Ibid.,* 432.

Interior Department intended to remove the Ponca without their consent. Commissioner J. Q. Smith replied on the same day: "Removal of Poncas will be insisted upon. Spotted Tail and Red Cloud must move this summer to Missouri River. Their presence will render further stay of Poncas at old location impossible." Under new orders, Kemble returned to the Ponca agency to proceed with his assignment.[37]

In the meantime, Rutherford Hayes succeeded Ulysses Grant; the new Secretary of the Interior was Carl Schurz of Missouri. Alfred L. Riggs, missionary of the American Board of Commissioners for Foreign Missions, wrote to Schurz on March 19 and pointed out the injustice which was pending. Riggs' letter was endorsed by prominent citizens of Yankton and by John P. Williamson, Presbyterian missionary at the Yankton agency. All requested an investigation prior to forcible removal. On April 3 a citizen of Niobrara, adjacent to the Ponca reservation, pleaded with the Secretary to intervene. "The Ponca Indians have been more protection to the settlers on the frontier of Nebraska than if a regiment of soldiers had been stationed there," he argued. "If we are to have Indians on our border, let them be friendly and not hostile." Telegrams were sent to the Interior Department calling attention to the content of these letters. Also, the commandant at Fort Randall, Lieutenant Colonel Lugenbeel, on March 26 advised the government that the Ponca agency was no place for the Spotted Tail Indians because numerous whiskey shops were being established near the bounds of the reserve in anticipation of business with the Sioux. General Sheridan forwarded Colonel Lugenbeel's letter to the Adjutant General of the Army on April 2; it was customary for the Departments of War and Interior to supply one another with copies of correspondence dealing with subjects of mutual interest.[38]

---

[37] *Ibid.*, 421 and 426.
[38] *Ibid.*, 428-34.

The government's position was adamant. Contemplating the moving of the Sioux to the Ponca reserve within a few weeks, the Commissioner of Indian Affairs instructed Kemble on April 12 to "Press the Removal." The Inspector and agent James Lawrence did their best, but only a small portion of the tribe could be induced to follow the supply train which was made up. Kemble then proceeded to Washington for a conference in which it was decided to employ military force. Two companies from Fort Sully were never used, but their availability no doubt helped break Ponca resistance. On May 16, with a token force of twenty-five cavalry as an escort, the Indians began the arduous trek to their new home.[39]

This is not the place to discuss that miserable journey, accompanied as it was by suffering and death, or to speculate about the number of Ponca who expired of "fever and ague" during the three years that followed. It is sufficient to remark that no preparations were made to receive the Ponca in the Indian Territory, that their agent was not given funds necessary to prepare suitable dwellings upon their arrival, and that agricultural implements belonging to the tribe were locked up in a shed on the Dakota reserve, leaving them without means of support.[40]

After nearly two years, Standing Bear and about thirty other Ponca could endure Indian Territory no longer, and in January 1879, with the body of that chief's dead son in a farm wagon, they trekked northward. By March this party, in an utterly exhausted condition, reached the Omaha reservation. Here, as they rested for the last lap of the homeward journey, troops arrived under orders to return the Ponca to Indian Territory.[41]

[39]*Ibid.*, 439, 441-42, and 448 ; Earl W. Hayter, "The Ponca Removal," *N. Dak. Hist. Quart.*, VI (1932), 269-70.

[40] Rpt. on Ponca Removal, *op. cit.*, xxiv.

[41] *Ibid.*, 16-17 ; Francis E. Leupp, *The Indian and His Problem* (New York, 1910), 252-53.

Placed under arrest, the band was temporarily confined in the fort at Omaha, where a humanitarian reformer and editorial writer for the *Omaha Herald* took up their case. Thomas H. Tibbles had been an abolitionist preceding the Civil War, and had participated in the Kansas free-state movement. After the war he studied for the Methodist ministry and became one of the most popular circuit riders in the West. In 1875 he settled in the Republican River Valley of Nebraska, and rendered a great service by collecting in the East some $85,000 plus several train loads of supplies for the relief of settlers whose crops were destroyed by the grasshopper plagues. He joined the *Herald* in 1876.

When the Ponca prisoners arrived in Omaha, Tibbles and two associates engaged the services of John L. Webster, a lawyer and former member of the Nebraska legislature. They procured a writ of habeas corpus from Judge Elmer Dundy of the U.S. District Court, and there developed the famous case of *Standing Bear* vs. *Crook,* in which the right of an Indian to bring suit was upheld. The Indians were freed and proceeded to their old reserve.[42]

The embellishment of Standing Bear's tragic account in the press and from the rostrum by Tibbles and others made the removal of the Ponca a public issue. Because anti-Indian sentiment at Omaha was unfavorable to the cause, Tibbles went to Springfield, Massachusetts in August 1879 to begin a lecture tour of the northeastern states. Bright Eyes, the educated daughter of an Omaha chief and later Tibbles' wife, participated in these lectures and attracted much attention before audiences of Boston, New York, Philadelphia, Wilmington, and Baltimore. Her romantic appeal evoked visions of Minnehaha in the public mind, and resulted in a legend that she was that same fair maiden. Longfellow had published *Hiawatha* in 1855,

---

[42] Rpt. on Ponca Removal, *op. cit.,* 17 and 47; Cohen, *Handbook,* 162; Hayter, *op. cit.,* 272.

while Bright Eyes was only twenty years of age in 1879. Nevertheless, the speeches of this couple, accompanied as they were by the stoic presence of Standing Bear, soon had the north Atlantic seaboard bubbling with enthusiasm for Indian rights.[43]

Agitation of the Ponca case prompted the Merchants' Exchange of Boston to organize an Indian reform committee, with Governor John Davies Long as chairman. Long, who later became William McKinley's Secretary of the Navy, was also an advocate of prohibition, women's suffrage, and world peace. Most prominent among his associates on the Indian committee were D. A. Goddard, editor of the *Boston Daily Advertiser,* and William H. Lincoln, president of the New England Ship Owners' Association. Judging from the volume of correspondence, the latter appears to have been a key figure, and very likely made use of his many official capacities in Boston business to establish the committee. Interestingly enough, Lincoln was also president of the Board of Trustees for the Episcopal Theological School at Cambridge and secretary of the Boston Y.M.C.A.[44]

Mounting criticism from various reform groups moved the federal government to examine the Ponca difficulties. Although citizens around Omaha were mostly unsympathetic, Protestant missionaries there willingly joined the fight. Soon after the arrest of Standing Bear, representatives of the American Board of Commissioners for Foreign Missions, and of the Presbyterian and Protestant Episcopal churches, addressed a petition to President Hayes asking for the return of the tribe to Dakota Territory, or for their resettlement on the Omaha, Santee, or Yankton reservations. If neither of these alternatives could be

---

[43] Ann. Rpt. of Com. Ind. Aff., 1879, House Exec. Doc. No. 1, 46th Cong., 2nd Sess., Vol. 1, 179 ; *New York Times,* Dec. 13, 1879 ; Henry E. Alvord to Henry L. Dawes, Aug. 1, 1880, and D. A. Goddard to Dawes, Nov. 23, 1880, Dawes Papers.

[44] Tibbles to Dawes, Jan. 19, 1880 ; Lincoln to Dawes, May 28, 1880 ; Goddard to Dawes, Nov. 29, 1880, Dawes Papers.

granted, they requested the appointment of a commission to determine a better solution. No special commission was appointed at this time, but the Northern Cheyenne committee of the Senate, which was investigating the removal of that tribe to Indian Territory, decided to consider the Ponca matter as well. Senator Henry L. Dawes of Massachusetts, a member of the committee, was just the sort of connection which the reformers needed in Congress. He had in 1876 offered assistance to the American Board of Commissioners for Foreign Missions in the furtherance of Indian work, and now, with the sentiment of his home state rising in support of the red men, he could afford, politically speaking, to take up the cause of Indian rights. Writing the majority report of the Ponca investigation in May 1880, Dawes proposed legislation to return the tribe to the Dakota reserve. This recommendation was based upon interrogation of the Ponca chiefs, one of whom stated a preference for imprisonment to continued residence in Indian Territory. Senator Samuel J. Kirkwood of Iowa wrote a minority report and summed up his arguments with the query: "Shall we break faith and go to war with the Sioux because we have already broken faith with the Poncas?" Expediency had been the reason for removing the Ponca in 1876, and it apparently was still an important consideration in the Congressional mind, even though the Sioux were now subdued. It happened that the Senate recessed before action was possible on the Dawes bill, but it was given priority on the agenda of that body for the new session beginning in December.[45]

While Protestant reform groups were clamoring for return

[45] Undated petition of John P. Williamson, Joseph W. Cook, Alfred L. Riggs, *et al.*, including statement that "some thirty persons were recently taken back, by troops, from Omaha Agency who had clandestinely returned that far." April 1879, Bur. Ind. Aff., Ltrs. Rec'd. N. G. Clark, Sec. of A.B.C.F.M., to Dawes, Apr. 5, 1876, and copy of Dawes to Hayes, Nov. 24, 1880, Dawes Papers. Rpt. on Ponca Removal, *op. cit.*, xviii, xxiv, 1 and 235.

of the Ponca to Dakota, the Interior Department took action.
Inspector William J. Pollock and an aide were sent to the
Indian Territory to survey affairs on the Ponca reservation.
They reported that the agency was being managed in the
interest of agent William H. Whiteman and his friends, and that
the Indians were demoralized. Inspector Pollock assumed
charge, and houses of better quality than the tribe had ever
known were built on the high ground, away from the malarial
lowlands. The Ponca were provided with schools and were
given a liberal supply of agricultural implements and stock
cattle. Sanitary conditions were improved so that sickness and
death among them decreased. Consequently, the changed attitude of tribal members was remarkable. Chiefs who had in
March spoken vigorously against remaining in the Indian Territory proposed in October that they come to Washington and
sign away their Dakota lands.[46]

To the Boston committee and to Senator Dawes it appeared
that the Interior Department was endeavoring to present
Congress with an accomplished fact. The Senator wrote to
President Hayes on November 24 and requested a stay of proceedings. It was unfair for Secretary Schurz to forestall Congress, "when he himself claims that Congress directed him to
do what he has done." The good name of the administration
would require assurance that the Ponca were acting of their own
free will.[47]

Indian rights committees of Boston and Omaha combined to
press for the appointment of a special commission of inquiry,
and President Hayes chose Generals George Crook and Nelson

---

[46] E. Pugh at Ponca agency, Ind. Terr., to Com. Hayt, Dec. 27, 1879,
Bur. Ind. Aff., Ltrs. Rec'd. ; Ann. Rpt. of Sec. Interior, House Exec.
Doc. No. 1, 46th Cong., 3rd Sess., Vol. 1, 23 ; Rpt. of Ponca Commis-
sion, Dec. 18, 1880, Senate Exec. Doc. No. 30, 46th Cong., 3rd Sess.,
Vol. 1, 41.

[47] Goddard to Dawes, Nov. 15, 1880, and copy of Dawes to Hayes,
Nov. 24, 1880, Dawes Papers.

Miles, together with William Stickney of the Board of Indian Commissioners and Walter Allen, a nominee of the Boston group. They were directed on December 18 to visit the Indian Territory and possibly Dakota to ascertain what justice and humanity required the government to do for the Ponca.[48]

Circumstances made it unnecessary for the commissioners to proceed immediately to the reservations because the Ponca chiefs, by invitation of the Interior Department, arrived in Washington. The inquiry was therefore begun on the spot, and some of the testimony given was of considerable interest. White Eagle, the head chief, explained the Ponca change of mind and attitude in this way:

... but from last spring up to this time we have not had sickness. We had made a turn in our course; turned over a new leaf, and we think now ... that we'll have better times. A bad agent and sickness ... were very hard to bear, but we have now a good agent and are doing better. ... For five winters I've been looking for some one to help me, and now the sickness is going away. ... I said to my agent, ... the land we had I'll sell, and I will dwell in this land.[49]

Thus spoke the Indian who less than ten months earlier, before the Northern Cheyenne committee, had said that nothing less than a return to the old reservation would satisfy his people. One must ask whether White Eagle's testimony explained why the Ponca changed their mind. Up to a point it probably did, but Standing Buffalo, the chief who earlier declared a preference for imprisonment to continued residence in the South, was more precise: "We think that if we went back to Niobrara we'd receive no tools and no rations, and so we'd prefer to remain here." The Ponca had their new houses, farm implements, schools, and stock cattle in the Indian Territory. A bird

---

[48] Goddard to Dawes, Nov. 25, 1880, Dawes Papers. According to Hayter, *op. cit.,* 272, members of the Omaha committee were R. H. Clarkson, A. W. Partridge, A. F. McGeorge, P. L. Perrine, Levi Barnum, and William Yates.

[49] Rpt. of Ponca Commission, *op. cit.,* 16.

in hand was better than two in the bush. Why rely on the seldom-kept promises of a government which had already caused so much grief? For them, the matter was closed. Thus, the chiefs signed a declaration on December 27 expressing a desire to remain in Indian Territory and to relinquish all rights to the reserve formerly inhabited by the Ponca tribe. Standing Bear would have to make terms with Washington as necessity required.[50]

What might happen to Standing Bear's band, which had grown in number through an underground railroad operated by the Omaha committee, was a major concern of the Indian rights group. It lay at the foundation of their antipathy toward Carl Schurz, who ordered White Eagle and Standing Buffalo to Washington upon learning that the Ponca chiefs were willing to surrender the Dakota reserve. Lincoln declared the proceeding diabolical, and together with Goddard worried about the fate of Standing Bear. The Boston committee was instrumental in having the special commission of inquiry appointed by President Hayes visit the Ponca in Dakota Territory as well as those in the Indian Territory. The affair ended happily when the commissioners recommended that each man, woman, and child of the tribe should select 160 acres of land at either place and should receive a patent to the same, inalienable for thirty years, and further that money should be appropriated to provide the Dakota Ponca with improvements comparable to those already made in the Indian Territory. The President was amenable to these proposals, and Congress, with the exception of the patents, made them law. A delegation of Sioux was brought to Washington in August 1881, and surrendered all claim to the Ponca's Dakota reserve.[51]

---

[50] Rpt. on Ponca Removal, *op. cit.,* 203-204; Rpt. of Ponca Commission, *op. cit.,* 1, 25 and 26.

[51] Hayter, *op. cit.,* 272 and 274; Rpt. of Ponca Commission, *op. cit.,* 3-5; Goddard to Dawes, Nov. 15, 1880, and Lincoln to Dawes, Nov. 24, 1880, Dawes Papers; 21 U.S. Stat., 422.

Meanwhile the battle between Schurz and the Ponca sympathizers raged in the press, and the Secretary was interrogated by the Northern Cheyenne committee. The congressmen learned that when Schurz took office there was a widespread assumption that the placing of as many tribes as possible in the Indian Territory would be advantageous to both white and red races; where they had lived formerly was considered unimportant. The Northern Cheyenne and the Ponca were relocated on this basis. Different criteria, however, determined federal policy following the arrival of these tribes on the great southern reservation. Attempts of white parties to make settlements there had given rise to a precarious situation; troops were having difficulty keeping them out. For the government to begin returning tribes to former locations would weaken the concept of an exclusive domain for Indians, whereupon the problem of discouraging intruders would become even more troublesome. Moreover, the exodus of a few tribes might cause a wholesale migration. In the Secretary's opinion, white encroachment would continue unless every square mile of Indian Territory were settled by red men holding firm titles to the land.[52]

Although Schurz's explanation seems adequate, the evidence demonstrates that he did not become enthusiastic about the Indians' welfare until criticism was leveled at the Interior Department during the Ponca controversy. The Secretary was preoccupied with efforts to rid civil service of the spoils system and to pacify the South, which had suffered long under carpetbag government. Indeed, his report for 1878 did state that "the case of the Poncas seems entitled to especial consideration," did recommend allotment of land in severalty, did propose a legal system for reservations, did encourage greater emphasis upon education; yet Indian affairs were on the periphery of

---

[52] Rpt. on Ponca Removal, *op. cit.*, 358-60.

Schurz' interests. In his own apt phrase, the red men were "on his hands," and nearly all of the recommendations attributed to him had become monotonous through repetition in annual reports of the Indian Bureau during a decade and a half prior to Schurz' term of office.[53]

The Ponca controversy focused attention upon the need for recognition of Indian rights. In Boston, where Standing Bear's pathetic story caused influential citizens to demand the return of his people to Dakota Territory, it was soon realized that lack of legal status lay at the bottom of injustice toward red men. They must have privileges of citizenship, protection of law, and individual land patents, the same as Anglo-Americans. New Englanders approached the problem in a spirit of moral urgency which was suggestive of the abolitionist movement. George A. Jackson, a young minister from Swampscott, wrote in April 1880: "It is fitting that Massachusetts, foremost in putting an end to the servitude of the black men, should now be foremost in putting an end to this worse servitude of the red men." William H. Lincoln was of the same mind. "We want New England solid on this question," he declared in November. "We have destroyed slavery and were punished severely while doing it. It remains now to rid the land of a system that will surely bring a curse upon us if we continue it."[54]

---

[53] Ann. Rpt., House Exec. Doc. No. 1, 45th Cong., 2nd Sess., Vol. 8, viii-xii ; Frederic Bancroft, ed., *Speeches, Correspondence and Political Papers of Carl Schurz* (New York, 1913), Vol. 3, 416. The Schurz Papers in the Library of Congress were examined for the years 1877 through 1880.

[54] Jackson to Dawes, Apr. 19, 1880, and Lincoln to Dawes, June 21, Nov. 30, and Dec. 29, 1880, Dawes Papers.

IX

Organization and Reform

UNTIL THE PONCA story broke in 1879, it had been impossible to create a national reform organization of an enduring and effective character. The American Indian Aid Association was formed in 1857 with headquarters in New York City, but was so inactive that it was necessary to reorganize in 1873. In that year the Association persuaded President Grant to prevent the execution of two of the six Modoc prisoners who had been sentenced to death after Captain Jack's hardy band was finally forced to surrender, but this was the only known accomplishment. The Association, in addition to being organized and reorganized during a period when the general public was out of sympathy with the red man, helped assure its own defeat by adopting the impossible aim of protecting and assimilating all Indians on both of the American continents.[1]

Besides the missionary boards which participated in the "Peace Policy," there were several local societies, such as the Indian Hope Association of Philadelphia, all pleading the Indians' cause in their own way. For the most part, these were made up of Christian women who had been stirred by the speeches of such notables as Bishop Whipple, Bishop Hare, and William Welsh, or through numerous articles on the Indian which appeared in religious periodicals. Lacking coordination, they made no discernible contribution to the reform movement except that of helping keep it alive through the years of trouble.

In the spring of 1879 a Baptist school teacher, Mary L.

---

[1] W. C. Gould, Sec. of Amer. Ind. Aid Assn., to Pres. Grant, Nov. 28, 1873, Bur. Ind. Aff., Ltrs. Rec'd. Directors of the Association were Tappen Townsend, Charles Sears, Henry Case, Joseph Lafume, Jesse Keen, Samuel Leavit, J. K. Ingalls, L. T. Warner, and R. J. Hallock.

Bonney of Philadelphia, who was aroused by the Ponca tragedy, perceived that there could be no legislative reform unless the people generally demanded it, and therefore determined to organize the Christian women of the nation for the purpose of mobilizing public opinion. Operating with only a few volunteer workers, her group presented a petition to Congress in February 1880, signed by 13,000 men and women from fifteen states. From that time forward the organization expanded rapidly, assuming several titles before it became, in 1883, the Women's National Indian Association. By 1884 there were eight Protestant denominations represented on the executive board, and in 1886 eighty-three branches had been organized in twenty-eight states and territories. During 1884 the general secretary, Amelia S. Quinton, addressed 102 meetings, nearly half of which were in the northeastern states; but she also spoke in Kansas, Nebraska, Minnesota, Indiana, Michigan, Wisconsin, Illinois, and Ohio, where auxiliary associations were organized. Very little was done in the South, although Maryland and Georgia did have branch associations in 1885. Generally the methods employed by this organization to stir public sentiment in the Indians' favor were circulation of leaflets and petitions, publication of articles and letters, and speechmaking before religious gatherings, which often culminated in the creation of auxiliaries.[2]

A counterpart to the women's group was the Indian Rights Association which was also founded at Philadelphia, in December 1882, upon the instigation of Herbert Welsh, who followed in the footsteps of his uncle William as an Indian reformer. The object of this organization was to create such public feeling that congressmen would be compelled to secure for the Indians civil rights, law on reservations, education, and citizenship—all conducive to their assimilation. A massive effort was

[2] Ann. Rpts., 1883-1886.

launched by persuading religious denominations in the principal cities of the nation to form branches; even Albuquerque, New Mexico had an auxiliary of the Indian Rights Association. These branches were kept in close communication with a central board at Philadelphia, from which they received information concerning all important events and issues in which the Association was interested. Agents of the Board visited the Indian reservations and collected data which was circulated through newspapers, pamphlets, public addresses, and private correspondence. Such data was also used in preparing remedial legislation, and the bills written were followed through by Professor Charles C. Painter, who represented the Association in Washington. Painter's services were invaluable, for at the focal point of the reform movement, he was an effective lobbyist and a reliable source on Congressional proceedings.[3]

A third organization, established by Alfred Meacham and Theodore Bland in 1885, was the National Indian Defense Association. It did not have much effect on Indian legislation of the middle eighties. However, Meacham, who was badly wounded in the Modoc conspiracy of 1873, had contributed to reform by taking a delegation of Modocs on tour in 1874 and by founding, at Washington in 1878, *The Council Fire*, a monthly publication dedicated to the Indians' protection and assimilation. Bland became associate editor of this organ, which ran for ten years and expounded the view that the Indians should be consolidated and protected upon large reservations such as the Indian Territory, and that individual allotments of land should not be made until the Indians were far enough advanced to request citizenship with some understanding of what was involved.[4]

Two books recounting the long series of Indian massacres

---

[3] Ann. Rpts., 1883-1884. New Mexico was then a territory.
[4] Sec. of Interior C. Delano to Com. Ind. Aff. E. P. Smith, Nov. 6, 1874, Bur. Ind. Aff., Ltrs. Rec'd. ; *The Council Fire* (Aug. 1881).

and broken treaty promises had an impact upon the public. George W. Manypenny, who had been Commissioner of Indian Affairs in the fifties and who had served as chairman of the Sioux commission of 1876, in 1880 published *Our Indian Wards*. His volume was influential because he wrote with authority. In 1881 Helen Hunt Jackson, who had taken no part in the reform movement prior to 1879, published *A Century of Dishonor*. Although she denied the charge of "feeble sentimentalism," hers was an appeal to sentiment:

There is but one hope of righting this wrong. It lies in appeal to the heart and the conscience of the American people. What the people demand, Congress will do. It has been—to our shame be it spoken—at the demand of part of the people that all these wrongs have been committed, these treaties broken, these robberies done, by the Government. So long as there remains on our frontier one square mile of land occupied by a weak and helpless owner, there will be a strong and unscrupulous frontiersman ready to seize it, and a weak and unscrupulous politician, who can be hired for a vote or for money, to back him.[5]

Because of ill health, Helen Hunt had spent the winter of 1873-1874 at Colorado Springs, where she met William Jackson, a banker and a member of the Society of Friends, whom she later married. Having observed the destitution of Indians, her sympathy for them reached a climax upon hearing Tibbles and Bright Eyes lecture on the wrongs of the Ponca at Boston in 1879. Working in the New York Library, she completed *A Century of Dishonor* in May 1880, and persuaded Bishop Whipple to write the preface. Though not so intended, the book has been regarded as a poetical view of the Indian question. Yet it had an important role in arousing the public in favor of the legislation that was to be passed by Congress in the middle eighties. Congress itself recognized Mrs. Jackson in 1882 by appointing her a special commissioner to study conditions

---

[5] (Boston, 1881), 10-11 and 30.

among the mission Indians of California. This experience furnished material for a second book, *Ramona,* which became better known as a romance of the tragic ending of semi-feudal Spanish culture than as a contribution to the Indian reform movement.[6]

With many organizations and individuals clamoring for reform, there was yet needed some means of coordinating the whole effort. It occurred to Albert K. Smiley, a Quaker educator who was appointed to the Board of Indian Commissioners in 1879, that the annual one-day gatherings of religious representatives at Washington were too much subject to interruptions in that environment. Having purchased an old inn on scenic Lake Mohonk in New York State, he conceived the idea of a three-day conference in which differences of opinion could be resolved, "so that all should act together and be in harmony, and so that the prominent persons connected with Indian affairs should act as one body and create a public sentiment in favor of the Indians." The first meeting in 1883 was sparsely attended, but in 1885 nearly everyone of importance to the movement was present, including Senator Henry L. Dawes of Massachusetts.[7]

All of the Mohonk reformers were agreed that citizenship, including the suffrage, was necessary to the Indians' assimilation, but there were differences of opinion concerning the rapidity of the acculturation process. Dr. Lyman Abbot, editor of the *Christian Union* and the most extreme advocate of drastic action, wished to terminate the reservation system immediately, distribute patents for land in severalty, provide implements of industry and education, endow the Indians with all the rights enjoyed by white citizens, and say to them: "You

---

[6] Helen Jackson to Henry B. Whipple, May 22 and Oct. 29, 1880, Whipple Papers; Helen Jackson to Henry L. Dawes, Dec. 30, 1880, Dawes Papers.

[7] Ann. Rpt. of Bd. Ind. Com. (1885), 69 and 109-10.

must take care of yourself and confront the civilization of the nineteenth century." Professor Painter was more sensible than Abbot, but regarding the suffrage it was his view that since no educational qualifications were required of immigrants who became citizens, there should be no objection to extending "the ballot to such Indians as you can chase down, lasso, and bring to the polls." In principle Painter believed that certain literacy qualifications should be required for all who voted, but concurrently he did not suppose that fifty thousand enfranchised Indians scattered over the whole country would do any great damage to American institutions, while the right to vote might offer them some advantage locally. Writing from Arizona, even General George Crook advised that the ballot would eventually be the Indians' best means of defense; and, if one may judge by the platforms which were adopted, a majority of the Mohonk conferees were in agreement with ex-Justice of the United States Supreme Court William Strong, who in 1885 made the following statement:

The immediate admission of the Indians to all the rights of citizenship, including suffrage, I cannot agree to that. I am in favor of their being admitted to citizenship as rapidly as there is any degree of fitness for it. I believe all those Indians, who have lands in severalty, ought to be admitted to citizenship; but whether to admit them to the suffrage is another question. I am greatly in favor of education. Suffrage is not an indispensable requisite of citizenship.[8]

Those who held, as did Dr. Theodore Bland of *The Council Fire*, that the Indians must be allowed to make up their minds whether or not they wanted all of the privileges and obligations which the Mohonk reformers meant to procure, were given very little hearing. In any event, such arguments were unrealistic because there was no possibility of the Indians making a choice of cultures. That issue had already been settled by the

---

[8] *Ibid.*, 83 and 96.
[9] *Ibid.*, 85 and 93-94; Crook to Herbert Welsh, Nov. 24, 1884, is quoted in Ann. Rpt. of Indian Rights Assn. (1884), 15-16,

onslaught of western European civilization. As Carl Kraenzel
has wisely observed, Indian culture could not find expression
under conditions imposed by the advancing frontier. Vast un-
fenced territory with itinerant buffalo herds and other wild
game had determined the character of primitive plains institutions. With the rapid settlement of the West between 1860 and
1890, the environmental base of plains Indian culture disappeared. Since tribal bonds were weakened by white contact
and since the Indians demonstrated little capacity for self-
government, especially after their reservations were surrounded
by settlements, the need to proceed according to the theory of
wardship was obvious. Neither treaties that guaranteed them
reservations in perpetuity nor individual certificates of occupancy were adequate to protect the Indians' land, which was
being swallowed up through the pressure and the cupidity of
frontier population. How to save the red men's remaining
patrimony and how to afford them the possibility of adjusting
to the culture which was displacing their own, was the problem. Carl Schurz, who agreed with the majority of the Mohonk
reformers point by point, and who took a very active part in
the movement from 1880 onward, expressed this when he
wrote: "We must not expect them . . . to evolve out of their
own consciousness what is best for their salvation. We must in
a great measure do the necessary thinking for them, and then
in the most humane way possible induce them to accept our
conclusions." Equality before the law, vocational as well as
academic education, and a firm title to their lands were primary
requisites of Indian assimilation.[10]

---

[10] Schurz to Whipple, Apr. 5, 1880, Whipple Papers; Carl Schurz,
"Present Aspects of the Indian Problem," *North American Review*,
CXXXIII (1881), 23. Carl Kraenzel, *The Great Plains in Transition*
(Norman, Okla., 1955), 25-26, has portrayed the effect of the westward
movement upon Indian culture as follows: "The nation's Indian reservation policy spelled the doom and destruction of a culture—for two
reasons. First, the bison disappeared, and in his place came slaughtered

By 1880, all Indians on western reservations were feeling insecure because of agitation to have these remaining lands opened to settlement. American Horse of the Oglala Sioux said: "We do not wish to dispute with the Great Father, but we wish to talk about our country and our prospects for living permanently upon it." White Cloud of the White Earth Chippewa wrote: "Petitions are being extensively circulated . . . asking the Great Father to open for settlement by white people the fine agricultural lands north of our reservation, which were reserved for those Indians who chose to remove from other reservations." He added: "We wish the land to remain as it is until it is known that no Indian will need it." A movement in 1878 to consolidate the reservations of Oregon and Washington Territory at Yakima without compensation to industrious Indians for their improvements not only threatened an uprising but produced bitter opposition from Washington settlers, who felt that if instead the Indians were

---

beef, meted out at the trading post. How was the Indian to make love to his maiden now, and to show his personal feats and abilities? How could the youth become the brave? Whom could one worship, and by what ritual? What would a strong male Indian do to occupy his time, and what were the responsibilities of the Indian woman? What was a man to tell his children so that they might be proud of him? How was a man to hold his family, his clan, and his tribe together? How could a brave become a chief, exert authority, exhibit leadership? Under these conditions could an Indian—male or female—be anything but a 'ward' or a 'cultureless creature'?

"The second destructive blow to the Indian was his confinement to a restricted area. The reservation limited mobility, and it placed severe restrictions on the use of a horse. It 'fenced in' a large number of 'cultureless creatures.' It forced groups of human beings, whose culture had been suddenly destroyed, to live next to one another. No wonder they tried to escape from the reservation. And no wonder they just sat. In the face of such frustration, the use of opiates, especially as exhibited in Peyotism and the 'Red Messiah' religion, became a favorite form of withdrawal behavior." See also J. S. Slotkin, *The Peyote Religion* (Glencoe, Illinois, 1956), 12.

given lands in severalty where they were, peace could be maintained, while a large amount of good land would be left over for white claimants. The Congregational Association of Oregon and Washington went to the defense of the more advanced Indians in the Northwest, urging that homestead titles be granted to those of industrious habits before their reservations were consolidated. So it was that both land-grabbers and humanitarians favored individual allotment.[11]

Although the plan to allot land to Indians individually was adopted in 1854, as witnessed in treaties from that date, and gained momentum in the early sixties with the urgent recommendations of Commissioner William Dole, the essence of the Dawes Act did not emerge clearly until 1869, when the Board of Indian Commissioners said in their first report that the Indians "should be taught . . . the advantage of individual ownership of property, and should be given land in severalty, . . . and . . . the titles should be inalienable from the family of the holder for at least two or three generations." In 1874, Commissioner Edward P. Smith drafted and sent to Congress a bill which would have made it possible for individual Indians to become citizens by proving in a court of record that they had "sufficient intelligence and prudence" to manage their own affairs, that they had "adopted the habits of civilized life," and that they were capable of self-support. Since white settlers in Washington Territory were contesting a provision in the regulations of the General Land Office allowing Indians to file

---

[11] A. Hand at Dayton, Washington Terr., to Gen. O. O. Howard, Mar. 2, 1878 ; Myron Eells, Clerk of Cong. Assn. of Oreg, and Wash., to E. A. Hayt, July 16, 1878 ; agent V. T. McGillycuddy at Pine Ridge, Dak. Terr., to Com. Ind. Aff., Jan. 10, 1880, with copy of American Horse to H. W. K. Heath at Philadelphia, Jan. 9, 1880, enclosed, Bur. Ind. Aff., Ltrs. Rec'd. White Cloud to Bishop Whipple, Feb. 17, 1882, Whipple Papers. Apparently many Indians thought the distribution of land in severalty desirable: Supt. R. H. Milroy to Felix R. Brunot, Sept. 9, 1872, Bd. Ind. Com., Ltrs. Rec'd.; Acting Com. Ind. Aff. to Sec. Interior, Mar. 17, 1881, Sec. Interior, Ltrs. Rec'd.

claims under the Homestead and Pre-emption Laws, Smith's bill would protect Indians who had taken advantage of this rule from claim-jumpers. Although the measure as a whole did not become law, Congress confirmed in the following year that all heads of Indian families over twenty-one years of age, who had abandoned or who should in the future abandon their tribal relations, could make homestead entries outside of reservations subject to the provisions of the law of 1862.[12]

In July 1877, Alfred Riggs, missionary of the American Board of Commissioners for Foreign Missions to the Santee Sioux, declared that the time had come to make reservation Indians independent by giving them both land in severalty and citizenship. He stated that the Santee and Sisseton Sioux had desired to take allotments for many years, and presented a copy of the latest Santee petition to the President as evidence that the Indians of this tribe had not changed their mind. Near the close of the same year, Riggs rejected a bill sent to him by the secretary of the Board of Indian Commissioners and drafted a new one which provided that the two tribes might make homestead entries under the general provisions of the Homestead Act within their reservations, and that whenever any such Indian had perfected his homestead title and could read and write either his own or the English language, he might become a citizen by taking an oath to support the Constitution of the United States. The provisions of Riggs' bill were to be extended to other reservations in Nebraska and Dakota Territory whenever, in the judgment of the Secretary of the Interior, the occu-

---

[12] Ann. Rpts. of Com. Ind. Aff., Senate Ex. Doc. No. 1, 37th Cong., 2nd Sess., Vol. 1, 647, and House Exec. Doc. No. 1, 38th Cong., 1st Sess., Vol. 3, 130; Indian Citizenship Bill, House Exec. Doc. No. 228, 43rd Cong., 1st Sess., Vol. 16; Ann. Rpt. of Bd. Ind. Com. (1876), 4-5; 18 U.S. Stat., 420. W. A. Buckingham at Norwich, Conn., to E. P. Smith, Sept. 29, 1873, Bur. Ind. Aff., Ltrs. Rec'd., suggests that a law of Connecticut which conferred citizenship upon the Mohegan Indians was used as a model.

pants were prepared for it; and no part of any reserve to which the proposed legislation was applied might be opened to white entry for a period of ten years following the date of application. The reason for limiting the bill to Nebraska and Dakota was that its author wished "to avoid raising that hornets nest down in Indian Territory [Five Civilized Tribes] and also because circumstances might require other arrangements there and elsewhere." Riggs knew the situation in his area as well as if not better than anyone else. He thought it very important "to get the homestead wedge into all . . . Nebraska Reserves" for the reason that unless the Indians became homesteaders and citizens, public opinion would require their removal from the state. The provision which would have closed the Santee reserve to white entry for ten years aroused the latent antagonism of the adjacent Niobrara community, which demanded that the tribe be removed immediately to the Great Sioux Reserve in Dakota Territory, and managed to get a resolution through the Nebraska legislature to that effect. In the meantime all three of the missionary groups represented at the agency presented a solid front in favor of Riggs' bill, and in March 1879 the A.B.C.F.M. recommended it to Senator Dawes. At the same time, the Board of Indian Commissioners responded to a request for support with a resolution to President Hayes that "legislation to provide for titles to lands for all Indians desirous of occupying and tilling them is very much wanted." It was pointed out that nearly a dozen treaties made since 1854 had provided for patents, but that these had seldom been issued to those Indians who had selected allotments. The wisdom of such allotments had been placed in question because of weaknesses in the inalienability provisions, and the Commissioner of Indian Affairs had stopped issuing patents to the Shawnee in 1870 because the Indians were not holding the land after it was assigned to them. Riggs' bill never became law, but it was important for the clauses dealing with allotment, citizenship, and, in effect, with inalienability; these made it a predecessor of the Dawes Act.[13]

From 1879 onward, numerous unsuccessful allotment measures were introduced in Congress, some of them drafted almost wholly in the interest of white settlers. For example, a bill proposed to the House of Representatives in 1882 purported to provide "for the support and civilization of the various tribes of Sioux Indians" on the Great Dakota Reservation, but its content called for negotiations with the Sioux tribes, looking to the cession of all their land north of the White River—the portion of the reserve most suitable for agriculture. In the event that such negotiations failed, lands could be allotted individually anywhere within the reserve, with inalienable patents, for a specified period, and the Indians receiving them become subject to the laws of the territory or state of Dakota. Since nothing was said about the residue of the lands after allotments had been selected, it was presumed that the ultimate purpose was to have them opened for white settlement. Clearly, this was an attempt at diplomatic subterfuge; whether the Indians negotiated or not, they would likely lose most of their reservation.[14]

The organizations represented at the Mohonk Conferences were strongly opposed to schemes of this type, and were important in blocking their adoption. Although the Conference favored the sale of a portion of the Great Sioux Reserve and the breakup of the remainder into smaller separate reservations which should ultimately disappear, its members were generally

---

[13] Riggs to N. G. Clark, Sec. of A.B.C.F.M., July 6, 1877; Riggs to E. Whittlesey, Sec. of Bd. Ind. Com., Dec. 4, 13, 1877, and June 8, 1878; Riggs et al. to E. A. Hayt, Apr. 20, 1878; Clark to Whittlesey, Mar. 19, 1879, Bd. Ind. Com., Ltrs. Rec'd. Clark to Henry L. Dawes, Mar. 19, 1879, Dawes Papers; William Stickney, Sec. of Bd. Ind. Com., to Hayes, Nov. 15, 1879, Sec. Interior, Ltrs. Rec'd.; Acting Com. Ind. Aff. to R. T. Van Horn, June 27, 1870, Bur. Ind. Aff., Ltrs. Sent.

[14] Com. Ind. Aff. to Sec. Interior, June 12, 1882, Bur. Ind. Aff., Rpt. Book.

much concerned that the Indians should receive greater compensation for their land and adequate preparation for assimilation before these things were accomplished.[15]

Following the principles of Riggs' bill, the first Conference
recommended that "the Indians be admitted to . . . citizenship
so soon, and only so soon, as they are fitted for its responsibilities," and that "all Indians who are ready and anxious to
receive titles to separate homesteads, and are capable of taking
care of property, should be empowered to do so by proper legislation, which shall, at the same time, secure the lands so allotted
from alienation and incumbrance for a period of twenty-five
years. . . ." Under pressure from the Mohonk conferees, the
Senate during the winter of 1883-1884 passed the Coke bill,
which had been revised and amended since its introduction
by the Texas Senator in 1881; but this measure failed in the
House of Representatives. In final form, it would have given the
tribes inalienable title to their reservations for a quarter of a
century, and would have permitted separate allotments of 160
acres to the whole tribe if the President deemed it advisable and
if two-thirds of the adult male Indians gave their consent. But
it would also have allowed individual Indians to take land in
severalty upon request if the tribe as a whole did not favor it,
and would have extended the jurisdiction of the civil and criminal laws of states and territories to the Indians upon completion of allotments, while prohibiting the passage of statutes by
local governments denying Indians equal protection of the law.[16]

The difficulty with the Coke bill stemmed from the fact that
it was framed to favor the interest of the Indian rather than of
the western land-grabber. Professor Painter, the representative
of the Indian Rights Association at Washington, informed the
Mohonk Conference in 1885 that unless reform legislation

---

[15] Ann. Rpt. of Bd. Ind. Com. (1883), 39-41.
[16] Ann. Rpt. of Mohonk Conference, House Exec. Doc. No. 1, 48th
Cong., 2nd Sess., Vol. 12, 715-17 and 722-23.

could be identified with the interests of white citizens it could not be successful. As if to prove the rule, one exception to this was the passage in 1884 of a bill which allowed Indians to avail themselves of the provisions of the Homestead Law outside of reservations, with inalienable titles for twenty-five years and without the payment of fees."

The Individual Allotment Act, which became law in February 1887, was dependent upon Western land-hunger to carry it into effect. Western congressmen were unwilling to vote for a land-in-severalty law as a straightforward humanitarian measure, and until the Indian reform movement assumed national proportions, with its best support in Massachusetts, even Senator Dawes was skeptical of the propriety of such a statute. Early in 1882 Stephen Riggs wrote to him persuasively: "Now, my dear friend, let me say that God has placed you in a position, as chairman of the Indian Committee of the Senate, in which you can do more for the uplifting of the Indians than any other man in the world. Embrace your opportunity." The authorship of this allotment and citizenship measure cannot be fixed upon any single person. Alfred Riggs of the A.B.C.F.M., E. Whittlesey of the Board of Indian Commissioners, and Charles Painter of the Indian Rights Association collectively drafted amendments which were adopted. Professor Painter was responsible, against the opposition of Dr. Theodore Bland of the National Indian Defense Association, for striking out a provision in the bill which would have closed all reservations to white settlers for twenty-five years. Beyond this it is certain that the Massachusetts Senator was often in conference with these reformers and that he spent some time at Riggs' house in Washington during the winter when the final bill was before Congress. That Dawes was a front man for national organizations and that he was, at least in part, prompted to assume that

---

" Ann. Rpt. of Bd. Ind. Com. (1885), 74-75 ; 23 U.S. Stat., 96.

role because of the popularity of Indian reform among his constituents, is an inescapable conclusion.[18]

The Dawes Act gave the President power, at his discretion
and without the Indians' consent, to make all reservation
Indians, with the exception of the Five Civilized Tribes and a
few others, landowners in severalty and citizens of the United
States with all the privileges and responsibilities attendant
thereon, including the suffrage. The right of citizenship accompanied the ownership of land. Heads of families were to receive
a quarter section with a patent inalienable from themselves or
their heirs for twenty-five years. Single persons over eighteen,
and orphans under that age, were to obtain eighty acres. All
other persons under eighteen who were born prior to a Presidential proclamation directing allotments were to secure forty
acres. If the land should be suitable only for grazing, the acre-
age was to be doubled in all cases. Should any Indian neglect to
file a real estate claim within four years after the President had
directed the allotment of land on a particular reservation, the
Secretary of the Interior could direct the Indian agent to make a
selection for him. As in the Coke bill, Indians became subject to
the laws of the state or territory of their residence, with protection against discriminatory legislation, upon completion of allotments. With tribal consent, the federal government could sell
surplus land to white settlers in 160-acre tracts, and hold money
from such sales in trust for the Indians' benefit. All Indians
living apart from their tribes and having "adopted the habits

---

[18] Stephen R. Riggs at Carlisle Barracks to Henry L. Dawes, Jan. 16,
1882, Dawes Papers ; C. C. Painter to Herbert Welsh, Jan. 8 and May 6,
1886, Indian Rights Assn. Papers, Pa. Hist. Society, Philadelphia ;
Dawes at Pittsfield, Mass., to E. Whittlesey, Ap. 24, 1887, Bd. Ind. Com.,
Ltrs. Rec'd. ; James B. Thayer, "The Dawes Bill and the Indians,"
Atlantic Monthly, LXI (1888), 317. Passage of the Dawes Act was
delayed by a discussion of oleomargarine: *Proceedings of the Lake
Mohonk Conference* (1886-1890), 1. Stephen R. Riggs was the father of
Alfred ; both were Dakota missionaries.

of civilized life" became citizens at once.[19]

Dawes and those whom he represented did not favor giving Indians any of the privileges or responsibilities of property-holders and citizens without preparation to assume them. For this reason the Senator decried the House amendment which immediately made citizens of all those who had previously, under any tenure, taken individual allotments, and he called upon "the constructive genius" of the Indians' friends to "meet the exigency" at the following session of Congress.[20] Dawes expected that Presidents would withstand Western pressure which might break up the reservation system prematurely, but in this the Senator was also disappointed. Speaking at the Mohonk Conference eight months after the law was passed, he made the following statement:

President Cleveland said that he did not intend, when he signed this bill, to apply it to more than one reservation at first . . . which I thought was very wise. But you see he has been led to apply it to half a dozen. The . . . greed of the landgrabber is such as to press the application of this bill to the utmost. This will come most rapidly, —too rapidly, I think. The greed and hunger and thirst of the white man for the Indian's land is . . . going to press it forward too fast.[21]

In order to get the approval of Congress, the Dawes Act compromised some of the finest humanitarian ideals of the nineteenth century with the realities of American politics, and was perverted by the latter. Professor Painter's pragmatic assumption that the bill must appeal to the white man's interests had enabled it to become law, but in consequence the assimilation of Indians remained almost as remote as before.

The Dawes Act virtually condemned reservation Indians to poverty for many generations. For this, weaknesses in the law

---

[19] 24 U.S. Stat., 388-91. The Burke Act of 1906 withheld citizenship until land titles were free of the inalienability provision.

[20] Dawes to Whittlesey, Apr. 24, 1887, Bd. Ind. Com., Ltrs. Rec'd.

[21] *Proceedings of the Lake Mohonk Conference* (1886-1890), 67.

itself were responsible, together with the failure of Congress to pass much other reform legislation needed to accomplish assimilation. It would have been better had the government allowed most of the tribes to form stock-raising associations, because most of them were on land better suited to animal husbandry than to agriculture. Furthermore, in the middle eighties the Indians still possessed huge reservations which could have been converted to profitable ranches with little cost to the public. Instead, Congress directed in 1886 that many northern reserves be reduced in size, and negotiations were begun for the surrender of the larger share of those Indians' lands. For example, the Blackfeet, Blood, Gros Ventre, Piegan and River Crow of Montana gave up 17,500,000 out of 21,651,000 acres to be sold for their benefit! Cattlemen and Indians alike had to make way for white farmers, who were superior in number and needed plenty of land to divide among them. The same fallacy which underlay the Homestead Act of 1862 influenced the Individual Allotment Act both in its content and in its administration. In the subhumid and semiarid west, a quarter section of land did not make a worthwhile farm; yet the government ostensibly set out to make farmers of Indians by allotting them 160-acre tracts of the least desirable land in the region. Though ninety-eight per cent of the Lower Brule Sioux Reservation was "properly classifiable for grazing purposes," it was distributed in quarter sections, "violating every canon of good land use." Surplus land there was ceded for white settlement in 1904 and 1907, reducing the original reserve from 446,500 to 234,653 acres. As everywhere, nothing was withheld for future allotment in the event of an increased Indian population. In the view of humanitarians, the reduction and ultimately the abolition of reservations was justifiable because the Indians were to be incorporated into the body of Anglo-American citizenry; in the view of white farmers looking for a piece of Western land the same process was justifiable because the Indians were a dying race. But the majority neither assimilated nor died out, and grinding poverty and parasitical existence were consequently their fate. Lewis Meriam was mistaken in supposing that "the government assumed that some magic in individual ownership of property" was enough to acculturate the Indians. It was rather a case of meritorious assimilation measures being out of harmony with the selfish desires of white citizens.

Moreover, the passage of any legislation involving the tribe as a whole was delayed by a false concept, promulgated by the Senate Judiciary Committee in 1870, that such measures would be unconstitutional. Ex-Commissioner Francis Walker argued in 1874, with no effect, that the examination of unexpired treaties revealed nothing that would "prevent the United States from establishing a magistracy and a code of laws for the government" of Indian tribes. And in the same year, Commissioner Edward P. Smith prepared a bill which upon the request of a superintendent or agent would have given United States district and circuit courts jurisdiction over offenses committed by Indians against Indians within reservations, and which would have authorized United States marshals to make arrests in such cases. Had the bill passed, it would have been a tremendous boon to the agents, whose authority was always subject to question; certainly discipline was absolutely essential to rapid assimilation.[23]

The need to set up a system of government for those tribes

---

[22] Ann. Rpt. of Com. Ind. Aff. (1887), xxix ; 24 U.S. Stat., 44 ; Oliver La Farge, ed., *The Changing Indian* (Norman, Okla., 1942), 89 and 92 ; Lewis Meriam, *The Problem of Indian Administration* (Baltimore, 1928), 7. Besides the tribes of northern Montana Territory, those affected by the act of 1886 were the Sioux of Ft. Berthold, Dakota Territory ; the Chippewa in Minnesota ; and the Pend d'Oreilles, Coeur d'Alene, and Spokane in Idaho and Washington Territories.

[23] Rpt. of Senate Judiciary Com., Senate Rpt. No. 268, 41st Cong., 3rd Sess., 9 ; Rpt. on Lands in Severalty, House Rpt. No. 1576, 46th Cong., 2nd Sess., Vol. 5 ; Bill to Extend Jurisdiction of U.S. Courts

who were incapable of governing themselves was stressed again and again. As Smith's successor pointed out:

Civilization even among white men could not long exist without the guarantees which law alone affords; yet our Indians are remitted by a great civilized government to the control, if control it can be called, of the rude regulations of petty, ignorant tribes. Year after year we expend millions of dollars for these people in the faint hope that, without law, we can civilize them. That hope has been, to a great degree, a long disappointment, and year after year we repeat the folly of the past. That the benevolent efforts and purposes of the Government have proved so largely fruitless, is, in my judgment, due more to its failure to make these people amenable to our laws than to any other cause, or to all other causes combined.[24]

Bishop Whipple confirmed this analysis in 1877 with the comment: "We expect to accomplish civilization for wild Indians under circumstances which would wreck any civilized nation on earth."[25]

In an effort to correct this situation an elaborate bill, which excepted the Five Civilized Tribes from its provisions, was drawn up and presented to Congress in 1878 by the Associated Executive Committee of the Society of Friends. It would have given all Indian agents magisterial powers within the jurisdiction of their agencies, so that they could hear and determine all minor civil and criminal cases arising on reservations, whether Indians or white persons, or both, were involved. Upon demand of the defendant, the agent acting as a magistrate might summon a jury of five Indian men who understood the English language, or partly of such Indians and partly of agency employees, to try the case. For major cases and appeals the bill

over Indian Reservations, House Exec. Doc. No. 200, 43rd Cong., 1st Sess., Vol. 12; Francis A. Walker, "Indian Citizenship," *International Review,* I (1874), 319-20.

[24] Ann. Rpt. of J. Q. Smith, House Exec. Doc. No. 1, 44th Cong., 2nd Sess., Vol. 4, 387-88.

[25] Henry B. Whipple to Pres. Hayes, Sept. 28, 1877, Bur. Ind. Aff., Ltrs. Rec'd.

the first consideration in making appointments to the Indian
service. Following the advent of the Cleveland administration
in 1885, new agents were appointed for more than fifty out of
fifty-eight agencies, and although a few possibly deserved employment on the basis of merit, most of them did not. It was
tragic that men "of unflinching courage . . . and splendid executive ability," such as Dr. V. T. McGillycuddy of the Pine Ridge
agency, had to make way for any of these. Agent McGillycuddy
had managed six thousand of the wildest and most warlike of
the Oglala Sioux from 1879 until 1886 without ever calling
upon the aid of the Army. He depended wholly upon fifty
Indian policemen, and his own ability, to maintain the respect
of the progressive and orderly element, which in turn held Red
Cloud and his trouble-making entourage in check. Agent H. D.
Gallagher, a Democrat, had sense enough to resign in 1890
when an uprising, caused mostly by a reduction of the beef
issue, seemed imminent. With Benjamin Harrison in the White
House, politics called for a Republican successor—a party
devotee. That he lacked the qualities which usually character-
ized a good agent—"experience, force of character, courage,
and sound judgment"—was not an important consideration.
D. F. Royer got the job.[28]

The plight of the Sioux at the end of the eighties was pathetic. Their herds of cattle were diminished by black leg in 1888;
their crops failed in 1889 and 1890; epidemics of measles,
grippe, and whooping cough struck their camps with devastat-
ing mortality. In the same period they were pressured by a com-

House Exec. Doc. No. 1, 48th Cong., 2nd Sess., Vol. 12, 724-25 ; 23 U.S.
Stat., 385 ; 118 U.S. Rpts., 375-85 ; Cohen, *Handbook,* 148 ; James B.
Thayer, "A People Without Law," *Atlantic Monthly,* LXVIII (1891),
686-87. The seven crimes were murder, manslaughter, rape, assault with
intent to kill, arson, burglary, and larceny.

[28] James Mooney, *The Ghost-Dance Religion and the Sioux Outbreak
of 1890* (14th Ann. Rpt. of the Bureau of Ethnology, Part 2, Washington, D.C., 1896), 844-48.

proposed the establishment of eight judicial dis...
ing the reservations within the states and terr...
Michigan westward. With the advice and consent of...
the President would appoint eight judges who migh...
juries of twelve men made up in the same way as ...
juries. Each judge was to visit and hold court at each...
agencies within his district annually, and upon special occ...
when notified by an agent. These judges were to have al...
powers "prescribed by law for judges of Territorial courts...
the United States and those known to common law." Law e...
forcement would have been effected through the appointmen...
of special white marshals and Indian constables.[26]

Although Senator Dawes became interested in this measure
in 1879, and although similar bills were prepared by the Indian
Rights Association and the Mohonk Conference, it was impossible to get congressmen to pass them, with the result that
no such court system on Indian reservations was established.
Consequently, agents were left to meet the exigency as best they
could by arbitrarily creating native tribunals, called Courts of
Indian Offenses. By 1885 Congressional misgivings over authority to legislate for the tribes had waned, and a federal statute
named seven major crimes which, if committed by one reservation Indian against another, would be subject to trial in the
same courts and in the same manner, with the same penalties, as
if they had been committed by other persons within the jurisdiction of the United States. The constitutionality of this
measure was immediately challenged and upheld in the case of
the *United States* vs. *Kagama,* thereby clearing the way for the
Dawes Act itself.[27]

During the eighties, as in the sixties, political patronage was

[26] Josiah W. Leeds at Philadelphia to Pres. Hayes, Apr. 29, 1878, with
copy of proposed bill, Bur. Ind. Aff., Ltrs. Rec'd.
[27] Abstract of proposed bill, Mar. 1879, Dawes Papers ; Ann. Rpt. of
Indian Rights Assn. (1884), 16-17 ; Ann. Rpt. of Mohonk Conference,

mission to surrender eleven million additional acres of their land, and did so in 1889 after repeated assurances that the government would continue rations according to treaty. They had no more than signed when Congress cut the beef ration at Pine Ridge to less than half of what the treaty called for. Already brooding over their desperate condition, a new generation of warriors who had grown up since the humiliating defeat which followed the Custer affair was easily persuaded to test the fighting qualities of white soldiers. With an agent of McGillycuddy's stamp at Pine Ridge, they would never have been given the opportunity which Royer's call for troops afforded. This attempt of the Army to disarm a remnant of the greatest tribe of the plains resulted in the Wounded Knee massacre near the agency on December 29, 1890—a well-known event because it was the last of a series of such massacres and because it was associated with the Ghost-Dance Religion, in which the Indians placed a futile hope for the revival of their lost culture.[29]

From 1866 onward the national Indian rights organizations worked to secure the extension of the principles of civil service reform to the Indian service and asked the advice and cooperation of such prominent members of the National Civil Service Reform League as Dorman Eaton, Carl Schurz, and George Curtis. But the spoils system, which had been firmly re-established after its interruption during Grant's two administrations, was not easily overcome. Congressmen were so jealous of the prerogative of naming agents that the reformers thought it unwise to attempt an application of civil service rules to that office. Both strategy and time were required to attain the desired end. By Executive order, Indian school personnel and physicians were placed under classified civil service in 1891, and minor employees were included in 1896. Meanwhile an act was passed in 1893 authorizing the Commissioner of Indian Affairs,

---

[29] *Ibid.*, 826-28,

with the approval of the Secretary of the Interior, to give school superintendents control of agencies. A decade and a half elapsed before this provision was applied throughout the service, and the influence of politics upon the appointment of Indian agents was remedied only through the elimination of the office itself.[30]

As of 1890 the assimilation of the Indians was scarcely begun. At that time an unusually competent Commissioner of Indian Affairs, Thomas J. Morgan, was making an extraordinary effort to improve the reservation schools. Morgan, a former professor of church history at the Baptist Union Theological Seminary in Chicago, was a keen student of past Indian management and believed that compulsory education in a well-coordinated public school system, including industrial training, was the best means of preparing Indian youth for life in Anglo-American society. It was to his credit that the practice of making contracts with religious denominations for the maintenance of Indian schools ended as public facilities were provided between 1892 and 1901. The Superintendent for Indian Schools at Washington, an office created in 1882, had formerly exercised little authority, but the Division of Education, with the Superintendent at its head, assumed a central position within the Bureau of Indian Affairs during the Harrison administration. In 1889 Superintendent Daniel Dorchester, a Methodist clergyman, dismissed from the school service many incompetent and otherwise undesirable persons whose appointment was due to political patronage. As has already been noted, other blows at the spoils system came in 1891 with the subjection of school personnel to civil service rules, and in 1893 with Congressional authorization to place school superintendents rather than politically appointed agents in charge of reservations. Thus, educa-

---

[30] Ann. Rpt. of Indian Rights Assn. (1886), 7-8 ; 27 U.S. Stat., 614 ; Laurence F. Schmeckebier, *The Office of Indian Affairs* (Baltimore, 1927), 83-84.

tion won a strategic position which was well suited to the purpose of Indian administration.[31]

For those who agreed that assimilation was a desirable solution to the Indian problem there was, aside from the emphasis upon agriculture, much wisdom in the program adopted during this period. That it was largely ineffective was the fault of Congress, which did not appropriate enough funds to allow the employment of an adequate, qualified educational staff. The assimilation policy which had at last received some legislative support still lacked, as it always had, the willingness of Congress to carry it through. This deficiency grew out of the self-interested orientation of public opinion. Because of the egocentric nature of men, political democracy has seldom been humanitarian in its motivation. Political democracy has always best served the interests of powerful groups, and has neglected weak minorities. This perhaps was the most important reason why a policy intent upon the acculturation of the 325,000 Indians on reservations in 1890, had not reduced significantly the number of those living apart from Anglo-American society at the middle of the twentieth century.[32]

[31] Ann. Rpts. of Com. Ind. Aff. (1889), 3 and 95 (1890), 5-6 (1892), 9 (1900), 26-27 (1901), 26 ; C. C. Painter to Herbert Welsh, Oct. 2, 1886, Indian Rights Assn. Papers ; Morgan to Sec. Interior, Nov. 25, 1889, Benjamin Harrison Papers, National Archives.

[32] Lewis Meriam, *Problem of Indian Administration,* 8 ; "Resident Population on Indian Reservations, 1950," Dept. of Interior Pamphlet based on U.S. Census for 1950 ; "Indians on Federal Reservations in the United States," Dept. of Health, Education, and Welfare Pamphlet (Washington, 1959), vi. The emphasis upon the tribal relationship under the Wheeler-Howard Act of 1934 may now be regarded as an interlude in the effort to assimilate the Indians ; enthusiasm for the Wheeler-Howard policy waned in the forties and gave way during the fifties to advocacy of termination of federal responsibility for Indian affairs and absorption of Indians into urban life. Indian population in the 240 federal reservation areas, excluding Alaska, has increased sharply since 1950 and has currently reached a total of approximately 350,000. A good summary of Indian administration since 1890 is found in William T. Hagan, *American Indians* (Chicago, 1961).

Bibliography

I. PRIMARY SOURCES

A. Private Papers

American Board of Commissioners for Foreign Missions Papers, Houghton Library, Harvard University.

Archives of the Bureau of Catholic Indian Missions, 1873-1895, Washington, D.C.

Grover Cleveland Papers, 1885-1889, Library of Congress.

Henry L. Dawes Papers, 1870-1887, Library of Congress.

Charles Ewing Papers, 1867-1883, Library of Congress.

John B. Garret Papers, Quaker Collection, Haverford College, Haverford, Pennsylvania.

U. S. Grant Papers, 1865-1877, Library of Congress.

Benjamin Harrison Papers, 1876 and 1888-1893, Library of Congress.

Rutherford Hayes Papers, 1877-1881, Library of Congress.

Enoch Hoag Papers, Quaker Collection, Haverford College, Haverford, Pennsylvania.

Indian Rights Association Papers, 1883-1887, Historical Society of Pennsylvania, Philadelphia.

James E. Rhoads Papers, Quaker Collection, Haverford College, Haverford, Pennsylvania.

Carl Schurz Papers, 1877-1880, Library of Congress.

William T. Sherman Papers, 1865-1871, Library of Congress.

Henry B. Whipple Papers, 1859-1886, Minnesota Historical Society, St. Paul, Minnesota.

Thomas S. Williamson Papers, 1863, Minnesota Historical Society, St. Paul, Minnesota.

B. Federal Documents (Unpublished)

Board of Indian Commissioners, Letters Received and Letters Sent, 1870-1890, National Archives.

Bureau of Indian Affairs, Letters Received, Letters Sent, and Report Books, 1860-1890, National Archives.

Secretary of the Interior, Letters Received and Letters Sent, 1860-1890, National Archives.

War Records, Selected Letters and General Orders, 1860-1880, National Archives.

C. Federal Documents (Published)

1. General

Annual Reports of the Board of Indian Commissioners, 1870-1890.

Annual Reports of the Commissioner of Indian Affairs, 1860-1890, and selected reports for an earlier period.

Annual Reports of the General of the Army, 1860-1880.

Annual Reports of the Secretary of the Interior, 1860-1890.

Congressional Globe.

Congressional Record.

Kappler, Charles J., ed., *Indian Affairs: Laws and Treaties*, 2 vols. (Washington, 1904).

Laws of the United States, IX (New York, Gould & Banks, 1839).

Richardson, James D., ed., Messages and Papers of the Presidents, 1789-1897, 10 vols. (Washington, 1907).

United States Reports of Cases Adjudged in the Supreme Court.

United States Statutes at Large.

2. Special

Bill to Extend Jurisdiction of United States Courts over Indian Reservations, House Exec. Doc. No. 200, 43rd Cong., 1st Sess., Vol. 12 (1874).

Estimates of Deficiencies in Appropriations for the Indian Service, House Exec. Doc. No. 56, 46th Cong., 3rd Sess., Vol. 18 (1881).

"Indians on Federal Reservations in the United States," Dept. of Health, Education, and Welfare Pamphlet (Washington, 1959).

Letter Requesting Appropriations, C. Delano, Secretary of the Interior, to James G. Blaine, Speaker of the House of Representatives, Mar. 17, 1874, House Exec. Doc. No. 186, 43rd Cong., 1st Sess.

Memorial of John Beeson to Congress on Improvement of the Indian Tribes, Senate Misc. Doc. No. 94, 43rd Cong., 2nd Sess. (April 1, 1874).

Memorial of the Choctaw Nation, Senate Misc. Doc. No. 90, 41st Cong., 2nd Sess. (March 17, 1870).

Memorial of Yearly Meeting of Friends on Treatment of Indians, House Misc. Doc. No. 29, 40th Cong., 3rd Sess., Vol. 1 (Jan. 21, 1869).

Message of President on Indian Treaties, Senate Exec. Doc. No. 57, 41st Cong., 2nd Sess., Vol. 2 (March 8, 1870).

Petitions of the Cherokee Tribes, House Misc. Doc. No. 76, 41st Cong., 2nd Sess. (Feb. 1870).

Plan of E. S. Parker to Establish Peace with the Indians, House Misc. Doc. No. 37, 39th Cong., 2nd Sess., Vol. 1 (1867).

Report of Deficiencies in Appropriations for 1869, Senate Exec. Doc. No. 62, 40th Cong., 2nd Sess., Vol. 2.

Report on Difficulties with Indian Tribes, House Exec. Doc. No. 240, 41st Cong., 2nd Sess., Vol. 2 (April 6, 1870).

Report of Indian Disturbances on the Sioux Reservation, Senate Exec. Doc. No. 52, 44th Cong., 1st Sess. (April 22, 1876).

Report on Indian Hostilities, Senate Exec. Doc. No. 13, 40th Cong., 1st Sess. (July 13, 1867).

Report on Consolidation of Indian Tribes, Senate Report No. 131, 41st Cong., 2nd Sess. (April 27, 1870).

Report on Items Omitted and Changes Made in Indian Appropriation Bill for 1869, Senate Exec. Doc. No. 62, 40th Cong., 2nd Sess., Vol. 2.

Report of the Joint Special Committee of Congress on the Condition of the Indian Tribes, Senate Report No. 156, 39th Cong., 2nd Sess. (Jan. 1867).

Report on Lands in Severalty for the Indians, House Report No. 1576, 46th Cong., 2nd Sess., Vol. 5 (1880).

Report of the Ponca Commission, Senate Exec. Doc. No. 30, 46th Cong., 3rd Sess., Vol. 1 (Jan. 25, 1881).

Report on the Removal of the Ponca, Senate Report No. 670, 46th Cong., 2nd Sess., Vol. 6 (May 31, 1880).

Report of the Sioux Commission, Senate Exec. Doc. No. 9, 44th Cong., 2nd Sess. (Dec. 18, 1876).

Report of the Senate Judiciary Committee, Senate Report No. 268, 43rd Cong., 3rd Sess. (1870).

Report of the Commission to Investigate Charges Against E. P. Smith, Dept. of Interior Pamphlet (Washington, Feb. 2, 1874).

"Resident Population on Indian Reservations, 1950," Dept. of Interior Pamphlet Based on U.S. Census for 1950.

Resolution on Expediency of Establishing a Territorial Government over Certain Tribes, House Misc. Doc. No. 21, 41st Cong., 2nd Sess., Vol. 1 (Jan. 13, 1870).

Resolution of the Kansas Legislature on Indian Removal, Senate Misc. Doc. No. 55, 41st Cong., 2nd Sess. (Feb. 16, 1870).

Resolution of the Kansas Legislature on Indian Removal, Senate Misc. Doc. No. 69, 41st Cong., 3rd Sess., Vol. 1 (Feb. 18, 1871).

Welsh, William, *Report of a Visit to the Sioux and Ponka Indians on the Missouri River* (Washington, D.C., July 1872).

D. *Publications of Reform Organizations*

Annual Reports of the Indian Rights Association, 1883-1890.

Annual Reports of the Women's National Indian Association, 1883-1890.

The Council Fire, 1878-1887.

Proceedings of the Lake Mohonk Conference (1886-1890). The Proceedings for earlier years were published in the Annual Reports of the Board of Indian Commissioners.

E. *Newspapers*

Arizona Citizen (Tucson, Ariz. Terr.), Library of Congress, 1871.

Bismarck Weekly Tribune (Bismarck, Dak. Terr.), Minnesota Historical Society, St. Paul, Minnesota, 1876.

Cheyenne Daily Leader (Cheyenne, Wyo. Terr.), Library of Congress, 1870.

New York Herald (New York, N.Y.), Library of Congress, 1878.

New York Times (New York, N.Y.), Library of Congress, 1869, 1878, and 1879.

Omaha Republican (Omaha, Neb.), Library of Congress, 1874.

Oregon Statesman (Salem, Oreg. Terr.), Library of Congress, 1876.

Providence Journal (Providence, R.I.), Library of Congress, 1878.

Rocky Mountain Daily News (Denver, Col.), Library of Congress. Numerous issues throughout the 1870's were studied but no materials were selected.

Saint Paul Pioneer (St. Paul, Minn.), Minnesota Historical Society, 1862.

Saint Paul Press (St. Paul, Minn.), Minnesota Historical Society, 1862.

Saint Paul Daily Press (St. Paul, Minn.), Minnesota Historical Society, 1873.

Saint Paul and Minneapolis Pioneer-Press and Tribune, Minnesota Historical Society, 1876.

Washington Chronicle (Washington, D.C.), Library of Congress, 1870.

Wyoming Weekly Leader (Cheyenne, Wyo. Terr.), Library of Congress, 1875.

F. *Books*

Bancroft, Frederic, ed. *Speeches, Correspondence and Political Papers of Carl Schurz*, 6 vols. (New York, 1913).

Beeson, John. *A Plea for the Indians* (New York, 1858).

Jackson, Helen H. *A Century of Dishonor* (Boston, 1885).

Manypenny, George W. *Our Indian Wards* (Cincinnati, 1880).

Palladino, Lawrence B., S. J. *Indian and White in the Northwest* (Baltimore, 1894).

G. *Articles*

Abbott, Austin. "Indians and the Law," *Harvard Law Review*, II 1888-1889), 167-79.

Butler, E. "A Glance at the Indian Question," *Catholic World*, XXVI (1877), 195-203.

Canfield, George F. "Carl Schurz on the Indian Problem," *Nation*, XXXII (1881), 457-58.

Cox, J. D. "The Indian Question," *International Review*, VI (1879), 617-34.

Girard, P. "Our New Indian Policy and Religious Liberty," *Catholic World*, XXVI (1877), 90-108.

Godkin, E. L. "The Indian Difficulty," *Nation*, VII (1868), 544-46.

——— "Our Indian Wards," *Nation*, XXIII (1876), 21-22.

Harsha, William J. "Law for the Indians," *North American Review*, CXXXIV (1882), 272-92.

Head, F. H. "Our Ishmaelites," *Overland Monthly*, IV (1870), 105-11.

Linn, J. M. "The Relation of the Church to the Indian Question," *Presbyterian Review*, I (1880), 677-93.

Lowe, Charles. "The President's New Indian Policy," *Old and New*, III (1871), 487-504.

Mallery, G. "Otis's Indian Question," *Nation*, XXVII (1878), 13-14. A review of Lt. Col. Elwell S. Otis's *The Indian Question* (New York, 1878). It is of value as an Army point of view.

Miles, Nelson A. "The Indian Problem," *North American Review*, CXXVIII (1879), 304-14.

Morgan, Lewis H. "The Hue-and-Cry Against the Indians," *Nation*, XXIII (1876), 40-41.

———. "The Indian Question," *Nation*, XXVII (1878), 332-33.

Riggs, Alfred L. "What Shall We Do With the Indians?" *Nation*, V (1867), 356.

Riggs, Stephen P. "The Indian Question," *New Englander*, XV (1857), 250-72.

Schurz, Carl. "Present Aspects of the Indian Problem," *North American Review*, CXXXIII (1881), 1-24.

Thayer, James B. "The Dawes Bill and the Indians," *Atlantic Monthly*, LXI (1888), 315-22.

———. "A People Without Law," *Atlantic Monthly*, LXVIII (1891), 540-51, 676-87.

Walker, Francis A. "Indian Citizenship," *International Review*, I (1874), 305-26.

———. "The Indian Question," *North American Review*, CXVI (1873), 329-88.

II. Secondary Works

A. Books

Abel, Annie H. "The History of Events Resulting in Indian Consolidation West of the Mississippi," *American Historical Association Annual Report, 1906*, I (Washington, 1908), 233-450.

Alvord, Clarence W. *Mississippi Valley in British Politics*, 2 vols. (Cleveland, 1917).

Anderson, Harry. "History of the Cheyenne River Agency and Its

Military Post at Fort Bennett," *South Dakota Historical Collections*, XXVIII (1956).

Athearn, Robert G. *William Tecumseh Sherman and the Settlement of the West* (Norman, Okla., 1956).

Atwater, Isaac, ed. *History of Minneapolis*, 2 vols. (New York, 1893).

Beeson, Jasper L. *Beeson Genealogy* (Macon, Ga., 1925).

Byrne, P. E. *The Red Man's Last Stand* (London, 1927).

Carley, Kenneth *The Sioux Uprising of 1862* (St. Paul, 1961).

Cohen, Felix S. *Handbook of Federal Indian Law* (Washington, 1942).

Connelley, William E. *History of Kansas*, 5 vols. (Chicago, 1883).

Dale, Edward E. *The Indians of the Southwest* (Norman, Okla., 1949).

Eastman, Elaine G. *Pratt: The Red Man's Moses* (Norman, Okla., 1935).

Fuess, Claude M. *Carl Schurz: Reformer* (New York, 1932). Mr. Fuess, in the chapter entitled "Schurz and the Indians," gives Carl Schurz far too much credit as an Indian reformer.

Hagan, William T. *American Indians* (Chicago, 1961).

Haines, Francis. *The Nez Percés* (Norman, Okla., 1955).

Harmon, George D. *Sixty Years of Indian Affairs, 1789-1850* (Chapel Hill, N.C., 1941).

Hodge, Frederick W., ed. *Handbook of American Indians North of Mexico*, 2 vols. (Washington, D.C., 1907-1910).

Hyde, George E. *Red Cloud's Folk: A History of the Oglala Sioux* (Norman, Okla., 1937).

Kelsey, Rayner W. *Friends and the Indians, 1655-1917* (Philadelphia, 1917).

Kraenzel, Carl. *The Great Plains in Transition* (Norman, Okla., 1955).

La Farge, Oliver, ed. *The Changing Indian* (Norman, Okla., 1942).

Leupp, Francis E. *The Indian and His Problem* (New York, 1910).

McLaughlin, James. *My Friend the Indian* (New York, 1910).

Meriam, Lewis *The Problem of Indian Administration* (Baltimore, 1928).

Mohr, Walter H. *Federal Indian Relations. 1774-1788* (Philadelphia, 1933).

Mooney, James. *The Ghost-Dance Religion and the Sioux Outbreak of 1890* (14th Ann. Rpt. of the Bureau of Ethnology, Part 2, Washington, D.C., 1896).

Morgan, Lewis H. *Ancient Society* (Chicago, 1877).

Murray, Keith A. *The Modocs and Their War* (Norman, Okla., 1959).

Osgood, Ernest S. *The Day of the Cattleman* (Minneapolis, 1954).

Paxson, Frederic L. *The Last American Frontier* (New York, 1910).

Payne, D. P. *Captain Jack* (Portland, Oregon, 1938).

Priest, Loring B., *Uncle Sam's Stepchildren* (New Brunswick, 1942).

Rahill, Peter J. *The Catholic Indian Missions and Grant's Peace Policy, 1870-1884* (Washington, 1953).

Rister, Carl C. *Border Command, General Phil Sheridan in the West* (Norman, Okla., 1944).

Rushmore, Elsie M. *The Indian Policy during Grant's Administration* (Jamaica, N.Y., 1914).

Schmeckebier, Laurence F. *The Office of Indian Affairs: Its History, Activities, and Organization* (Baltimore, 1927).

Slotkin, J. S. *The Peyote Religion* (Glencoe, Ill., 1956).

Stewart, Edgar I. *Custer's Luck* (Norman, Okla., 1955).

Swanton, John R. *The Indian Tribes of North America* (Washington, D.C., 1952).

Tappan, Daniel L. *Tappan-Toppan Genealogy: Ancestors and Descendants of Abraham Toppan of Newbury, Massachusetts, 1606-1672* (Arlington, Mass., 1915).

Textor, Lucy E. *Official Relations Between the United States and the Sioux Indians* (Palo Alto, Calif., 1896).

Wissler, Clark. *Indians of the United States: Four Centuries of Their History and Culture* (New York, 1940).

B. Articles

Briggs, Harold. "The Black Hills Gold Rush," *North Dakota Historical Quarterly*, V (1931), 71-99.

Byrne, P. E. "The Custer Myth," *North Dakota Historical Quarterly*, VI (1932), 187-200.

Carter, Clarence E. "British Policy toward the American Indians in the South, 1763-1768," *English Historical Review*, XXXIII (1918), 37-56.

Davenport, T. W. "Slavery Question in Oregon," *Oregon Historical Quarterly*, IX (1908), 189-253 and 309-73.

Farrand, Max. "The Indian Boundary Line," *American Historical Review*, X (1905), 782-91.

Hayter, Earl W. "The Ponca Removal," *North Dakota Historical Review*, VI (1932), 262-75.

Santee, J. F. "Edward R. S. Canby, Modoc War, 1873," *Oregon Historical Quarterly*, XXXIII (1932), 1-24.

Way, Royal B. "The United States Factory System for Trading with the Indians, 1796-1822," *Mississippi Valley Historical Review*, VI (1919), 220-35.

Wemett, W. M. "Custer's Expedition to the Black Hills in 1874," *North Dakota Historical Quarterly*, VI (1932), 292-301.

Index

Abbot, Lyman, editor, 202

Agencies assigned to churches, 76-79

Aldrich, Cyrus, Congressman from Minnesota, 41

Alemany, J. S., Archbishop of California, 95

Allen, Walter, Ponca commissioner, 194

American Horse, Oglala chief, 205

American Indian Aid Association, 198

Annuities: as cause of Minnesota massacre, 42; foster indolence, 18, 31; and fraud, 27, 144, 158-60; just payment advocated for, 28, 39-42; 46, 65; Kiowa and Comanche await payment of, 70; military officers inspect, 121; their payment reformed, 157; their payment supervised, 44

Apache Indians: condition of, 32; confined, 112; defended, 71; make treaty, 63; Western attitude toward, 117, 119; whiskey sold to, 21

Appropriations inadequate, 56, 68, 74, 135, 136, 138

Arikara Indians, 173

Arizona Citizen, reflects Western viewpoint, 116

Armstrong, Samuel C., principal of Hampton Institute, 164

Arny, W. F., Navajo agent, 145

Aspinwall, Ruffee, and Nash, contractor, 50

Assiniboin Indians: Army asked to subsist, 137; attacked by Sioux, 173

Augur, Gen. C. C., peace commissioner, 63

Austin, Horace, Governor of Minnesota, 28

Bannock Indians, 113

Bassett, Joel, Chippewa agent, 50

Bayley, J. Roosevelt, Archbishop of Baltimore, 93

Beeson, John, reform advocate, 34-38

Bennett, Capt. F. T., Navajo agent, 149

Bent, Col. William; and Cheyenne and Arapaho Treaty, 60; and Indian hostilities, 30

Big Horn Association, demands Sioux hunting grounds for settlement, 171

Big Horn Mountains: Powder River road there provokes Sioux, 61, 63; settlement there threatens Sioux hunting grounds, 128, 171

Bismarck Weekly Tribune, comments on Custer massacre, 176

Black Eye, Yanktonai chief, 22

Blackfeet Indians: attacked by Sioux, 173; reservation reduced, 214

Black Hills: and gold rush, 173; invaded, 125

Black Hills Mining and Exploring Association, demands Sioux reservation for settlement, 172

Blair, Frank, Benton's heir, his political influence, 26

Blanchet, F. N., Archbishop of Oregon, reacts to "Peace Policy," 88-91

233